Infrastructure Finance

An Inside View

Martin Blaiklock

Author
Martin Blaiklock

Managing director
Sian O'Neill

Infrastructure Finance: An Inside View
is published by

Globe Law and Business Ltd
3 Mylor Close
Horsell
Woking
Surrey GU21 4DD
Tel: +44 20 3745 4770
www.globelawandbusiness.com

Infrastructure Finance: An Inside View

ISBN 9781787420830
EPUB ISBN 9781787420847
Adobe PDF ISBN 9781787420854
Mobi ISBN 9781787420861

Table of contents

Acknowledgements 7

About the author 8

Preface 9

Sources 11

Glossary 13

Part 1: Principles 21

What is infrastructure? 23

- Introduction and context
- Recent history
- History – Europe and the rest of the world (excluding North America)
- History – North America
- What are PPPs?
- Impact of the financial crisis on PPPs

Financial structures 35

- The project company
- Funding structures – government guarantees
- Funding structures – corporate guarantees
- Project finance (cash flow) structures
- PPPs
- Types of PPP
- Balance sheet issues
- Not-for-profit companies/PICs

Options for governments 53

- Which funding structure to adopt?
- The gateway decision-making process
- Value for money – public v private
- Advantages/disadvantages of such structures
- Other features to note

Risk 69

- What is risk?
- Measuring risk
- Risk analysis – identification and mitigation
- Risk mitigation – the role of insurance
- Concluding remarks – cross-sector financial structures

Sources of finance 87

- Introduction
- Equity
- Debt

Quantitative analysis 117

- Measures used by developers and investors
- Measures used by lenders
- Cash flow model – practical comments
- Cash flow model – an example

The contractual framework 131

Corporate identities and issues

Key project documents

The project engineer

The project process 151

Project/public-private partnership unit

Planning structure

Business plan/PIM

Financial adviser

Bid preparation and notices

Procurement laws and infrastructure

Timetable and bid costs

Innovative proposals

Raising the funds

Mandate letter

Due diligence

Project monitoring

Standards of probity and conflicts of interest

Part 2: Practice and experience 161

Transport – roads and highways 163

Key features

Key risks for highways

Risks for other road-related sectors

Transport – bridges and tunnels 177

Key features

Key risks

Case histories

Transport – rail 183

Key features

Key risks for inter-city/HSR

Case histories

Key risks for rolling stock and vehicles

Transport – metros, mass transit, light rail and trams 189

Key features

Key risks and case histories for metros and mass transit

Key risks and case histories for light rail and trams

Transport – ports 195

Key features

Key risks

Case histories

Transport – airports 201

Key features

Key risks

Case histories

Air traffic control

Power generation – thermal (coal, oil, gas) 207

Key features

Key risks

Case histories

Power generation – hydropower 215

Key features

Key risks

Case histories

Power generation – nuclear 221

Historical features

Key features

Future prospects

Power generation – renewables (wind, solar, geothermal, biomass) 225

Kyoto Protocol

Renewable energy projects

Case histories

Oil, gas and power transmission and distribution 239

Key features

Power transmission – applications and experiences

Power and gas distribution – applications and experiences

Oil and gas pipelines – case histories

Conclusion

Water and waste management 245

Key features

Water projects

Waste management projects

Miscellaneous government services – schools, health, housing, offices, information technology, stadiums, prisons, defence 253

General features

Case histories

UK infrastructure – issues and challenges 261

Introduction

UK privatised utilities and the Regulatory Asset Base model

Case history 1 – Thames Water and Thames Tideway Tunnel

Case history 2 – Heathrow Airport Expansion (Runway 3)

Case history 3 – Hinkley Point C and other UK nuclear power plants

Case history 4 – HS2

Concluding comments 283

Index 285

Acknowledgements

I would like to thank all those colleagues who, directly or indirectly, have made their contributions – knowingly or not! – to a corner of the financial markets that ever continues to fascinate.

In particular, I would like to thank Globe Law and Business and their team for providing the opportunity to shed some light onto an area of finance that is vital to the sustainability of the global economy.

I would also like to thank those friends and family who, through their forbearance and patience, have provided the support needed for me to arrive at this point, when I have put pen to paper. It may not have been such fun for them, but I hope they appreciate the output!

About the author

Martin Blaiklock has over 40 years' experience of structuring, developing, evaluating and implementing the funding of public and private sector projects – that is, private finance initiatives (PFIs), public-private partnerships (PPPs) and so on – in infrastructure, energy and the process industries throughout the world and, particularly, in emerging markets.

Uniquely, Mr Blaiklock has worked for extended periods in an investment bank (Kleinwort Benson Ltd), a commercial bank (HSBC) and a development bank (the European Bank of Reconstruction and Development – the EBRD – as director of power and energy utilities).

Since 1995, he has operated as an independent consultant and was an expert witness for the Parliamentary Inquiry into the London Underground PPP.

Over the past six years he has undertaken over 120 training seminars on project finance/PPPs for the World Bank/International Finance Corporation, the EBRD, the African Development Bank, governments, contractors, utilities and commercial banks in over 40 countries.

He is also a member of Independent Port Consultants (www.port-consultants.com), a London-based association of independent port development specialists.

Preface

In my nearly 40 years working as a banker in infrastructure and energy project finance, I have been fortunate to have worked alongside many experts in the field, negotiated with many across the table and travelled the world to see the products of my travails. It has undoubtedly been a rich experience and, generally, great fun!

There came a time, however – not least when a colleague at a City Christmas party suggested that I might be the "longest serving member of the project finance community in London" – when it felt appropriate and useful to record these events and experiences.

The fundamentals of project financing have remained largely unchanged over the years. While lawyers, consultants, accountants, financial advisers and investment bankers (as opposed to merchant bankers whose word was their bond – sadly now a dying, even extinct, breed) are forever attempting to create ever more complex project structures, it is actually simple funding structures which form the basis for successful project finance.

However, at times the excitement of creating a new project can overtake common sense, resulting in over-complexity. Thus, the concession agreement for the London Underground public-private partnership (PPP) was reportedly over 3,000 pages long (maybe reflecting the fact that no one had ever undertaken a PPP before for a major city and suburban metro system anywhere in the world). More recently, a surge of UK high-value project proposals, such as London's 'Super Sewer' (£4 billion), the HS2 fast-rail link (estimated at £50 billion), Hinkley Point Nuclear Power Plant (£18 billion), Heathrow Northwest Runway Expansion (£18 billion) and Barrages in the Severn Estuary (estimated at £25 billion), has demonstrated that vanity also pervades Whitehall.

Such projects also provide great business opportunities for lawyers and advisers, with fees paid for creating the 'monster' in the first place, with yet more fees incurred when project managers need help when matters go wrong. But that aside, are these infrastructure projects, taken as a whole, sensible ventures? Will they deliver the value for money expected?

As a scientist by first degree, I perceive project financing and the use of private capital for investment in public service assets such as PPPs as similar to process engineering. It is like building a brick wall. One needs a lot of bricks which, if suitably assembled, will withstand the weather over a long period. The technology is simple, but the multiplicity of the component parts makes it a complex task. Nevertheless, the secret of a wall's strength and its longevity lies in the quality of the mortar holding the bricks together and the skills of the architect and builder.

Arising out of the mass of detail that these infrastructure transactions demand is the fact that no one person can manage and have all the expertise for all aspects of a deal. Project finance, and PPP, is the ultimate team game in the financial sector. Typically, one needs a core team comprising a banker, a lawyer, a technical expert, an environmentalist and proposal manager, plus probably the support of a computer modeller, to bring a deal to a successful conclusion. Furthermore, the team needs to be politically aware, as the infrastructure assets form the basis for a public service for which, ultimately, the relevant government has to carry responsibility.

Another consideration for all involved is that putting these deals together is time consuming. It can take months, if not years, to move from project concept to financial close. As part of this process, colleagues can become friends. The camaraderie of the project teams that I have worked with, forged through hours of preparation and negotiation and thereafter project monitoring, is one lasting pleasure that I have had over my many years in this business. The sector may not make many millionaires, but it certainly sustains many long-lasting friendships.

In preparing this book, I have drawn on much of the experience I have learnt from others, as well as the reports, as are available in the market, as to project successes and failures.

Many of the examples in this volume are UK based, but then the United Kingdom has undertaken many (over 800) PPP-type concessions for infrastructure development over the past 25 years.

To the extent possible, I have endeavoured to relay the facts as they have been reported, and to be fair and objective, particularly when describing projects which have not proceeded quite according to plan! It is from those occasions, however, that one learns how to avoid mistakes in the future.

That said, one of the difficulties has been that many of the details of specific project finance or PPP deals remain confidential to the parties involved. Furthermore, given most deals' complexity, there is usually more than one version of what the 'true' facts are about a particular deal! Pardon, in advance, to those who disagree with my assumptions and interpretations of events.

There are two principles, however, that I have stood by over the years, and which I commend:

- Learn when to say "no"! Project promoters are naturally optimistic, and as a financier one has a responsibility to sort out the jewels from the chaff. A better proposal might cross your desk next week; and
- Enjoy the experience. Take time off to travel to where a proposed project is to be implemented. Understand the project promoter's aims and objectives, and the culture within which the project is to be implemented. Infrastructure deals have to be seen to benefit local populations. Successful projects are, indeed, partnerships.

Martin Blaiklock
July 2017

Sources

The basic material for this book has been derived from training courses on infrastructure and energy project finance undertaken by the author over the past seven years in over 40 countries.

With respect to project descriptions, the information has either been gathered from public sources or derived from the author's direct experience. The main public sources have been as follows.

Publications:

- *Project Finance,* a monthly business magazine published by Euromoney Institutional Investor plc; and
- *Project Finance International,* a fortnightly business magazine published by Thomson Reuters.

Topical reports:

- UK National Audit Office Reports (www.nao.gov.uk);
- UK Parliamentary Committee Reports (www.parliament.uk); and
- Reports by ratings agencies Standard & Poor's, Fitch and Moody's.

Internet sources, in particular:

- www.hm-treasury.gov.uk;
- www.ebrd.com;
- www.imf.org;
- www.partnerships.vic.gov.au;
- www.world-nuclear.org; and
- www.worldbank.org/icsid (regarding international arbitration).

In describing projects which have been undertaken or implemented, the author has made 'best efforts' to report the facts as fairly and, to his knowledge, as accurately and objectively as possible.

However, as project financings are highly detailed and complex transactions, and many such deals are cloaked by confidentiality agreements, it is inevitable that some commentators will have differing views or opinions as to facts and events. Nevertheless, any such differences that do arise will hopefully not undermine the arguments presented in the text.

Glossary

Commonly used acronyms

Acronym	Description	Explanation and purpose
ADSCR	Average debt service cover ratio	A measure of the capacity of a borrower to service debt over a period
BAFO	Best and final offer	Part of the bidding process
BLT	Build, lease and transfer	Concession type
BOO	Build, own, operate	Concession type
BOOT	Build, own, operate, transfer	Concession type
BOT	Build, own and transfer	Concession type
CERs	Carbon emission reductions	'Carbon credits' as used in the renewable energy sector
CfD	Contract for differences	Contract between two parties (buyer and seller) where the seller agrees to pay the buyer the difference between the price of an asset (eg, electricity) when the contract is struck and the market price at specific future date(s). If the difference is negative, the buyer pays the seller the difference, and vice versa. By agreement, the strike price may be adjusted over time by inflation.

continued on next page

Acronym	Description	Explanation and purpose
CP	Conditions precedent	The contractual conditions which must apply before a contract becomes effective
DBFO	Design, build, finance and operate	A type of PPP concession used, on occasion, for road projects
DBFM	Design, build, finance and maintain	A type of PPP concession used, on occasion, for road projects
DSCR	Debt service cover ratio	A measure of the capacity of a borrower to service debt at a specific date
DSRA	Debt service reserve account	An account, kept in trust for the borrower, to cover debt service costs, at least in the short term, arising from future unforeseen events
EBITDA	Earnings before interest, tax and debt amortisation	A measure of the ability of cash flows generated to cover fixed cost
ECA	Export credit agency	Governmental support schemes to support national exports of goods and services
EFW	Energy from waste	Renewable energy
EOI	Expressions of interest	An initial stage in the bidding process
EPC	Engineering, procurement and construction (contract)	Description of a construction contract
FBC	Full business case	Comprehensive feasibility or business report

continued on next page

Acronym	Description	Explanation and purpose
FIT	Feed-in tariff	The price paid by a buyer for (renewable) energy generated
FM	This means either: * Facilities management; or * *Force majeure*	The first interpretation for this acronym refers to the contract for managing accommodation-type PPP concessions. The second interpretation refers to unforeseen events, under a contract.
GHG	Greenhouse gases	Gas emissions referred to in relation to renewable energy in particular
IFI	International financial institution	Multilateral international development banks
ILOC	Irrevocable letter of credit	A form of bank guarantee
InsRA	Insurance reserve account	An account, kept in trust for the borrower, to cover project insurance costs, at least in the short term, arising from future unforeseen events
IPO	Initial public offering (market sale of shares)	Issue of shares on a stock exchange
IPP	Independent power producer	Private power generation project
IRR	Internal rate of return	A measure of profitability
JV	Joint venture	A type of corporate structure
LLC	Limited liability company	A type of corporate structure
LLCR	Loan life cover ratio	A measure of the capacity of a project's cash flow projections to cover debt service costs over the project's life

continued on next page

Acronym	Description	Explanation and purpose
MRA	Maintenance reserve account	An account, kept in trust for the borrower, to cover project maintenance costs, at least in the short-term, arising from future unforeseen events
NPV	Net present value	The value of a cash flow expressed in today's prices
OBC	Outline business case	Part of the bidding process
PE	Private equity (funds)	Type of investor capital
PERM	Project early repayment mechanism	A mechanism, imposed by lenders, to provide borrowers with an incentive to repay a loan earlier than originally agreed
PFI	Private finance initiative	Type of UK PPP
PIC	Public interest company	Not-for-profit enterprise
PIM	Project information memorandum	A document providing a comprehensive description of a proposed project
PPA	Power purchase agreement	Sales contract for a power project
PPP	Public-private partnership	A concession awarded to a private party to invest in assets and to deliver a public service for a fixed period
PSC	Public sector comparator	The present value of the costs of undertaking an investment in public service assets and delivering therewith a public service, as an alternative to a PPP concession

continued on next page

Acronym	Description	Explanation and purpose
PV	Present value	The value of assets expressed in today's prices
RFP	Request for proposals	Initial stage of a bidding process
RO	Renewables obligation	A unit of subsidy provided by the UK government to support renewable energy projects
ROC	Renewables obligation certificates	The certificate representing the unit of subsidy provided by the UK government in support of renewable energy projects
SOE	State-owned enterprise	Type of corporate structure for the project company
SPC	Special purpose company	A company with a specific purpose (ie, to build and operate a project)
SPV	Special purpose vehicle	Alternative name for SPC
SWF	Sovereign wealth funds	National investment funds owned and controlled by the host government
VfM	Value for money	A measure of the value of an asset or contract to the public or investor

continued on next page

Commonly used phrases

Phrases	Description
Assignment	Transfer of rights over project assets
Availability	Ability of a PPP project to provide a service
Bankable	A (project finance or PPP) proposal acceptable to lenders
Benchmarking	Comparison with similar activities in another area or sector
Cascade	Agreed priority for cash flow allocation or payment
Cash sweep	Use of surplus cash to pre-pay debt, instead of distributing such cash to investors as dividends
Concession	Provision of a (PPP) service for a fixed period, after which the project assets revert to the state
Capacity charge	Payment made to the (project finance or PPP) service provider for making capacity available for use
Deficiency agreement	Undertaking to make up shortfalls if funds are insufficient to service debt
Dividend stop ratio	A level of DSCR below which dividends cannot be paid
Equity bridge	A (junior or subordinated) loan provided during construction as an injection of equity
Equity kicker	A right for lenders to acquire equity in the project company at a later date
Escrow account	A bank account held in trust for the project company (the beneficiary)
Financial close	When all commercial and financial contracts are signed and conditions precedent met

continued on next page

Phrases	Description
Hard PERM/ hard bullet	Long-term loan with increasing margins, but if refinancing not executed by an early date, then default arises, and lenders can confiscate assets
Hell-or-high water Take-or-pay	Contractual commitment to pay whether or not the goods or service are delivered
Life cycle	Period of PPP concession or project from start to finish
Limited liability partnership	Company where partners are liable in proportion to the money that they have invested
Limited/non-recourse	The (limits of) liability that a parent company assumes to underpin obligations and commitments of the project company
Merchant	(Power sector) projects/PPPs operating in a deregulated or open market
Offtake	Output from sales contract or service delivered
Reserve cover ratio	Similar to LLCR, but taken over the life of the reserves (eg, oil/gas projects)
Reserve tail	Proven reserves after all debt has been repaid
Soft PERM/soft bullet	Long-term loan maturity with increasing interest rate margin, plus cash sweeps; possibly 100% sweep after a few years
Unitary charge	Periodic PPP payment for service provided (eg, monthly availability payment)
Wrapped bonds	Credit-enhanced bonds guaranteed by a credit insurance company such as a US monoline insurance company

Part 1: Principles

Part 1 starts out by defining what is meant by 'infrastructure' and its relationship with public services, and describes the essential building blocks, or features, which must be put in place for a successful and sustainable financing to be achieved.

In particular, Part 1 covers:

- how the use of private capital has been harnessed to fund infrastructure over recent decades, and the context of public-private partnerships (PPP);
- the advantages and disadvantages of the financial structures used to fund infrastructure;
- how governments should choose to harness private capital, and when not;
- the evaluation of project risk, or uncertainty, and its impact on funding structures;
- the sources of capital available for funding infrastructure: terms and conditions;
- the quantitative criteria and analysis used for assessing value for money of available project options;
- the legal and contractual framework, within which the technical, commercial and financial conditions and requirements are reflected to achieve financial close; and
- the commercial and financial procedures to be adopted in the preparation and implementation of infrastructure projects.

What is infrastructure?

1. Introduction and context

'Infrastructure' can have a number of definitions and interpretations.

In the context of this book, 'infrastructure' has been assumed to mean the underlying framework of fixed assets required to deliver a public service.

Within that interpretation, however, exist a number of grey areas, in particular with regard to what constitutes a 'public service'.

In most economies, services such as power, transportation, water, health, education, and municipal and governmental administration are seen as essential public services which the economy and population require for sustaining economic growth and development.

As these services are key to the well-being of the economy, a public interest requirement will inevitably underpin them such that they must, at least, achieve acceptable standards and quality of service, and represent value for money.

Alternatively, if the public are paying directly for the service provided (eg, for a toll road), the tariffs charged must represent acceptable value to users, otherwise users will go elsewhere. In this context, such services are usually controlled by the imposition of a regulatory regime under which service providers are licensed, and tariff levels are determined by a regulator which monitors and ensures that the standard and quality of service are maintained.

It is thus immediately apparent that the delivery of public services, whatever the boundaries of one's definition, will always be made against the backdrop of subjective, and not solely objective, criteria and judgements. Political influence and, possibly, interference is never far away.

In addition, some services may be deemed marginal in some countries and essential in others (eg, tourism facilities or sports stadiums). Similarly, in some sectors, such as telecommunications, the mode, or technology, of delivery of a specific public service (eg, for mobile phones) may change so rapidly that investment in fixed assets is very short term and could be deemed as a 'current', as opposed to 'capital', expenditure. By contrast, some components of the delivery of such services may be deemed as arguably 'long term' (eg, mobile phone masts) and therefore investment in such assets is treated as 'infrastructure'.

A third marginal infrastructure project type can be found in pipelines, which may be both constructed and operated for one dedicated user or beneficiary, or alternatively built and operated with open access – that is, available for use by third-party customers or beneficiaries. Pipeline financing, therefore, has many of the characteristics of infrastructure project funding, whichever its type, and therefore has been included here in the definition of 'infrastructure'.

In the table below, project investments are identified either as regulated (ie public services) or non-regulated (ie projects operating in open and competitive markets).

Figure 1.1: Project types

Regulated (public services, some of which may be monopolies)	
Sector	**Description**
Air transport	• Airports • Air traffic control (ATC)
Land transport	• Roads • Rail, metros and light rail (LRT) • Tunnels and bridges • Bus lanes
Municipal and government	• Schools, hospitals, offices • Defence • Municipal and waste management
Oil and gas pipelines	• Oil/gas pipelines: open access
Ports	• Container ports/terminals • Bulk handling/oil terminals • Cruise terminals
Water industry	• Water treatment and desalination • Irrigation
Non-regulated (projects operating in competitive markets)	
Sector	**Description**
Oil, gas and mining	• Exploration and development • Single-user pipelines
Process industries	• Cement, steel, aluminium • Petrochemicals and refineries • Agro-industries

continued on next page

Property	• Hotels, tourism and stadiums • Offices and housing
Telecommunications	• Satellites • Mobile phones • Broadband infrastructure

Source: author

The prime focus of this book is on the regulated projects listed above, which embrace infrastructure assets for whatever public service. Often such projects may, in the event, be in the form of public-private partnerships (PPP), but the underlying aim of the venture will be the same – namely, the creation of public service assets and delivery of a public service. On occasion, reference will be made in this book to projects in the non-regulated sector, when lessons can be learnt.

The fact is that the underlying financing structures for projects of both generic types, regulated and non-regulated, are largely similar. It is purely the internal balances within those structures that differ.

2. Recent history

Infrastructure project financing and PPP are, in essence, no recent phenomena. In the early 1800s a number of toll roads, turnpikes, railways and canals were funded as PPP-type concessions through the issue of shares to the public.

In 1854–59, the Suez Canal was funded using equity/shareholder funds, raised through a public issue to cover 51% of the costs, the balance coming primarily from the Egyptian government. This was then followed by a similar funding mechanism for the Panama Canal in 1878, although that project was overtaken by technical and environmental problems, leading to eventual completion being achieved only with the help of US government money. Similarly, many railway companies funded developments throughout Europe and North America by raising funds – debt or bonds, and equity – from investors.

Unfortunately, by the early 20th century many such projects had cost the investors dearly, so governments had to step in to fill the breach for investment in essential transportation infrastructure.

For the first part of the 20th century, infrastructure projects were largely funded by governments, or by public utilities as corporate financings. Developments thereafter in the second half of the 20th century followed differing paths in North America, and Europe and the rest of the world (see Figure 1.2).

3. History – Europe and the rest of the world (excluding North America)

In the first half of the 20th century, infrastructure projects outside North America were funded either using funds directly from the government's budget, or using loans raised against government guarantees. This process was seen as quick and straightforward. Even today, a large portion of investment in infrastructure is still funded this way.

Figure 1.2: History of infrastructure project finance

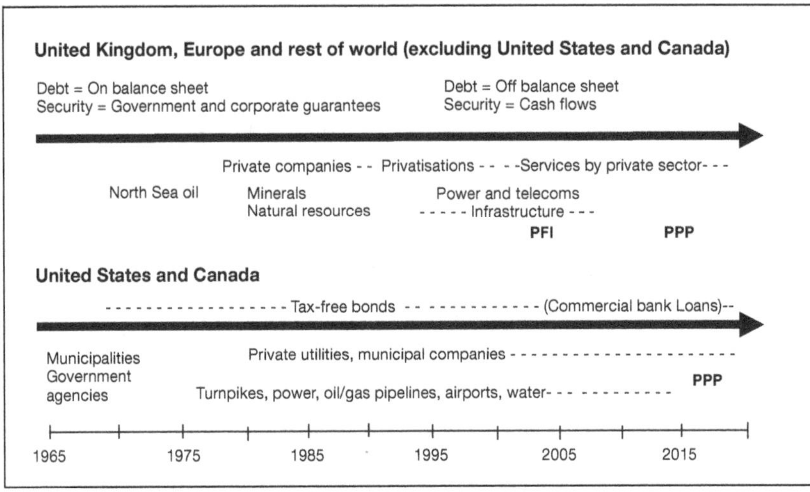

Source: author

The same applies to the industrial and commercial sectors, too. Much of the investment in capital assets by the large multinationals was funded through balance sheet or corporate debt financings, rather than using complex cash flow-based mechanisms. Indeed, this characteristic still applies today.

By the mid-1960s, North Sea oil and gas resources were beginning to be found and developed. Initially, the developers of such projects were large multinational oil companies, which funded these projects using the strength of their balance sheets (ie 'on balance sheet'). Over time, the governments around the North Sea wished to introduce competition, so licences were offered to smaller companies, often in consortium with the larger developers. However, the smaller companies did not necessarily have the balance sheet strength enjoyed by their partners, so struggled to raise their portion of the project funding required.

Faced with this problem, City bankers came up with the concept of raising the debt required against the security provided by the cash flows that the projects were going to generate. After all:

- the demand and price for oil and gas in the European market were relatively stable and predictable;
- the technology of extracting oil and gas from under the sea was well understood and within experience;
- the companies involved with constructing, completing and operating the projects were substantial and experienced; and
- lenders could take security not only over the project assets (ie drilling and production rigs) during the period when their loans were outstanding (ie not fully repaid), but also over the oil and gas reserves in the ground which as yet had not been extracted.

Cash flow financing was reborn!

Before long, as more deals were implemented as above, the same technique was applied to natural resources – namely, iron ore, zinc or copper mines. Furthermore, not only were commercial banks involved as lenders, but also, in time, development banks (international financial institutions or IFIs) and export credit agencies (ECAs) were prepared to lend on such terms too. However, such deals were between private sector industrial companies and their bankers, so quite often the terms and conditions remained confidential to the parties.

After some years, particularly in the United Kingdom, government policies were moving towards more private sector participation in the delivery of public services. Margaret Thatcher's government privatised the telecoms, power, water, airports and ports sectors, so that any new investment in these sectors had to be undertaken as private sector deals. Projects such as the Channel Tunnel (Eurotunnel), the Dartford Bridge and others were brought forward. In Southeast Asia a number of toll roads were promoted as build, operate and transfer (BOT) or build, operate, own and transfer (BOOT) projects, with others also following suit, for instance in Turkey and Mexico, with mixed success.

By the early 1990s over 20 countries were considering the use of private capital for investment in public service assets, but there remained many question marks over the value for money generated by such deals and their public acceptability.

In the United Kingdom, such deals were often termed as 'private finance initiatives' (PFIs) – which today might be described as PPPs – and a specialised unit in Her Majesty's Treasury was set up to pioneer and sponsor the mechanism throughout government. Indeed, for any investment over a specific value (eg, £20 million), the privately funded or PFI route had to be considered by all UK government ministries or agencies against the alternative of using public money (see further the chapter on government options).

There was an added potential advantage of such PFI-type deals in that, suitably structured, the financial obligations for the host government could be kept 'off balance sheet', which offered some attraction for those responsible for government budgets. However, such off balance sheet funding is tantamount, in effect, to using a credit card – and we all know how easy it is to overspend on credit cards.

When the Labour party came to power in the United Kingdom in 1997, a number of PFI-type deals were either operational or in the pipeline. While the new government was attracted by this concept for the procurement of public service assets, it felt that a name change was needed and the term 'public-private partnership', or 'PPP', emerged.

Taken literally, this is, however, a misnomer. The underlying framework of any PPP transaction is contractual: when there is a dispute, usually under such a framework there is a winner and a loser, with not much sharing or 'partnering' in the outcomes. Nevertheless, the term 'PPP' remains fixed and, superficially at least, the name and concept are very attractive for politicians.

Now between 80 and 90 countries worldwide are developing, implementing and operating PPP-type deals for capital investment in assets for the delivery of public services, some with more success than others. In the United Kingdom, PPP deals are still often referred to as 'PFIs', but the differentiation between acronyms and types is often blurred. Other countries now use different acronyms, such as 'P3' or '3P' in North America and 'PSP' in Southeast Asia. Generically, all these structures, however, are PPPs.

The PPP concept has taken hold not only in developed economies, but also in emerging markets, sometimes with negative effects. After nearly 25 years of global experience of the mechanism, one can arrive at two key conclusions:

- Infrastructure PPP deals are not free – their cost is merely delayed. Like credit cards, they allow the beneficiary – the government or taxpayers – to pay for the investment in public service assets at a later date. Unfortunately, as the financial obligations for PPP-type transactions can be kept off balance sheet, outside the watchful eyes of the International Monetary Fund (IMF), some emerging markets' governments have overspent on their PPP credit card. Regrettably, too, the guidelines as to whether any specific PPP is on or off balance sheet are somewhat imprecise and open to abuse, although in recent times the authorities have been tightening up on the interpretation; and
- Those countries which have been using the PPP mechanism as one option for investing in public service assets and have achieved the greatest success are those with either a long-term local capital market or an indigenous raw material (eg, oil or gas) which they can export for hard currency revenues, thereby providing a foreign exchange hedge against revaluations or devaluations of the domestic currency versus world markets.

This conclusion should come as no surprise as:

- PPP infrastructure concessions typically have a lifespan of 20 to 30 years. They are long-term deals;
- the underlying capital assets require a long cost recovery period and need to be funded with long-term debt and equity funding;
- much of the capital cost and, probably, much of the operating costs too, will be denominated in local currency. After all, such PPP concessions are delivering a public service locally; and
- in emerging markets in particular, the only source of long-term funds which can justify and support financial viability of the PPP will be denominated in hard currency.

Hence, any possible foreign currency fluctuation between the local currency and world markets for dollars, euros or yen can have a very significant impact on the PPP project's sustainability and ability to service its debts, in particular.

The conclusion, therefore, is that the development of PPP in any national environment ideally should proceed hand-in-hand with the development of local capital markets – that is, pensions funds and life insurance, among others.

Alternatively, if the country has a hard currency-generating export, then such revenues, often via some form of sovereign wealth fund, can be used as a foreign exchange hedge or buffer against such currency fluctuations, in support of PPP developments.

Here are two examples:

- As mentioned earlier, in the 1990s a number of Southeast Asian countries (eg, Malaysia, Indonesia and Thailand) embarked on PPP-type deals, often called BOOT in those days, particularly for toll highways and power projects. Such PPP projects were built and operated, for a time, quite satisfactorily.

  In the late 1990s recession hit the region. The Thai baht and Indonesian rupiah devalued sharply, putting their PPP deals into jeopardy, in some cases terminally, as it was impossible to increase tariffs to compensate for the devaluation. Malaysia, for its part, weathered the storm thanks to its oil and gas exports, which cushioned the Malaysian ringgit from significant devaluation, thereby protecting PPP-type revenues.

  Similar events have hit PPP-type deals in Argentina, Mexico and some Central European countries, too, over the years. Whereas the underlying PPP concession contracts may include clauses requiring tariff changes in the event of devaluation of the underlying currency, bolstered by international arbitration proceedings to enforce them, it can be politically unacceptable for host governments to impose such tariff rises on their populations.
- By contrast, countries such as South Africa and Chile have enjoyed the benefit of sizeable and long-term local capital markets, which have been available to fund most of such PPP-type deals, thereby avoiding the foreign exchange risks inherent in such funding structures.

4. History – North America

In the early days of the 20th century, the United States was in a similar position to Europe concerning the state and development of its infrastructure services.

After the depression of the 1930s, however, suddenly the demand for investment in new roads, bridges, rail connections, etc, flourished, not least because of the success of the mass-produced cars made by Ford and General Motors. Unfortunately, the municipalities and individual states sponsoring such infrastructure projects were short of funds to build the assets.

In response, the federal government recognised that the potential support for financing such assets over the long term would require participation from the private sector and, in particular, from the life insurance and pension fund industries, where fund managers took both a long- and short-term investment perspective and were seeking profitable, but low risk, investments for their funds.

To make such investments more attractive than those in commercial or industrial companies, investors in infrastructure ventures were not limited by amount and exposure, as for some industrial revenue bonds, and furthermore investors in such bonds did not pay tax on the interest that they received. Thus, states, municipalities, utilities or specific project sponsors could issue long-term bonds in support of infrastructure investments, giving investors this tax-free exemption. Today, we would call such tax-free bonds 'infrastructure bonds', which governments around the world sponsor to support infrastructure development.

A review of the US market for infrastructure developments today show that around 90% of the debt financing comes from this market source (ie, bonds, rather than bank loans). Furthermore, the US bond market, which is at least twice as large in value as any other regional market, can provide more longer-term funding, both in terms of cost to the borrower and maturity, than is available in the commercial banking sector.

With the Canadian market closely linked to the US financial markets, the same characteristic can largely be found in Canada also.

It comes as no surprise, therefore, that the use of PPP as a procurement option for investment in public service assets was slow to take off in the United States compared to other countries, and there remain many US commentators who doubt the real benefits of using PPP in their market.

Canada, by contrast, has been using the PPP mechanism for some years, with seemingly significant success. However, its public service sector has traditionally and proportionally been much larger than in the United States, so the balance sheet benefits of PPP may count more heavily.

By the mid 2000s, the terms and conditions for long-term debt financing between the North American and European markets were quite comparable. However, the onslaught of the 2007–2009 financial crisis and the impact of Basel III on bank lending thereafter have severely curtailed the development of PPP in Europe and most emerging markets. It is only recently that banks have been prepared to lend once more for the long-term periods that PPPs require, even though the bank loans so provided contain embedded incentives for the borrowers to re-finance their debt before maturity.

In North America, the long-term bond markets have largely recovered, and against the backdrop of the good performance of project financed and PPP-type deals through the financial crisis, with few, if any defaults, cheaper, longer-term debt finance is more readily available there than in the rest of the world.

5. What are PPPs?

As inferred earlier, over the past 20 to 25 years the PPP concept has been discussed and promoted widely by governments, politicians, development banks and aid agencies throughout the world. Regrettably, what PPP represents has, at times, been misinterpreted. Figure 1.3 summarises the possible range of private sector participation in the delivery of public services.

The first two columns show short-term contractual arrangements with minimal capital investment. If there is such investment, then the host government provides.

The next two columns describe medium-term contractual arrangements, typically some kind of lease, whether the assets are funded and provided by private sector entities or by government. Such arrangements have prevailed, particularly for vehicles in the public transport sector, for many years, but do not involve fixed or permanent assets.

The final two columns summarise what financiers usually describe as 'PPPs', where the capital investment and risk transfer from the public to private sector are significant, with the funding provided by private sector resources. Usually such arrangements are for a fixed concession period (eg, 20 to 30 years), but on occasion it can be indefinite – that is, until the underlying asset becomes economically unsustainable, for instance for a private power station.

Figure 1.3: The range of PPPs

Type	Services Contract (cleaning)	Management Contract (outsourcing)	Public Lease (buses)	Private Lease (trains)	PPP Concession (motorway) (IPP* + CfD** or FiT***)	'Stand-alone' PPP concession (toll bridge or IPP*)
Asset ownership	Public	Public	Public	Private	Private	Private
Duration	1–3 year	1–5 year	5–12 year	5–12 year	20–30 year	20–30 year (even potentially indefinite)
Capital investment	Public	Public	Limited	Limited	High	High
Risk transfer	Minimal	Low/part	Moderate	Significant	Yes/high	Yes/high
Operation and maintenance risk	Public	Public	Shared	Private	Private	Private
Payment structure	Unit prices	Fees, plus incentives	Operator pays rent to government	Operator receives payment from government for financial costs	Availability payments or guaranteed tariffs	(Regulated) unit payments from customers
Mobilises private capital	No	No	No	Yes	Yes	Yes
Features and issues	Promotes efficiency, but requires underlying legal regime	Promotes efficiency and commitment, but requires underlying legal regime	• Easier than PPP • Public/private conflicts possible	• Easier than PPP • Public/private conflicts possible	• Promotes efficiency and VfM • Complex and time-consuming to arrange • Not for small projects	• Promotes efficiency and VfM • Complex and time-consuming to arrange • Not for small projects

* IPP: Independent power producer ** CfD: Contract for differences *** FiT: Feed-in tariffs

Figure 1.3 differentiates between those PPPs where the user pays and those where a government agency responsible for delivering the service to the public pays a periodic 'availability payment', where 'availability' is measured against fixed performance criteria.

6. Impact of the financial crisis on PPPs

Overall, PPP-type transactions have weathered the financial crisis with few, if any defaults for financial reasons. That does not mean to say that PPPs have not failed, but when they have failed, the reasons have been technical, commercial or political rather than the result of the underlying funding mechanism.

One can summarise the impact of the financial crisis on PPPs and infrastructure as follows:

- The number of commercial banks actively supporting infrastructure and PPP-type deals is today probably half the number doing so before the financial crisis.
- The cost (ie, the lending margin over base rate) of commercial bank loans for infrastructure and PPP-type deals is approximately twice as much as before the financial crisis.
- The availability of commercial bank loans with maturity greater than 10 years, which many infrastructure and PPP-type deals require to be sustainable, has also been significantly reduced. The imposition of Basel III and subsequent regulations have reinforced this aspect for most banks.
- To overcome this lack of long-term debt maturity, many banks support project early repayment mechanisms (PERMs), which are loans with increasing margin over time, such that by years 8–10 the loan becomes increasingly expensive for the borrower, incentivising the borrower to refinance its debt.

However, some lenders are nervous about applying such mechanisms, as they fear the consequences of any market conditions in years 8–10 not allowing a refinancing. If default arises in such circumstances, the lenders will claim their security (ie, take over the assets), which in the infrastructure and PPP sector may be a politically sensitive action to take. Lenders may be reluctant to take such action in the event. Indeed, 'cash sweeps' seem to be a preferable and alternative loan covenant with similar outcomes.

The consequence of the above has been that, particularly in emerging markets, development banks and ECAs have had to step up as the main source of long-term funds, in an attempt to plug the lending gap left by commercial lenders.

- Balanced against the above part-withdrawal by commercial lenders from the sector, the pension fund and life insurance industry has become alert to the potential investment opportunities in the infrastructure/public services sector, as has long been the case in North America. However, the mode of bond market participation is not an exact fit into the gap left by the banks.

  Typically, pension fund and life insurance investment managers will invest in corporate and project bonds (ie, PPPs and infrastructure) only post-project completion. This is due to the fact that bond investors and pension fund managers have both a short- and long-term perspective, as their customers are either already retired and are drawing their pensions today, or younger, employed people who will not need a pension for some years. Hence, pension funds need income 'today', generated from interest on bonds invested, to satisfy the existing pension holders.

Unfortunately, project bond issuers will not be in a position to pay interest until the project is completed and operational, generating revenues. Accordingly, there is a mismatch.

Ideally, the debt portion of project funding should derive from commercial loans, which are flexible in their use (ie, 'drawdowns'), and then, on project completion, such loans are refinanced with bond-type funding. To date, the perfect refinancing mechanism which can be put in place at the outset of project funding has not been achieved, although the two generic funding sources are getting closer! Recently, the debt for a PPP highway transaction in the Netherlands was provided by bank loans, which, on project completion, was 80% refinanced with pension-type bonds committed at the outset of project funding.

- Each year Moody's publishes a review of defaults on project bonds, covering all sectors – many of them US infrastructure issues – and these have shown that such bonds have performed well throughout the financial crisis and since.

  In this context, it should be mentioned that many of the US infrastructure project bonds issued in recent years have enjoyed the revenues from an existing and operational asset or public service during the construction period. Hence, the generally successful performance of such bonds has been seen throughout the financial crisis.
- Lastly, just as commercial banks are being constrained by Basel III in providing infrastructure projects with long-term loans, the same issue could also arise for the project insurance industry in due course.

Here are two anecdotes:

- Following the financial crisis, many economies suffered economic downturns, and governments sought to provide employment for their workers by investment in infrastructure projects, including PPPs.

  However, *prima facie*, under the Basel III guidelines lenders to infrastructure and PPP-type transactions have to make the same kind of risk assessment for determining the weightings, or provisions, against possible losses that they will have to make in their balance sheets as for corporate lending in general.

  Unfortunately, under Basel III infrastructure and PPP-type projects, which need long-term funding, seemingly receive no particular exemptions in this respect, notwithstanding their seemingly good track record.

  On enquiry with the Basel Committee at the Bank of International Settlements, Switzerland, it is understood that banks can, if they deem it appropriate for the underlying contractual structure for an infrastructure or PPP-type deal, adjust the weightings that they have to make in their balance sheets to reflect the underlying credit risk, although how large or how little an adjustment might be acceptable is not explicit.

Curiously, the Basel guidelines for such assessments are dated June 2006 and have not been updated following the financial crisis, notwithstanding the importance and demand for new investment in infrastructure by many governments.

- Shortly after the financial crisis, the author was assisting a client with the planning and preparations for raising the debt required for a UK PPP-type project. One of the candidate lenders was a bank which had unfortunately collapsed as a result of the crisis, and had had to be rescued by its national government.

  Following the governmental rescue, a new CEO was appointed. Within days, he employed a consultant to review all the bank's departments' performances. Within four weeks, the results were available: all the bank's departments had failed somewhat, except the project finance and PPP department, which had had no defaults.

  The conclusion drawn was that, although infrastructure project finance and PPP-type deals were complex and long term, and deal flow was erratic, the underlying credit quality of the lending was good and the CEO decided that the bank should do more!

  As mentioned above, today nearly 90 countries around the globe are actively pursuing and developing PPP-type financings for investment in infrastructure and public service assets in their countries.

  So, the anecdote above reflects a more general reality. Infrastructure project finance deals are complex and time consuming to prepare and implement, but rarely default. Part of that is due to the care and attention to detail that practitioners apply, and the due diligence undertaken by financiers in completing the transactions.

Financial structures

1. The project company

However a project is to be funded, it is common practice to set up a special purpose project company or 'vehicle', whether as a limited liability company, partnership or joint venture, to undertake the project. This assists in ring-fencing, or controlling, the inherent project risks and uncertainties, and gives financiers, both investors and lenders, some comfort that the funding that they provide will be used to implement the intended project – and not diverted away to some other purpose.

Figure 2.1: Special purpose company structure

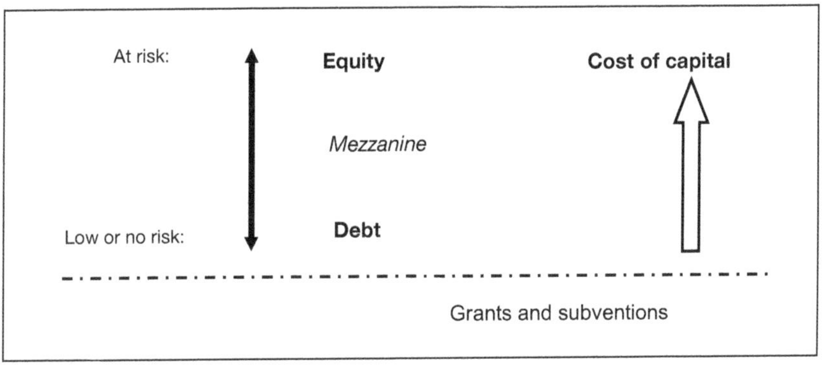

Source: author

Typically, such project company will comprise a component contribution by shareholder equity (ie, risk capital) and a component of debt (ie, low risk, or no risk, capital).

The lenders providing the debt will take security over the project company's assets. Thus, in the event that the project company goes into liquidation or is declared bankrupt, the lenders will have first call on the company's assets. If, after paying off any outstanding debts, there are any assets or value in the company left, then such assets or value will be for the shareholders.

Given that the lenders are taking lower risk, their funding will be cheaper than that provided by shareholder equity. In other words, the cost of equity capital will be higher than debt.

Accordingly, project developers, when assembling the funding for the project company, will seek to maximise the amount of debt that can be raised as it will be cheaper than equity. How much debt can be raised will depend on the assessment made by lenders as to how risky, or uncertain, the project company's business is. The higher the risk, the more equity will be required proportionately in the project company's funding structure, and vice versa.

As relatively low risk businesses, infrastructure and public services such as public-private partnership (PPP) concessions can often command debt-to-equity ratios of 70:30 in emerging markets, and 80:20 in more developed economies. In the heyday of the early 2000s, before the financial crisis, debt-to-equity ratios of 90:10 or even higher were seen in some markets. In themselves, they perhaps tell a tale.

Indeed, a review of some projects which have failed financially, such as the Channel Tunnel, reveals that quite often the initial debt-to-equity ratio, or leverage, was too high. In other words, the funding contained too much debt proportionately, reflecting either over-enthusiasm by lenders to lend, or poor risk assessment by lenders. Some might argue that the inherent incentive schemes underpinning bankers' salaries might also have had a role to play in such scenarios.

On occasion, particularly in emerging markets or in sectors which enjoy wide public support (eg, renewable energy projects), the project company may have access to cheap or concessionary (ie, subsidised) funding, or even grant monies. *Prima facie*, such funding might be attractive, but inevitably it comes with terms and conditions attached that the project developers must review to ensure that they are acceptable for the successful implementation of the project and its subsequent operations.

In the early stages of project development, it is normal for the evaluation of the inherent risks and rewards which a project proposal might generate to be based on a simple project structure comprising just equity and debt. By the time many such projects reach financial close, however, the funding structure often takes on a 'wedding cake' structure with layers of subordinated debt, debentures and shareholder loans representing some of the shareholders' equity. Such instruments are usually designed to improve lender returns and to optimise the taxation status of the project company, thereby benefiting shareholders as well.

Lastly, in some sectors – particularly when social issues such as health, education or safety are present (eg, in certain types of transport project) – governments have preferred to set up project companies on a non-profit making basis as public interest companies (PICs). In such cases, the funding is provided 100% by debt and no dividends are paid – in effect, there are no shareholders.

Examples of such structures can be found in Scotland in recent years under the Scottish Futures Trust programme, which has been particularly applied for schools and social housing PPPs. Some commentators opine that these structures remove the incentive for the project developer to perform, to build the assets to specification and to deliver the underlying PPP service. However, where the construction and operations of the underlying assets are simple and straightforward, with minimal uncontrollable risks, such structures may have some public and political merit.

Another example can be found in Wales where Glas Cymru, a not-for-profit utility, provides water supply and waste water management services, and arguably enjoys the best credit rating of all the United Kingdom's privatised water companies.

A further good example of a PIC is NavCanada, the Canadian air traffic control (ATC) system, created out of the Canadian provinces' ATC systems in 1995. The company has no shareholders, although institutionally it is answerable to the Ministry of Finance. It has to achieve an agreed annual return on capital, but is free to set tariffs at whatever level is required to achieve that target. The directors of the company cannot be elected officials or employees of government, significant ATC customers or equipment suppliers. Lastly, the company raises whatever funding it requires through the North American debt, mostly bond, market, effectively securitising future revenues, without any guarantee from the Canadian government. NavCanada enjoys a high investment grade rating accordingly.

Given the combination of technical and public safety issues related to NavCanada's business, this model certainly has merits, as well as the flexibility to adjust to changing market conditions.

2. Funding structures – government guarantees

Historically, the conventional structure for developing infrastructure projects has been through debt funding, with the support of government guarantees (see Figure 2.2).

Figure 2.2: Government guarantee structure

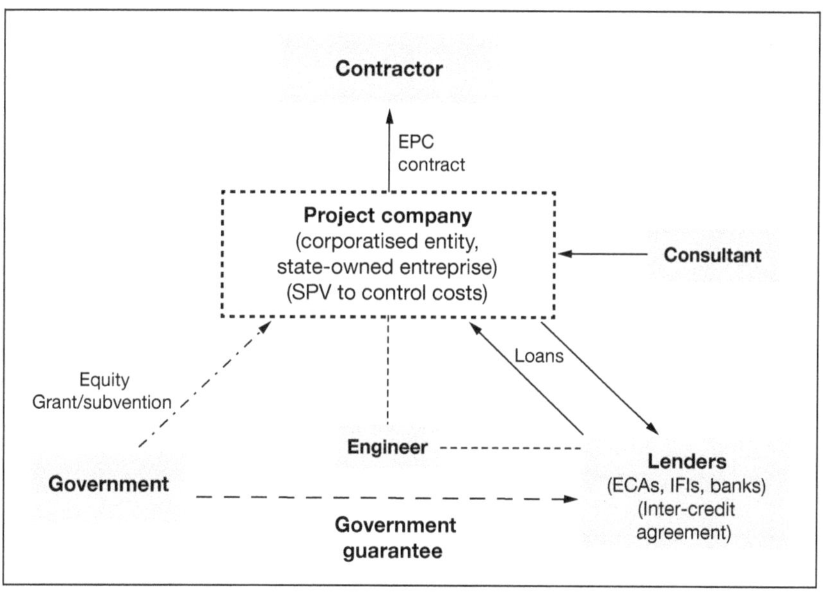

Source: author

The project company, which will be a corporatised entity (possibly a state-owned enterprise) will prepare, usually with the assistance of a consultant, an engineering, procurement and construction (EPC) contract, and award it to a contractor to build the project (infrastructure) assets.

To fund the construction, the project company will have access to both loans from development banks (international financial institutions or IFIs), export credit agencies (ECAs) and commercial banks, plus equity from the host government, as shareholder. Assuming that the project is completed and the project company operates the assets effectively, the project company will duly pay interest on, and repay, the loans. In the event that the project company is unable to service the debt, for whatever reason, the lenders could call on the government guarantee to repay the outstanding debt.

Such guarantees are sometimes called 'sovereign guarantees' and sometimes 'government guarantees'. The difference is primarily legal. A 'sovereign guarantee' enjoys the ratification of said guarantee by the host government's parliament, whereas a 'government guarantee' may be authorised by either the minister of finance, under the delegated authority from the host government, or parliament. In the world of project finance, the difference is minor and may have an impact only when IFIs are part of the funding package.

Notwithstanding the presence of the government guarantee, lenders may be nervous, however, to provide 100% of the amounts needed to pay the contractor under the EPC contract. For example, ECAs are constrained to fund only 85% of any export contracts. The theory is that if the government injects some equity, in whatever form, into the project company as prime shareholder, this will incentivise the government to ensure that the project is a commercial and economic success, thereby repaying its debts.

Lastly, it will be noted that the lenders enjoy the advice and support of an engineer. When the EPC contractor presents an invoice to the project company for payment, the project company may need to use, or drawdown, from debt to make such payment. Assuming that all conditions precedent for using the loan(s) have been achieved, then the engineer will check, on behalf of the lenders, that the work represented by the invoice has, in fact, been executed and will validate the invoice, thereby facilitating the use of the loan(s). The engineer's fees will be met as part of the fees attached to the loan(s).

The question, therefore, arises as to how strong, or weak, the underlying government guarantee is.

There is no perfect system for making such an assessment. It comprises both objective and subjective criteria. It is also reliant upon the quality of the underlying statistical data on the government, as guarantor, and its economy. Typically, the answers sought include those outlined below.

Economic measures:

- What are the historic growth patterns and future forecasts of the gross domestic product?
- What is the structure of the economy?
- Is the economy market-oriented, or a centralised economy?
- If a market economy, is it open or closed?
- What is the balance and nature of imports and exports?
- What is the balance of payments record of the government?

Financial measures:

- What is the level of national debt?
- What is the structure of such debt? Long or short term?
- Have there been annual budget deficits?
- What is the ability of the government to service its debt?
- What is the government's record on tax collection?
- Has the government a sovereign credit rating (eg, from Standard & Poor's)?
- Has the government managed the economy efficiently?

Political measures:

- What are the government's aims, policies and agendas?
- What is the timetable for future elections?
- Has the country a history of political stability?

3. Funding structures – corporate guarantees

Project funding structures where the debt is supported by corporate guarantees are in many respects very similar to those where the debt is support by government guarantees (see Figure 2.3).

Figure 2.3: Corporate guarantee structure

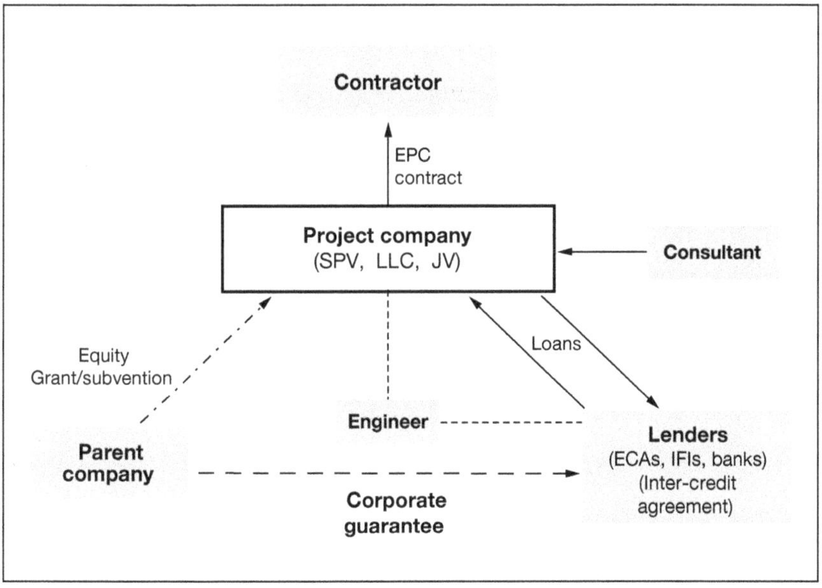

Source: author

The relationships between the participants are similar to those described for a government guarantee. The key question, though, relates to the strength of the corporate guarantee.

Many criteria and measures, both objective and subjective, can be used to assess the business and creditworthiness of a corporate guarantor. First, one might typically consider the points below from the guarantor's accounts.

Revenue analysis:

- Are company sales committed and occur on a regular basis, or is the company operating in a competitive, ie, uncertain, market?
- Are profit margins similar to those of other companies in the sector?
- What is the guarantor's market reputation and track record?
- How strong is its marketing ability?
- Is there close control and monitoring of revenues?
- Are sales made to repeat and/or bulk purchase customers?
- How are sales executives incentivised? Are they paid on a commission basis?

Production analysis:

- Are the production facilities modern and efficient?
- Is production capacity adequate for their business sales?
- Is there any spare production capacity?

Labour issues:

- Is the guarantor company over-staffed compared to sector peers?
- Is the guarantor highly unionised?

Company development assessment:

- Does the guarantor company allocate adequate funding for research and development?
- Have the projects that the guarantor has undertaken in the past been successful?
- Does the guarantor have the resources to undertake investments?

Financial evaluation:

- What are the current working capital needs of the guarantor company and are they met?
- What is its current borrowing structure? Is it over-borrowed?
- What is the level of debtors compared to collections?

A number of quantitative assessments might also be undertaken using data from the guarantor's accounts:

Gearing or leverage*	= balance sheet debt v equity
Debt interest cover ratio	= cash flow (EBITDA**)/interest
Debt service cover ratio	= cash flow (EBITDA)/interest and loan repayment
Return on capital	= cash flow (EBITDA)/(equity and debt)
Current ratio	= current assets/current liabilities (eg, >1.2–5)
Quick ratio	= 'cash' assets/current liabilities (eg, >1.1)
Earnings per share	= after-tax profits/number of shares
Inventory turnover	= (inventory/cost of sales) × 365 (days)
Receivables	= (debtors/sales) × 365 (days)
Investor ratings	= Standard & Poor's, Moody's ratings, if available

[**EBITDA = earnings before interest, tax, depreciation and debt amortisation]
[*Are deferred tax liabilities included as 'indebtedness'?]

Ultimately, the strength, or weakness, of any guarantee offered must be judged with caution and prudence.

Nevertheless, large multinationals often favour this corporate guarantee structure for their projects, because they have the creditworthiness to satisfy lenders, and because the alternative mechanisms available are more complex and time consuming.

In this context, mention should be made of the dangers of using EBITDA as a measure for valuing enterprises.

In recent years, a number of existing, operational state-owned infrastructure or public service assets (eg, ports and airports) have been sold to private investors in many countries. In order to value the underlying assets, a common approach is to:

- identify the EBITDA from the current accounts of the existing operations in the relevant sector;
- compare that with the market value of said assets to derive a multiple for EBITDA for those operations; and
- apply that multiple to the EBITDA identified from the accounts of the target company to arrive at a value of the enterprise.

Alternatively, analysts may:

- identify the current EBITDA from existing operations;
- assess how much debt such EBITDA might support; and
- compare that amount of debt to the existing debt, to arrive at the potential earnings an acquisition might achieve.

Unfortunately, these somewhat simplistic approaches have, on occasion, ended in disappointment for investors: the multiples so derived may be overstated, in some cases by twice what a prudent investor might expect. In particular, in emerging markets comparators may not exist to identify such multiples and, consequently, future prospects of the to-be-acquired businesses have been assessed too optimistically.

Investors, beware!

4. Project finance (cash flow) structures

When government or corporate guarantees are not available to support project debt, then the only alternative is to structure the project such that the inherent cash flows generated by the project service all the debt raised and provide shareholders with adequate dividends for the risks that they take. This is a 'project financing' structure, as shown below.

Figure 2.4: Project finance structure (eg, private power station or IPP)

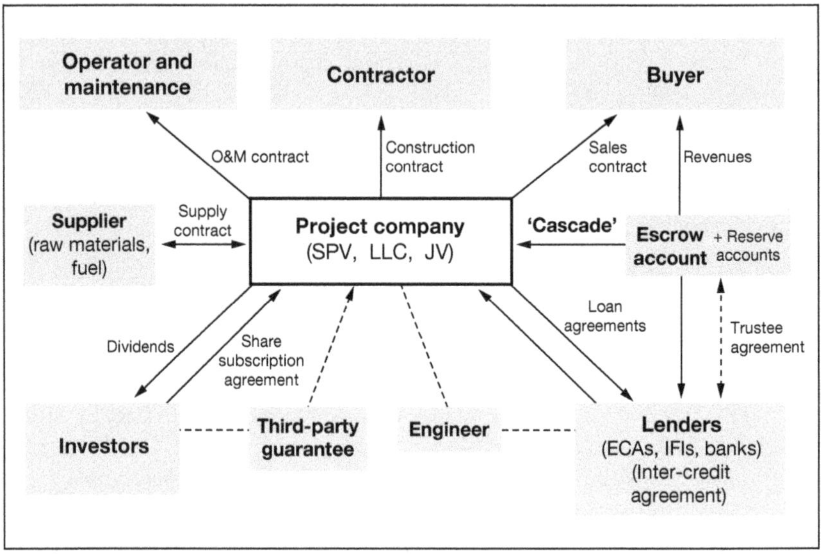

Source: author

The above structure has many similarities to the government/corporate guarantee structures, with the addition of a few contractual relationships.

- The project company is set up with debt and equity; it awards a contract to build the project assets. Payment for that contract will be derived from the debt and equity subscribed to the company.
- However, lenders are risk averse. They wish to ensure that the loans that they provide get repaid. The best way to ensure that this happens is for the project to be built according to specification, cost and timetable, and for operations to be commercially and financially successful. Accordingly, the full commitment of the investors, or shareholders, of the project company is required. Therefore, for the first payments to be made to the contractor, shareholder equity is used first and when that runs out, lenders will allow debt to be disbursed, or drawn down.
- That may appear harsh on investors, particularly for large projects when the construction period may span many years. On such occasions, lenders may accept that, after shareholders' equity is used to pay for, say, the first 10% of project costs, thereafter equity and debt are used, or drawn down, proportionately. However, lenders may require from the shareholders some sort of security with respect to the availability, when called for, of the shareholder equity – usually in the form of an irrevocable letter of credit (ILOC) or bank/corporate guarantee.
- A second issue for lenders will arise if any of the shareholders are financially weak. A key principle of project financing is that all the project funding, both equity and debt, is notionally committed and available at the outset – that is,

at financial close. Quite often, the shareholders in the project company may be a consortium made up of both strong and weak companies. If lenders perceive that any shareholder may not have the committed equity available, when called for, to inject into the project company, lenders may require some form of third-party guarantee, such as an ILOC.

- Once the project construction has been completed, the project moves into the operational phase. Contractual arrangements will have to be put in place to cover the management of operations, the supply of essential materials and other inputs, and arrangements made for the maintenance of the assets. Lenders will have to be satisfied that the project company has made such arrangements, which will ensure the best possible chance that the project will be a financial success so long as the loans are outstanding.
- The project company is now in a position to sell a product or a service to a buyer or customer, which hopefully will pay. Obviously, such buyer(s) has to be creditworthy too. Lenders will like to see some form of contractual arrangements put in place to cover both the volume and price of whatever is sold, for at least as long as their loans remain outstanding. Accordingly, long-term sales contracts are preferred.

  That may not always be possible, however – for instance, if the project company makes products which are sold into a competitive market rather than under contract. In such event, the underlying risks, or uncertainties, in the overall project framework increase, which will be reflected in the incremental costs of finance.
- The buyer receives the product or service, and pays accordingly. However, lenders will wish to ensure that the managers in the project company use the funds received in an appropriate manner, in the best interests of the company, and not for, say, a holiday in the Caribbean, or to buy a fleet of luxury cars for the senior executives.

  Hence, the lenders will set up an escrow, or trustee, account in the name of the project company, into which all revenues are paid. Technically, the money in said account belongs to the project company. However, the company cannot use that money until the lenders are satisfied and all loans have been repaid.
- Such escrow account is often managed by the trustee department of one of the lending banks as the trustee department and the loans department in the bank would operate completely separately.

  The lenders will then instruct the trustee to distribute the revenues received to the project company to meet certain specified costs and in a given priority. This is known as a 'cascade' (see Figure 2.5)
- The first priority for the trustee is to pass back enough funds to the project company to meet ongoing operational and maintenance costs, plus any taxes due – not least so the project company can continue in business.
- The next payment instalment is directed towards paying interest and any financial fees due on the loans.
- The next instalment is used to cover the periodic loan repayments.

Figure 2.5: Cash flow cascade

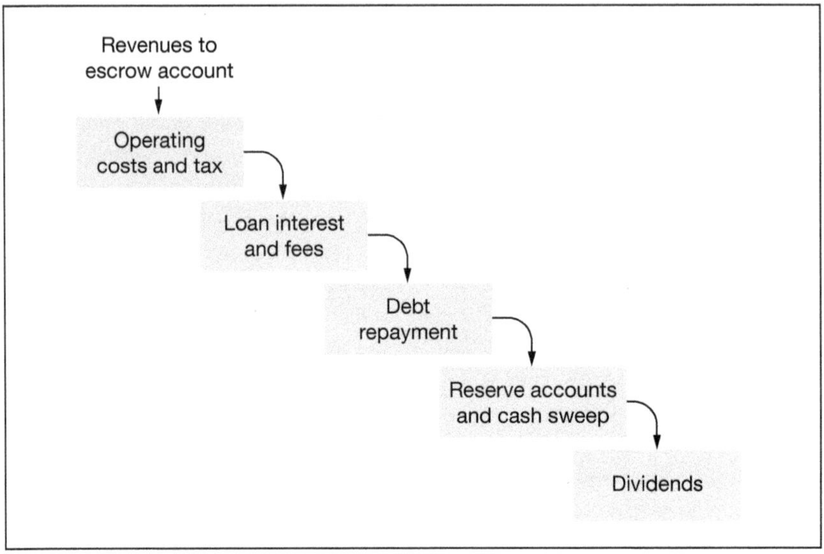

- The next instalment is to be used to top up any reserve accounts and to make early repayments of any loans under a cash sweep, if such condition is part of the loan arrangements.
- Lastly, any surplus cash can be distributed back to the project company to pay dividends to the shareholders.

  Such cascade arrangements are common in project financings in emerging markets, where the project risks may be deemed significant. However, in developed markets lenders may be more trusting in project company managers and their shareholders.
- One can see immediately that this 'project financing' structure is much more complex than the conventional government or corporate guarantee arrangement. Not surprisingly, the time taken to prepare the structure of such deals up to financial close – when all the underlying documents are signed, funding committed and available – is twice as long as via the conventional route.
- Similarly, it costs twice as much to prepare, as many advisers and experts must be paid to check the details. Hence, this funding structure is not cost-effective for small investment projects. It may also not be allowed by the timetable for meeting the service demand.
- With respect to security for lenders, then apart from the cash flows that the project, hopefully, will generate, lenders will also take security over the project assets via covenants in the loan agreement until their loans are repaid, as well as take assignment of bank accounts, shares, etc, in the project company.

  However, if for whatever reason a project-financed deal collapses, then usually the only way that the lenders will get their loans repaid is if remedies are put in place to restore the project back to operations again. To achieve that, the lenders may have to exercise their ownership, or 'step-in', rights, as dictated by the loan covenants.

- One of the main reasons for employing this mechanism, however, lies in the fact that the project structure is stand-alone – that is, it does not, at least in principle, rely on the financial support of a third party to raise and service its finance. Historically, such deals have been described as 'non-recourse'. On those occasions when the support, or part-support, of a third party is required, usually to satisfy lenders' risk aversion – for example, a minimum throughput commitment for a pipeline project – then such project could be described as 'limited recourse'. However, such terms are rarely heard today.
- Given the above, it is clear that such project, suitably structured as above, could be funded without having any financial impact on the project sponsors or shareholders. It is 'off balance sheet'. For many corporates, this may have some advantages. For governments, clearly the benefit could be significant if the government's finances are weak, but so could the risks.

5. PPPs

PPPs are an extension of the project finance structure. The key difference is that, first and foremost, the underlying specification as to what the project company builds and the service to be delivered to customers is defined by a concession agreement, which is, in effect, a licence or a franchise awarded to a private company by the host government.

In the infrastructure and public services sector, such a concession will typically extend over a period of 20 to 30 years.

For lenders, the concession period should be at least as long as any loans that they provide remain outstanding. Terminating a concession when loans remain outstanding is a messy process!

In theory the assets have to be handed back at the concession maturity date to government ownership in the condition that they were built, but the documentation and negotiation arising out of that condition can be complex.

In any event, if the concessionaire has been delivering a good service for 25 or 30 years, why not let it continue? If the concessionaire has failed, or been failing, in any respect during that period, then the concession grantor, or government, will always have had the right to terminate the concession.

Additionally, by the concession's maturity date, the government agency which might otherwise have provided the service, might not exist any more. If so, who is going to operate the assets after the maturity date?

Common sense suggests that the maturity date at least provides an opportunity to renegotiate the terms of the concession and adjust tariffs to reflect circumstances at the time. Such an approach also covers the issue of, for instance, having to buy new equipment in year 27 of a 30-year concession. In such a case, the concessionaire should be empowered to buy for the long term and not for just the subsequent three years, in order to provide best value for government and customers.

An example of this approach was the renegotiation in 2013 of the West Coast Mainline Rail Franchise in the United Kingdom, for the operation of the passenger train service between London Euston and Manchester and the Northwest, probably the busiest and most congested rail connection in the country. Initially, the government attempted to re-assign the franchise through a competitive bidding process, but for a variety of reasons, technical and managerial, that failed. In the end, Virgin Rail, the incumbent franchisee, had its franchise renewed through negotiation. Operating major railway systems is not straightforward and each operator will have its own detailed manuals and managerial procedures. Changing such arrangements without good cause rarely offers value for money.

Some concessions, indeed, have extended for more than 50 years (eg, the United Kingdom's Midlands Expressway toll road). However, not having a maturity date on a concession would be tantamount to the privatisation of a public service, which may be politically unacceptable. The Eurotunnel concession was extended until 2086 – that is, 100 years from the outset – when its funding was renegotiated in 2006!

6. Types of PPP

There are two main generic types of PPP concession (see Figures 2.6 and 2.7). Both are very similar, except for the source of revenues.

Figure 2.6: PPP structure (PPP service delivered to paying customer)

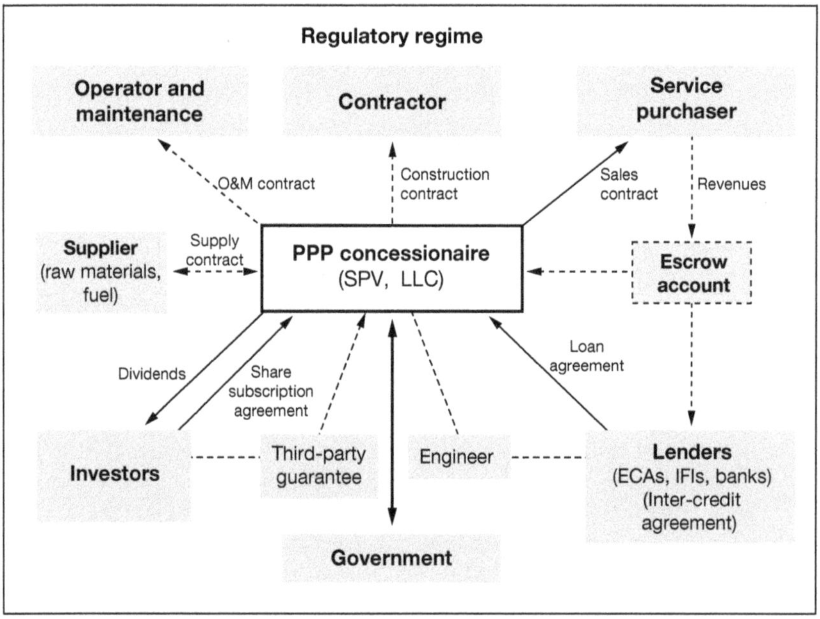

In Figure 2.6, the users of the service provided by the PPP concessionaire pay directly for that service – for instance, for a cash toll road or indeed a PPP power station. If the lenders have concerns about the managerial skills and integrity of the project company managers, then an escrow account arrangement may be set up, but that is rarely the case. Otherwise, the underlying financial structure is similar to a classic project finance deal.

Given that the underlying project represents the delivery of a public service, then the whole framework may be ring-fenced by a regulatory regime, ensuring standards of service and value for money if the concession agreement does not provide these conditions already.

Figure 2.7: PPP structure (PPP service delivered to the public free) (PPP concessionaire paid against availability)

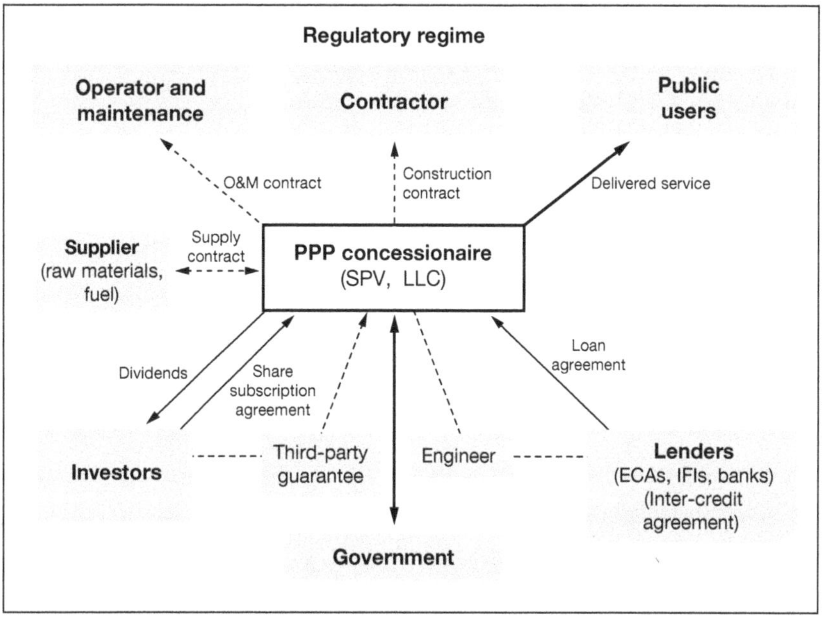

In Figure 2.7, the service is delivered to the public free of charge, and the concessionaire receives payments from the government or its agent, made against a performance regime based on making the underlying project assets 'available' for use. In this case, the PPP concessionaire is not taking a user, or traffic, risk. That risk is carried by the government.

In many ways, this latter structure is less complex than the former. User forecasts can, at times, be more of an art form than a science, as shall be demonstrated in the review of transport infrastructure projects (see Part 2 of this book). Furthermore, it is easier for lenders, which after all are usually providing the majority of funding for PPPs, to identify and accept the inherent risks in the structure.

Not only is this structure often applied for PPP roads, bridges, schools, hospitals, etc, it can also be used for pipelines such as Nord Stream, the gas pipeline from Russia to Germany under the Baltics Sea, where throughput forecasts were highly uncertain. By setting an 'availability' requirement, lenders were left with assessing:

- Will the project be built to time and cost conditions?
- Will it operate to the agreed performance criteria?
- What is the creditworthiness of the entity making the availability payments?

How much, or how little, gas was actually transported was not a component of the funding structure, other than transported volume could have some marginal impact on maintenance costs.

7. Balance sheet issues

It can be seen that, in the absence of corporate or government guarantees for lenders, the key criteria for implementing an acceptable financing framework using this mechanism is to be able to manage and control (ie ring-fence or isolate) the risks inherent in the underlying project. As a result, the structure becomes stand-alone.

The debts raised to fund the project will appear on the project company or PPP concessionaire's balance sheet, so it will be off balance sheet for the shareholders. The only exception to that could be when a majority portion of the shareholding in the project company or PPP concessionaire is provided by one entity, and the accounting regime in the host country requires that the project company or PPP concessionaire be classified as a subsidiary and its accounts be consolidated into the parent company's accounts.

One can immediately see that using a PPP structure makes it possible to remove away from the host government's balance sheet the financial obligations arising from the raising of debt to build the assets.

In effect, whichever PPP structure is adopted per Figures 2.6 and 2.7, it could well be off balance sheet for the host government. In other words, the financial obligations are moved from the host government's capital account, which would have been the case if the government had funded the project itself, and placed on current account, as for Figure 2.7 (just like a credit card) or removed completely, as in Figure 2.6.

The attractions for governments are obvious, particularly for those with limited financial resources. In Europe, it will be no surprise that before the financial crisis of 2007–2009 the governments in countries such as Spain, Portugal, Greece and Ireland, often supported by development funding from the European Investment Bank for instance, were all very active in the use of the PPP mechanism for investment in infrastructure and public service assets, relative to their overall national annual investment in such assets. But these countries were not alone, and many governments worldwide have been drawn to the political expediency of using the PPP credit card, when prudence might suggest greater constraint on public resources, whether for capital or current account.

Unfortunately, the accounting rules regarding whether such PPP structures should be on or off balance sheet remain somewhat elusive. The fact is that, for a structure as described in Figure 2.7, the 'availability' payment by the government to the PPP concessionaire represents a contingent liability for that government. It is often open to interpretation and prudence, however, whether such contingent liabilities are recorded in the national accounts. Some governments (eg, Poland) have traditionally taken the prudent view that all such PPP contingent liabilities are recorded as direct liabilities, so appear immediately in national accounts. Other governments have been more liberal in their interpretation.

A good example of this issue has been Network Rail, the private, not-for-profit company which owns and operates the UK railway infrastructure (ie track, tunnels, stations, etc) along which private railway franchisees operate passenger and freight services.

Over the past 10 to 15 years, Network Rail has borrowed significant sums (over £30 billion) to fund the rehabilitation of the country's railway system. The private operators pay a fee to Network Rail for use of the infrastructure, but Network Rail's revenues from that source represent only about 20% of the revenues that it needs to cover its costs. The balance comes from a direct UK government grant or subvention.

In 2002–3, when the initial loans for the rehabilitation programme were first raised, the UK Office of National Statistics (a data-gathering and analytical institution, which at that time also opined on government finances) decided, following liaison with the European Union, that Network Rail's debts were off balance sheet for the UK government. The Treasury was delighted!

This issue was reviewed by the UK government in 2013–14, not least because international accounting requirements are tightening up on such matters. It was announced that from 2014 Network Rail's debt will be assumed as on balance sheet for the UK government.

Of course, such an issue applies not just to the United Kingdom. It is facing all governments and the para-statal entities, power utilities, ports, airports, etc in their countries.

The International Monetary Fund has been aware of the problem for some years, particularly with respect to PPPs in weaker economies, but clear and transparent guidelines remain elusive.

In the European Union, on/off balance sheet issues are decided by Eurostat in Brussels. The main guidelines for PPPs have until recently been as follows:

- If the construction, or project completion, risk is carried by the concessionaire and if more than 50% of the revenues come from user fees, then the funding of the project is off balance sheet for the host government.

  By way of example, the 8 kilometres PPP road/rail toll bridge between Denmark and Sweden (the Oresund Bridge across the Oresund Strait) is owned 50/50 by the Swedish and Danish governments and cost the equivalent of approximately €3 billion. The finance consisted mainly of bank loans, but as the construction/completion risk and more than 50% of revenues arise from road and rail tolls, the debt is off balance sheet for the Danish and Swedish governments.
- If the construction, or project completion, risk is carried by the concessionaire, and if the demand or availability risk is also carried by the concessionaire, then the PPP can be deemed off balance sheet for the government paying the 'availability' payment.

The above guidelines are far from perfect. They do not consider at all the fact that under the covenants for most loans for PPP projects, in the event of default lenders have the right to take ownership of the assets and the host government cannot intervene unless it pays back the outstanding amounts on the loans. This contingent liability can be quite significant if default occurs during the early operational life of a PPP, when the maximum amount of debt is outstanding.

Such a situation arose, in effect, with the London Underground PPP in 2007/8. The PPP concession was terminated by Transport for London (TfL) (ie, the government) when the concessionaire still had outstanding a debt of £1.7 billion. Technically, lenders had, or at least should have had, a lien over the concession assets (ie, various London Underground tube lines) unless their debt was repaid by TfL/government. It is also likely that the lenders were not inclined to try to operate London's metro system themselves.

On the TfL/government side, £1.7 billion was a significant sum to find, and the normal source would have been the same banks that had lent to the PPP concessionaires in the first place in 2002/3. Consequently, a deal was negotiated behind closed doors.

Given the above, Eurostat has been requiring EU governments to follow the requirements of ESA 95 (Eurostat's system of national and regional accounts), now updated by ESA 2010, with respect to balance sheet issues for PPPs, albeit that the regulations remain somewhat open to interpretation. After all, risk and the allocation of risk, upon which ESA 95 is based, is a subjective value. Furthermore, the same rules that apply for PPPs should also apply to EU para-statals to ensure consistency.

ESA 2010 attempts to bring greater certainty to the assessments by focusing on control issues rather than risk issues. However, some confusion remains with interface conflicts arising between the accounting, in contrast to the statistical, application and treatment of the available data, depending on the intended final use of the outcomes by host governments.

The latest guideline recommends an analysis as to where the balance of financial benefit or reward lies, both for construction and during the operations or service delivery period. For the transaction to be deemed off balance sheet, 70% to 80% of the benefits should lie with the private developer for both elements. Within the European Union, Eurostat provides advice on such assessments.

8. Not-for-profit companies/PICs

In some sectors of infrastructure and public services, governments may consider that a not-for-profit company or PIC is a more appropriate corporate vehicle to provide certain public services, such as health, education, social housing (eg, Scottish Futures Trust PPPs) and transportation when safety is a critical issue. The aspects to consider include the following:

- Does the PIC structure, where there is no equity interest from participants, provide adequate incentive for contractors, developers and operators to perform to the specification and standards required?
- Is the PPP service to be provided essential and monopolistic, where the public, as customer, has no choice (eg, Glas Cymru, the Welsh water utility)?

- Is the PPP service being provided in a limited market (eg, an island economy)? On such occasion, a PIC may be seen as politically more acceptable.
- Is public safety a key issue (eg, NavCanada, an ATC PIC)?

A description of the NavCanada experience was provided in section 1 above. Indeed, the Crown Corporation model practised in Canada has many merits for public service utilities, even though it has not been widely adopted internationally.

Options for governments

1. Which funding structure to adopt?

All governments considering investments in infrastructure and public service assets must answer the same questions regarding funding: Should they fund the projects conventionally, using government budgetary resources or loans raised against the security of a government guarantee? Or should they employ private sector capital?

The answer is not necessarily straightforward (although the latter route will have less, or no, direct impact on the government's balance sheet and thus may seem advantageous).

Much depends on factors lying outside the financial arena, and experience has shown that governments' decision-making in this area is rarely optimal. Certain sectors of infrastructure, such as mass transit railways, are more complex and difficult to implement than other sectors, which in turn limits the chances of successful outcomes. Governments' choice as to when to use private capital does not necessarily take into account such characteristics.

To assist governments and their agents in assessing whether to use private capital or public finance for particular project opportunities, the 'gateway' decision-making process in Figure 3.1 is suggested.

2. The gateway decision-making process

It is the role and responsibility of governments to invest in infrastructure and deliver public services. Accordingly, government experts must determine where and when a demand for investment in new public service assets exists, and whether the cost-to-benefit ratio will be positive. Once these aspects have been considered, the question arises, as mentioned above, as to whether these assets should be funded with public (state) or private capital.

2.1 Gate 1

The starting point is usually based upon an economic feasibility study of the possible options to develop a particular aspect of public services and the need for new infrastructure to meet such demand.

Having identified the need for investment in infrastructure and/or public service assets, does the government have the financial resources to fund and undertake the project itself?

If yes, then it will do so. This may often be the chosen option in richer economies, such as Germany, where historically most infrastructure projects have

Figure 3.1: Gateway decision-making process

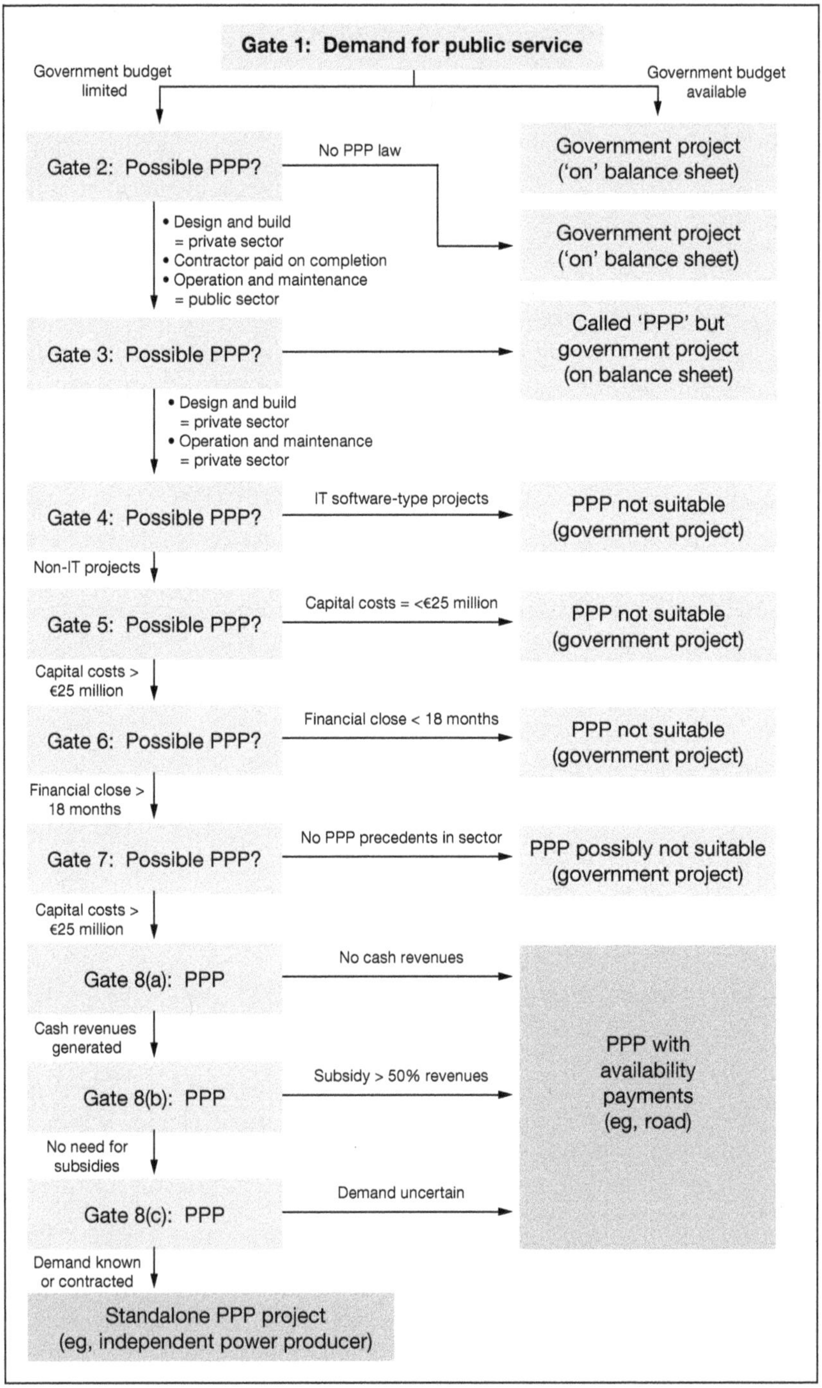

been government-funded. (It is only relatively recently that such countries have adopted public-private partnership (PPP)-type structures for such investments, and then only in specific sectors.)

If the government has limited financial resources, a PPP-type structure, employing private capital, may be preferable.

Go to Gate 2.

2.2 Gate 2

Is there a national PPP-type concession law or equivalent legal framework governing the licensing of private sector companies to build infrastructure and public service assets, and deliver public services?

If no such law or regulation exists, then any form of PPP concession is unlikely to be successful. Conventional government funding may be the only option.

If there is such law or regulation, then a PPP could be a possibility for the project.

Assuming the above requirement is met, go to Gate 3.

2.3 Gate 3

What is the role of the private sector?

Is the plan that the private sector will design, build and finance the construction of the project, and then upon project completion the government will repay the lenders and operate and maintain the project itself? Or is the plan that the private sector will design, construct, finance, operate and maintain the project, and receive payment for the agreed pubic services as delivered?

In the first case, some practitioners might call the project structure a PPP, but in essence it is construction financing. Such a funding mechanism is often employed in Gulf countries.

In the second case, then a PPP-type structure could be feasible.

Go to Gate 4.

2.4 Gate 4

Does the project involve the development of an IT software program or package?

If yes, then using some form of PPP-type funding structure is unlikely to be successful. Usually, such IT programs have to be developed and tailor-made to meet specific output demands, and there is a high likelihood of cost overruns. Experience has shown, particularly in the UK PFI programme, that it can be exceedingly difficult to define, and not to change at a later date, the output required of such programs, and no ready-made alternatives are available commercially. Some governments (eg, United Kingdom) now exclude IT projects from their PPP programmes.

By contrast, IT infrastructure (eg, telecommunication masts, broadband networks, etc) may be suitable for long-term PPP-type structures. However, care must be taken in assessing the useful life of the assets, given the ever-changing and rapid technological advances in this sector.

If the project does not involve the development of IT software programs, then go to Gate 5.

2.5 Gate 5

What are the capital costs of the project?

The high upfront costs for advisers, consultants and lawyers to undertake the due diligence required by lenders and investors mean that below a notional watershed value of around £20 million (or $30 million or €25 million), it is usually not cost-effective to employ PPP-type funding structures.

The watershed value will vary from country to country, but should not be ignored. A review undertaken by the United Kingdom's National Audit Office on the first four design, build, finance and operate (ie, PPP-type) road projects in the United Kingdom in 1998 highlighted this issue (HC 476, January 1998). Unfortunately, many potential PPP-type projects in the municipal and water sectors, as well as renewable energy, fall below the £20 million watershed value.

If the capital costs of the project are greater than £20 million or equivalent, then go to Gate 6.

Addendum: It is sometimes possible to aggregate a series of similar projects which individually fall below the watershed value, but which, when taken collectively, exceed the minimum value for PPP.

For example, in 2000 the Glasgow municipality approved a PPP-type concession for 29 schools, consisting of upgrading 17 existing schools and building 12 new schools within the city. Overall, the capital value of the PPP project was £225 million, well in excess of the watershed. Individually, it is probable that a number of such schools would have fallen below the watershed value for PPP.

A similar approach has been adopted elsewhere for projects which are relatively simple to build, operate and maintain, such as 49 Offenbach schools in Germany (2003).

2.6 Gate 6

Is the planned date for financial close (ie, when all the commercial, financial and legal documents are to be signed and funding finally committed) less than 18 months hence?

If yes, then complex PPP-type funding structures may not be appropriate.

Typically, a PPP-type transaction proposed by the government will take at least 12 months, possibly 24 or more months, to pass from decision to proceed with either private or public sector funding to financial close. The average time for such a process for the many PFI deals in the United Kingdom over the past 20 years is reportedly around 27 months, although some projects in other countries have been somewhat quicker (eg, 12–15 months).

Generally speaking, PPP-type transactions take twice as long and cost twice as much to prepare than conventional loan/guarantee-type deals. The extra time and costs stem from the need for financiers to undertake their due diligence of all the inherent project details before committing finance.

As a general rule (although there are always exceptions), for a project with a capital value of $100 million, the upfront costs of designers, engineers, environmental consultants, financial advisers and lawyers can amount to between 3% and 5% of project costs for a project funded conventionally with loans and third-party/government guarantees.

For a project funded as a type of private concession or PPP, such costs can amount to between 5% and 8% of project costs, depending on the sector and complexity. Such amounts can be significant for developers, as they are mostly to be paid before project construction commences. However, in the case of PPPs, financiers may allow some of the upfront costs (if fully justifiable) to be included as part of the capital costs. Accordingly, for a project costing $100 million, financiers would raise in excess of $105 million to cover such upfront costs.

Lastly, it should be emphasised that governments often overlook the timetable constraint imposed by PPP-type deals when considering which infrastructure projects to undertake and when.

With infrastructure projects often taking between two and three years, possibly longer, to build, adding the long preparation and negotiation period for private, PPP-type deals can often result in the overall execution period for such transactions to be longer than the host government stay in power between elections (eg, five years).

If financial close beyond 18 months is acceptable, then go to Gate 7.

2.7 Gate 7

Is this the first private sector, PPP-type deal in the infrastructure sector in the country?

If there are no precedents for PPP-type transactions or concessions for infrastructure developments executed to date in any specific market, investors and lenders will naturally be cautious. Indeed, some investors and lenders may prefer to wait and see how the PPP concession law or regulations operate in any given country before committing to deals of this type, reducing the funding options until national procedures and processes become established. Further, if the underlying project straddles the border between two or more countries, an international agreement or treaty will be likewise required before investors and lenders entertain funding proposals.

Assuming that there exist precedents to follow, go to Gate 8.

The three variations of Gate 8 below determine the optimal funding structure for an infrastructure PPP-type funding mechanism.

2.8 Gate 8

(a) Gate 8(a)

Does the service to be provided by the infrastructure assets generate cash revenues from user fees?

If no, then the private sector infrastructure PPP concessionaire will have to be paid periodic amounts by the government or PPP concession grantor to cover operations, maintenance and finance (ie, equity and debt) costs, measured against an 'availability' or performance regime.

Many highway PPPs in emerging markets, where traffic forecasts and tariff regimes may be unreliable, are structured this way. Furthermore, due to a number of failed toll-road projects in Southeast Asia and Mexico, among other places, in the 1990s, financiers are nervous about stand-alone PPP toll-road projects, preferring the availability structure, which:

- avoids traffic and tariff risks; and

- transfers the risk towards underpinning physical project performance and the payment risk onto the government concession grantor.

There exist a range of variants to this structure today, and these are discussed in Part 2 of this book in specific project case histories.

If the answer to the cash revenue question above is 'yes', go to Gate 8(b).

(b) *Gate 8(b)*

Do the revenues from user fees fully cover the PPP concessionaire's costs, or are subsidies or subventions required?

If the answer is 'no' and subsidies or subventions are required, then an availability payment mechanism for such PPP, as under Gate 8(a), may be more appropriate. To many financiers, subsidies represent political intervention into a project's operations, and government policies can change over the years (medium/long term) that infrastructure projects span.

If the answer is 'yes', go to Gate 8(c).

(c) *Gate 8(c)*

If the only revenues that the infrastructure PPP concessionaire receives are user fees from beneficiaries or customers, and traffic/demand forecasts are reliable or contracted, then a stand-alone PPP structure should be possible.

Stand-alone infrastructure projects, such as toll roads, toll bridges or tunnels, and private sector power stations in developed markets, fall into this category.

The above gateway mechanism can be a useful tool for governments in carefully choosing when to use private capital for infrastructure project implementation, and when not to.

3. Value for money – public v private

Once the possibility of structuring an investment in infrastructure assets using private capital has been identified, the next question is whether that investment represents value for money (VfM).

To answer this question, a comparison has to be made between the publicly funded option and the private sector alternative.

There are three principles to take into account:

- There is no perfect and objective methodology available to undertake this comparison;
- The VfM assessment is being made before, not after, bids may have been received from investors and potential concessionaires. Hence, the assessment is based on (hopefully, well-informed) estimates as to what the publicly and privately funded options might cost; and
- Both the publicly and privately financed options must be compared against the same timeline or project life cycle. Typically, the life cycle will be between 25 and 30 years, which is also the length of a PPP concession in many jurisdictions.

Figure 3.2(i): Costs of public sector procurement (government funding) Public sector comparator (excluding inflation)

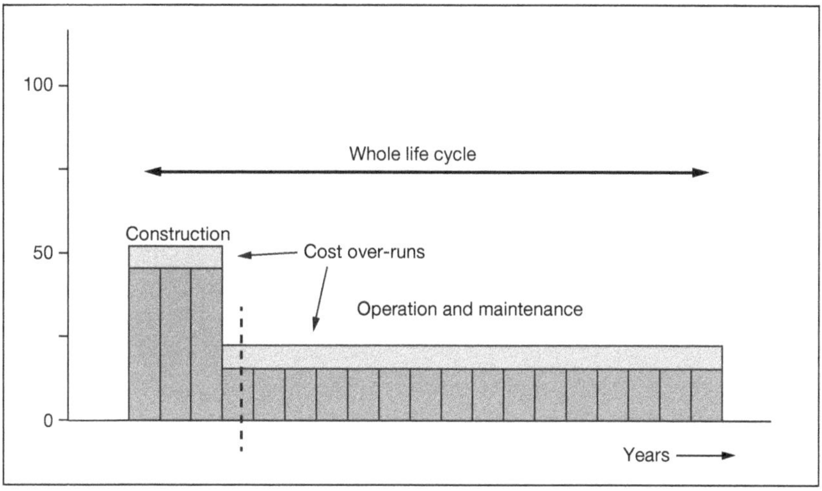

Source: author

Figure 3.2(ii): Costs of PPP procurement (excluding inflation)

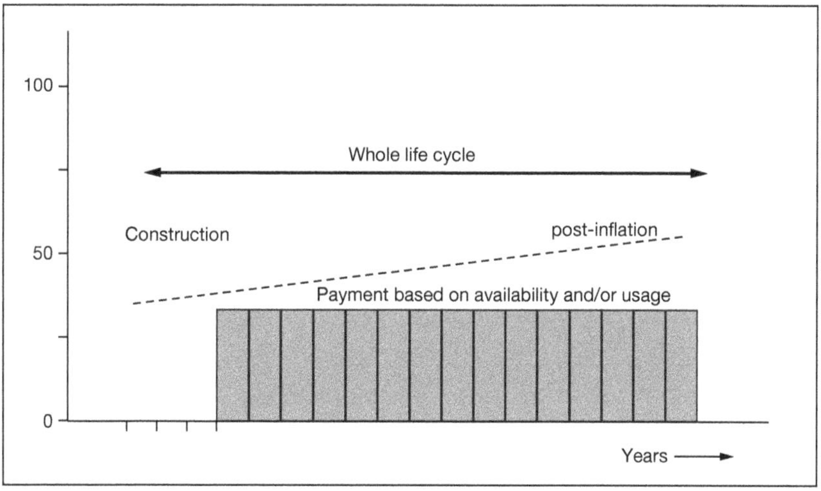

Source: author

Once the alternatives have been compared and a decision made as to which funding route to adopt, government sponsors should not turn back halfway through a subsequent bidding process and reverse that decision. Financiers in the market will note any such reverses, which could negatively affect their confidence in the host government's ability to keep to its decisions in respect of future similar transactions.

The underlying mathematics of the comparison process is simple and straightforward. It is based on the present values of the cost flows for either option (ie, compound interest applied to costs), working backwards.

Figures 3.2 (i) and (ii) show the cost profiles of the two options over the whole project life cycle. For the publicly funded option, the costs are all weighted into the early years of the cycle, whereas with the privately funded, PPP option the costs are weighted much later in the process. In many ways, the latter effect is comparable to using a credit card.

Hence, to assess the government- or publicly funded option, which is commonly termed the 'public sector comparator' (PSC), the government needs to:

- identify the demand for public service or infrastructure investment;
- define what the performance output should be of the completed assets;
- prepare cost estimates as to how much it will cost to build the assets and then operate and maintain them over the whole project life cycle;
- determine the source of revenues – either user fees or performance (availability) payments; and, if necessary
- impose a regulatory regime to ensure standards and quality of performance.

For the privately funded, PPP option, an estimate has to be made as to how much it will cost the private party or concessionaire to design, build, finance, operate and maintain the same assets over the same project life cycle as for the PSC. Furthermore, the private party will have to operate under the same regulatory regime that might apply.

Quite often, the government undertaking this comparative exercise will seek the help of a consultant or adviser in estimating such costs.

The two cost flows are then compared as present values (see Figure 3.3).

Figure 3.3: PSC v PPP (including inflation but before risk assessment)

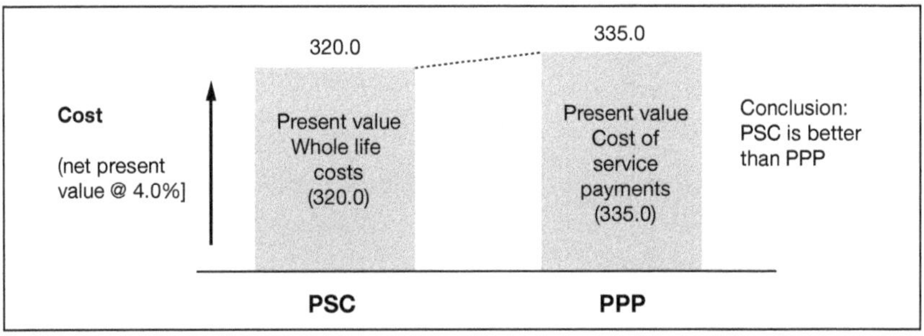

Source: author

Key to this calculation is the discount rate to use to arrive at present values for costs, which might spread over 25–30 years. Conventional investment analysis would suggest that the discount rate to employ should be the host government's long-term cost of capital.

For a developed country, one can obtain such data from the long-term bond yields in the international financial press. However, for emerging markets such rates may not be available and only 5 to 10-year bonds exist. In which case, one has to take the longest possible bond yield rate available, add a small amount to reflect political risk, and use the resulting rate.

However, this rate is only a 'guestimate'. A prudent analyst would use it for a base case analysis, then apply some sensitivity testing with different rates (eg, more or less 1% or 2%) and review the results.

As the underlying exercise is to compare one option against another, it is only when – by changing the discount rate from the base case to a different rate – the priority between the options changes that one then needs to review more closely the most relevant discount rate to choose.

In this context, however, it is worth remembering that this PSC v privately funded PPP option analysis is far from perfect and not an exact tool. Other considerations, which are more subjective than objective (see below), may carry more weight when deciding which option to choose.

Another contentious issue in such analysis is whether the cost data should be expressed in 'real' terms, which ignore inflation, tax and the cost of government funding, or in 'nominal' terms, where the cost estimates include such elements.

Conventional project investment analysis usually requires that such evaluations include assumptions for inflation, depreciation, tax and finance costs. After all, such assumptions represent key components of the make-up of the private sector's proposal for undertaking such projects.

However, some governments, such as the UK government through its Green Book guide for all ministries and government agencies, prefer to adopt a 'real' approach, excluding such assumptions. In such cases, the discount rate usually chosen is the 'social time preference' rate, which represents "the value that society attaches to present, as opposed to future, consumption". It is an economic, rather than financial, discount rate, and its derivation is based upon a series of arguably subjective judgements.

Notionally, such 'real' rate should be similar to the financial 'nominal' discount rate, less inflation, but that may not always be the case.

For example, for many years the 'real' discount rate chosen by the UK government was 6% 'real', whereas at the time the yield on government 30-year bonds was between 5.5% and 6% and inflation was between 2.5% and 3% – so the 'real' discount rate, as cited in the Green Book, was significantly higher than what might have been expected.

The net result was that the higher the discount rate, the more likely the present value analysis would favour the PPP-type option over conventional government funding. This is because PPP allows payments to be made for investment in infrastructure assets further out into the future.

Hence, some proposed infrastructure investments in the United Kingdom have been undertaken as PPP-type deals when nominal-type assessments would arguably have indicated they should not have been (see National Audit Office Briefing Paper to the Treasury Committee, October 2013).

Another consequence of using 'real' rather than 'nominal' values in the analysis is that if such projections of costs are later used by government sponsors of such investments for budgetary purposes, they could seriously underestimate the payments which will become due at future dates.

Many UK practitioners argue that this is the case for many of the NHS Trusts which have implemented PFI/PPP-type facilities and which now, five or 10 years later, find that their budgets are inadequate to cover the costs due.

Generally speaking, most governments undertake such comparisons using 'nominal' data.

The comparison is not complete, however, until one assesses risk, or uncertainty. With the private option, the possibility arises for many risks, which otherwise would be carried by the public sector, to be transferred to the private sector. Further, the value of such risks would be included within the estimates made for the cost of the private sector, PPP option.

To assess such risks, a 'risk matrix' is prepared.

Figure 3.4: Risk matrix PPP toll road (with tunnel) Weighted average method

Risk	Base cost (€ million)	Value of impact (%)	Event probability (%)	Value of risk (€ million)	Allocation to private sector (%)
Delays in land acquisition	320	10%	50%	16.0	10% (= €1.6m)
Delays in government approvals	320	10%	30%	9.6	10% (= €1.0m)
Geological risk	125	30%	20%	7.5	100% (= €7.5m) (capped @ €30m)
Completion	320	25%	10%	8.0	100% (=€8.0m)
Traffic volumes	320	25%	50%	Nil	PPP payment against availability (NB, payment risk?)
Design fault	320	10%	5%	1.6	90% (= €1.4m)
Construction materials fault	320	20%	5%	3.2	100% (= €3.2m)
Environmental risk	320	15%	15%	7.2	25% (= €1.8m)
Totals				53.1	£24.5m
		Risk = 17% of base cost			Retained risk = £28.6m

Source: author

Figure 3.4 gives an example matrix for a PPP motorway project that includes a tunnel. The analytical procedure is as follows:

- A list is made of the potential and significant risks that a project might face (in column 1);

- An estimate is made for the whole life cost, in present value terms, of the public option (column 2). In this example, where some specific risks may apply to the tunnel component but not to the balance of the project (eg, fire risk), then it might be prudent to evaluate that component separately;
- An estimate is made as to the financial impact on the project's value should such risks arise (column 3);
- An estimate is made of the probability, based on experience of similar projects in similar scenarios, of such risks arising (column 4);
- These values are multiplied together to arrive at an estimated value for each risk's impact on the project outcome (column 5). The total represents the aggregate value, in present value terms, of the possible risks that the project might face; and
- An assessment is then made as to how much of each individual risk can be assumed or carried by the private sector entity, should the project be undertaken as a PPP or similar structure, and a total is arrived at (column 6).

The results of the above process are then translated into the public v private sector comparison previously developed (see Figure 3.5).

Figure 3.5: PSC v PPP

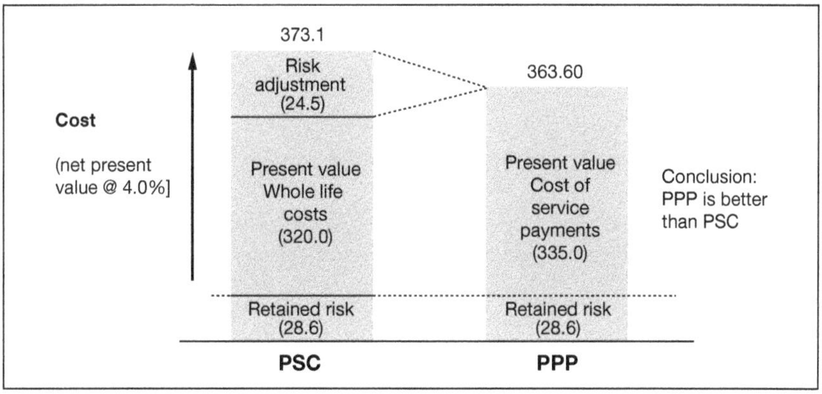

Source: author

For the comparison to be valid, the value of the risk (which can be transferred to the PPP private sector concessionaire) should be added to the public sector option too, as in estimating the value for the private PPP option such risks will already have been taken into account.

Lastly, there will always be some residual risk value which the public sector has to carry whichever option is chosen – whether public or private – to develop and fund the project, as shown in Figure 3.5.

Some caveats apply:

- The risk matrix methodology is not perfect. However, no better alternative has yet been developed to attach values objectively to the different options;
- The estimates of risk values and probabilities are inherently subjective. In

order to reach their conclusions, practitioners will often seek the advice and support of experts who have undertaken similar projects in similar circumstances; and

- The risk matrix is not the only criterion or tool which should be used to assess VfM for the different funding options available for infrastructure development.

4. Advantages/disadvantages of such structures

The following section highlights some of the other issues which should be considered when deciding whether to use private or public resources to develop an infrastructure project.

4.1 Completion and asset delivery

It is widely recognised that in most countries the private sector is more likely to build and deliver infrastructure project assets on time and to specification than the public sector.

4.2 Efficiency and operations

Just as for construction and completion, the private sector PPP option is more likely to deliver a public service to the quality and standards required than the public sector, particularly if the payments due to the private entity are attached to performance measures.

4.3 Transfer of technology

The private sector is more likely to employ the latest, but proven, technologies in undertaking any project. However, emphasis should be placed on the need to employ proven technologies; examples of international infrastructure projects abound where the technology employed was the latest, yet it later failed to match performance expectations.

4.4 Private sector investment

The private option for implementing projects entails inherently private sector capital investment, which otherwise might not take place in that country under the public alternative.

4.5 Institutional change

Many governments have, on occasion, used the PPP option of undertaking investment in infrastructure and public service assets to bring about institutional change and efficiencies in government ministries and agencies, which otherwise would have undertaken the projects themselves.

4.6 Maintenance regime lock-in

Under the private sector PPP option for infrastructure development, the private entity will usually receive payment only if the assets operate efficiently and to specification – that is, payments are made against performance measures. Naturally, therefore, the private entity will ensure that the underlying assets are kept in good condition at all times.

Under the public option, the maintenance regime, as planned, may be similar, but history shows that over time government or municipal budgets come under pressure. When that happens, invariably one of the first budget lines to be cut is that for the maintenance of public assets.

This maintenance advantage of the private, over the public, option is often overlooked. It is, however, key.

4.7 Timetable and complexity

The funding of private sector PPP infrastructure projects is inherently complex. These transactions consist of an intricate contractual structure, supported by a multitude of documents. As a result, it generally takes twice as long as for government-funded projects to negotiate PPPs and assemble all the agreements necessary to achieve financial close (the date when all the monies are committed and can be used).

Typically, when one expects a conventionally funded deal to take between 12 and 15 months from conception to financial close, an infrastructure PPP-type deal takes between 24 and 27 months. (There have, of course, been exceptions.)

Hence, timeframes and complexity must be taken into consideration when deciding which funding option to adopt. Privately funded, PPP infrastructure projects are not a quick fix, and may not fit the timetable of policymakers.

A consequence, often overlooked, in this respect is that the complexity of such deals can become a significant burden if the project is delayed for whatever reason, or adjustments have to be made to reflect changing circumstances. Renegotiating contracts can be time consuming and costly, and usually the private partner to such contracts starts out at an advantage.

4.8 Promotion of competition

The introduction of private capital and practices into the realm of public services was originally intended to enhance the possibility of more competition between potential contractors and operators, thereby reducing costs. If anything, history has shown the opposite to be the case.

A further negative influence on competition is that the inherent complexity of such deals is such that smaller companies are not prepared to risk their capital resources in bidding for such deals, which reduces the market only to those companies with large balance assets.

4.9 Employment issues

If the infrastructure project is built and operated by a private sector entity, then the possibility arises that this activity may displace those people who are currently employed by the public sector and who would have undertaken and operated the project if it had been publicly funded. This is a common occurrence in many markets.

However, whereas the private sector entity will most probably appoint its own project and senior management staff, the project will require many employees to undertake the day-to-day tasks. Consequently, many who had been employed by the public sector may well, in the event, be offered a job with the private entity, which can enhance career prospects.

Those countries which have been successful in introducing private investment and capital into infrastructure and public service investment have introduced not only laws or regulations to govern the conduct of public services being provided by private entities (eg, a concession law), but at the same time introduced regulations protecting the employment benefits and rights for any workers transferring from public to private sector employment (eg, the UK Transfer of Undertakings (Protection of Employment) Regulations 2006, known as TUPE Regulations).

5. Other features to note

5.1 Common contractual terms and documents

Ideally, common contractual terms, conditions and documents should apply across all sectors.

Unfortunately, this standard has rarely been achieved. That said, whereas the commercial and financial terms underpinning infrastructure project financings are similar all over the world, each lawyer will, to a certain extent (not least to meet local market demands) describe each component or event within such documents in his own words. General contract templates are available, but in the end each set of project documents has to be tailor-made to fit the circumstances.

5.2 Refinancing gains

The general perception for most projects is that the period of greatest risk is during construction. Once a project has been completed and moves into the operational period, risk diminishes. At this point, other debt sources may become available to the project company (eg, long-term bonds), which could be cheaper than the debt (usually loans) which had been used to fund costs during construction. Accordingly, the finance director of the project company or PPP concessionaire may wish to refinance existing debt.

Existing lenders will usually be receptive to such refinancing, provided that their risk exposure does not increase. However, the refinancing is rarely just exchanging $1 of bank loan for $1 of bond finance. Instead, $1 of bank loan may be refinanced with $1.05 of bonds, given that the overall risk profile of the project has decreased.

The net result of such refinancing is that the shareholders of the project company will generate a profit of $0.05 for every $1 refinanced with bonds. One might normally expect this windfall to be returned to shareholders as an extraordinary dividend.

However, under private sector, PPP-type deals in infrastructure, embedded in the concession agreement or licence for delivering the public service, there will be a clause stating that if the concession collapses, whether through fault of the private or public party, then before the assets can be returned to public ownership and control, lenders/creditors will demand repayment of their outstanding debt. This reflects one of the key principles of cash flow, project financing transactions: while lenders take prime security over the cash flows that the project generates, they also take a lien, or security, over the project assets for so long as their debt is outstanding.

Given the above and, in particular, the status of lenders and the host government, it is normal practice to share any such windfall gains 50/50 between the shareholders of the project company and the government counterparty. That does not exactly reflect the distribution of the underlying risks assumed by either party as the life of a project progresses, but it is taken as a norm in current PPP-type deals.

5.3 Short-term perspective of investors

Infrastructure projects are inherently long-term assets funded by long-term capital (debt and equity). However, many investors have only short- to medium-term investment horizons. For example, contractors and equipment suppliers, as investors, may well wish to sell their interest to a third party once they have completed the construction of a project and use their capital on another project elsewhere. Similarly, private equity-type investment funds often wish to turn round, or 'churn', their investments every five to seven years.

In private infrastructure and public service-type deals, lenders will usually have to approve any such sale. They will normally approve such sale, provided that the risk of the project to perform and repay its debts has not increased. The government may also have to approve such sale, particularly if the underlying asset is of strategic importance.

Over recent years, the arrival of pension and life insurance companies into the world of infrastructure and public service investment has demonstrated that there is no shortage of investors prepared to invest in, or refinance, such projects.

5.4 Institutional constraints in government

Private infrastructure deals require an understanding of technical, commercial, legal and financial issues, which most government-employed staff do not face through their normal work. Consequently, a skills shortage can arise. To overcome this issue, many governments set up a PPP unit to focus the expertise required by government to negotiate, implement and manage such deals (see further the chapter on the project process).

5.5 Conflicts of interest

Given the multinational nature of many infrastructure project finance deals, conflicts of interest can arise when consultants, advisers or auditors have ongoing and established relations with parties on either side of the transaction. Governments need to be alert to such conflicts and act to reduce them, wherever possible. Openness and transparency are demanded on such occasions. This can require, in some jurisdictions, the revocation of bids or licences, if rules about such conflicts of interest are transgressed.

5.6 Political life cycle

Governments will invariably be involved in any infrastructure project finance or PPP deal. Such deals are also long term. By the time the project is implemented or completed, those in government responsible for the go-ahead decision at the outset of project preparation will no longer be in office, and therefore unaccountable when problems arise. There is, unfortunately, no way of avoiding this problem.

5.7 National balance sheet issues

Reference was made to this issue earlier (in the chapter titled "What is infrastructure?"), but this can play a role in influencing government as to whether to use private capital or public funds to implement a specific project.

Lastly, it must be emphasised that none of the above issues and criteria, taken on its own, is sufficient to decide which funding option to adopt. There is no perfect mechanism to justify such decisions. Further, they are, to a degree, subjective.

However, once decision makers have selected the funding mechanism, it is essential that they do not change direction. As noted earlier in this chapter, financiers will take note of such changes of course. Considering how lengthy and complex the path to success is, maintaining investor and lender confidence in the process is key.

Risk

1. What is risk?

Risk is uncertainty. It is fundamentally a subjective issue. What is a risk to one person may not be to another. What represents a risk to investors may not be a risk to lenders, and vice versa. Hence, risk should not be described as having a definitive value. It will always be open to individual judgement.

That said, it is possible to:

- identify the risks associated with any specific scenario or project;
- assess the impact of such risks on the project's outcomes;
- recognise those risks which have the most impact on a project's outcomes and those which do not; and
- analyse further the probabilities of such risks arising, based on data assembled from similar projects undertaken previously in similar scenarios.

In the final analysis, risks are best allocated to those parties in a project best able to manage and carry them. Experience has shown, however, that project failure frequently stems from the inherent project risks not having been optimally distributed between the parties. In particular, lenders often assume what turn out to be equity, or investor, risks.

The importance of risk analysis cannot be underestimated. Comprehensive risk analysis will dictate:

- whether a specific project investment should proceed;
- whether it should be developed as a public or private venture; and
- what proportions of equity there should be in the funding structure relative to debt.

Three further features must be mentioned:

- Risk always exists. It cannot be avoided. It is akin to birth, death and taxes. It is inevitably present in whatever project;
- Risk changes over time. What may be a risk today may not be a risk tomorrow. In the context of projects, it is often assumed that risks during construction are greater than during operations. Accordingly, the costs of finance may be lower for the latter period than the former; and
- Risks can be managed, mitigated and shared between the parties to a project.

The process whereby a project's investors and lender assess the project risks is known as 'due diligence'. It is a key component of the process leading to a project's financial close.

2. Measuring risk

Given that risk is a subjective issue, attaching a value to any specific risk is of relevance only when compared with the value attained in a risk-free scenario.

Risk analysts will initially develop a base case, cash flow projection for a particular venture, using their best-efforts estimates for data.

Then, sensitivity testing will take place, whereby a range of values is applied to particular variables, which make up the projections. In particular, the values for capital costs, revenues and operating costs may vary (eg, more or less 10% or 20%), and the results of the projections compared against the base case.

This procedure may be undertaken for a wide range of data and variables, which make up the base case. Not only may capital cost, operating cost and revenue data be included in this exercise; inflation, taxation, financial terms (interest rates, repayment periods) and currency exchange rates may also be tested. The conclusion will be the identification of the risks that could have the greatest financial impact on a particular project.

The extent to which changes in any particular variable affect the outcomes to the base case projections will be noted from the perspective of the investors and lenders, and risk mitigation measures imposed to minimise the risk of such possibility arising.

The above process is not perfect, but from a practical point of view it serves its purpose. Risks can never be eliminated, but steps can be taken by prudent investors and lenders to limit their impact. Inevitably, some risks are hard to attach a value to (eg, environmental, social or technical risks), but measures exist which reduce their likelihood of being a problem (see below).

When data is available for the range of probabilities of any risk arising in a particular scenario, precedents from similar projects in similar scenarios may allow for a more sophisticated procedure to be adopted. For example, a probability range as applied in Figure 4.1 to the assumptions for revenues is evaluated in terms of a weighted average value for an outcome variable: the rate of return on investment.

An even more sophisticated approach to risk analysis is to attach statistical probabilities, defined mathematically as a 'mean' and 'standard deviation', to all the project variables making up the cash flow projection and reflecting their risk profiles (a procedure called 'stochastic analysis'). Software programs are available both to undertake such analyses and to produce the outcomes in means and standard deviations too.

There are, however, some inherent difficulties with such approach:

- Is there enough data to define the risk profile of each variable consistently?
- Once applied, are the underlying cash flow projections reliably representing the outcomes? (Note that it is extremely difficult to check the cash flow projections, or computer models, prepared on a stochastic basis.)
- Are the results of the analysis clearly understood? Many lending banks' investors and credit committees may not comprehend the conclusions.

Figure 4.1: Sensitivity test

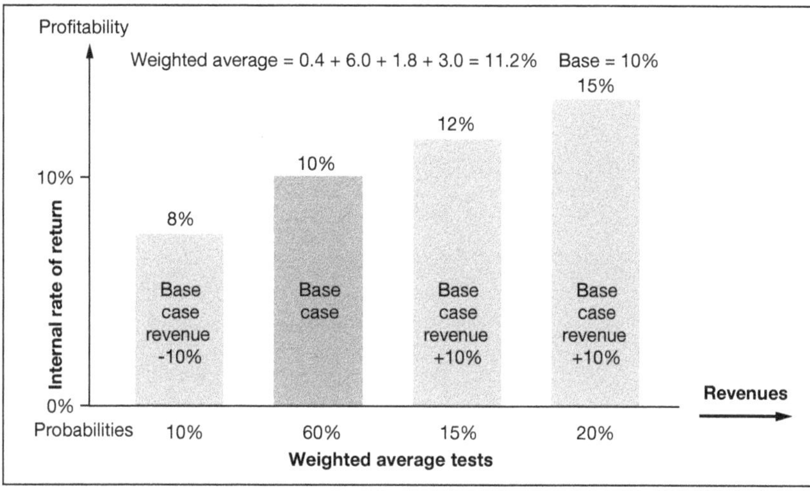

Source: author

Accordingly, this type of risk analysis has limited utility in project financing. Indeed, it has limited impact on the decisions of credit committees!

Risk valuations usually reveal that the prime risks or uncertainties found in infrastructure projects are:

- construction costs;
- operating costs;
- revenues forecasts; and
- currency fluctuations.

This latter risk is particularly important in emerging market infrastructure projects as:

- infrastructure projects are long-term ventures with long cost recovery periods. Hence, they need to be funded with long-term capital (debt and equity), which may be available only in 'hard' currency; and
- much of capital costs, operating costs and revenues may be in local currency because the project is infrastructure or a public service. This can create a significant long-term foreign exchange risk between the project's inherent currency of business and the currency of funding.

It comes as no surprise, then, that the nearly 80 countries worldwide that have successfully developed private-sector infrastructure or PPP-type projects are those countries that:

- have a long-term local capital market which can be used to fund such projects and eliminate the inherent foreign exchange risk; or
- have natural resources (eg, oil, gas, mineral) or a commodity which they can export for hard currency, thereby providing a foreign exchange hedge.

3. Risk analysis – identification and mitigation

A typical risk analysis for a project will usually categorise risks as:

- completion/construction;
- costs and revenues during operations;
- technical;
- environmental and social;
- financial;
- legal; and
- political.

3.1 Completion/construction risks

The main considerations under these risks are:

- Will there be cost overruns?
- Will there be delays to completion?
- Is the site available for the project to be built?
- Are utilities available at the construction site?
- What are the physical risks to the assets (fire, theft, etc)?

The main mitigation measures are as follows.

Negotiate fixed price, 'turnkey' contracts: The contractor has responsibility to build the project to time and specification, and to hand it over on completion to the buyer/project company as a ready-to-use asset.

In reality, it can be difficult to obtain a single turnkey contract for any specific project. However, every attempt should be made to ensure that between 80% and 90% of the works are covered by turnkey arrangements, and that those components which are not are easily managed and not essential to the successful completion of the project.

In addition, there is interdependence between cost overruns and delays; when there is a cost overrun, there inevitably is a delay, and vice versa. This is key when attaching values to such risks in any quantitative analysis.

Negotiate penalty and incentive clauses in the construction contracts: The level of penalty for under-performance in the construction contract will vary depending on jurisdiction and custom. If the potential penalty is too high, then the contractor will increase its initial price. However, the penalty should be large enough to compensate the buyer/project company for the time and effort needed to find a replacement should a contractor fail. Typically, such penalty clause may have a value of 15% to 20% of the contract value.

In some emerging markets it is customary for payments to the contractor during construction to include retention amounts, say 10% of the payment made, which is not paid to the contractor at the date of invoice, but is released within six to 12 months of project completion. Alternatively, buyers may impose performance bonds on the contractors, or, indeed, adopt a mix of these measures.

Ultimately, contractors will judge what they believe to be a reasonable penalty for the risks that they undertake and structure their bid accordingly. Likewise, the prudent buyer will wish to engender a competitive bidding process and receive the cheapest price for the project to be undertaken.

The balance can be difficult to achieve, the more so for infrastructure projects where the construction period may span a few years. A close, but not too close, relationship and cooperative understanding between buyer and contractor in a dynamic partnership are often the key to success.

By contrast, just as penalties should represent a key component of construction contracts, so should incentives. After all, if the project is completed and ready for use early, then revenues can be generated earlier, which will be of benefit to the buyer. The normal arrangement is that such benefits are notionally shared between the buyer and the contractor.

Keep the project specification fixed: Any buyer which, at any time after the signature of the construction contract, wishes to change the specification of the project being undertaken will be at a disadvantage in the negotiations with the contractor. Such change of scope has significantly increased the costs of a number of infrastructure projects – for instance, Eurotunnel over changes to the regulations covering fire hazard in the rolling stock during the construction period.

Buyers, and government buyers in particular, find it exceedingly difficult to define closely what they wish to buy and, in the world of public-private partnership (PPP), what service output they seek. It is for this reason that many IT-type PPP projects have failed (eg, the UK Libra Project Finance Initiative – an IT administration project for the Ministry of Justice).

Use experienced contractors: This is rather obvious. However, the key considerations for the buyer/project company when choosing a contractor are the following:

- Has the contractor undertaken such a project before? If so, where and when?
- Has the contractor all the resources needed to undertake construction?
- Has the contractor experience with the underlying project technology?
- Has the contractor the financial strength to assume all the risks allocated to it during the construction period?
- Has the contractor the capacity to uphold and comply with the performance warranties under the contract?
- Has the contractor a strong team to execute the project? (Reviewing the project manager's CV is essential.)

In seeking answers to the above, the buyer/project company may need to seek the advice of a technical/commercial consultant.

Consider site acquisition and access: For infrastructure projects which require significant tracts of land (eg, motorways, railways and pipelines), land acquisition can be both difficult and costly. Any concept defined, or announcement made, about a future infrastructure project can have a significant impact on the perceived value of the land that will have to be acquired for that project. On occasion, the land value may rise, whereas on others it may drop (eg, HS2 or the third runway at Heathrow in the United Kingdom). Private investors in such infrastructure projects will not wish to assume the risks of land acquisition, its availability and cost, and such risk will usually have to be carried by the host government.

Similarly, consideration in planning infrastructure projects should be given to 'access infrastructure'. A port or an airport will have limited commercial potential unless it enjoys good road and rail connections to allow passengers and freight to pass through the facilities. Likewise, adequate access from the sea needs to be ensured for a port. Is the port entrance deep enough? Does it require dredging (which is an expensive and continuous activity)?

Insure physical asset risk: Many governments and major corporations do not insure their assets, preferring to 'self insure'. However, project finance/PPP-type deals are inherently private, and lenders, which tend to provide most of the funding, will require insurance for the physical assets against fire, theft, etc (for details, see later in this chapter).

Not only do the premiums for such insurance add to operating costs, but it will be a condition precedent to any project loans that an acceptable insurance policy is put in place. Furthermore, the ability of the project company to continue to pay premiums will be embedded in the lenders' requirement for an insurance reserve account to be maintained by a trustee, with a balance sufficient to meet the next premium payment for so long as the loans are outstanding.

3.2 Risks during operations

The main risks are:

- revenues (in terms of prices, predictability and volumes);
- operating costs;
- project performance; and
- management failure.

(a) Revenue risks

Infrastructure and public service projects consist, in the main, of two types of revenue structure:

- direct payment by users, either under contract (eg, container terminal) or when used (eg, cash toll road); and
- payment made against performance (eg, 'availability' payments).

The first case involves two prime risks:

- What will be the unit price or tariff for the use of the asset or service provided?
- What volume or amount of usage will arise?

In some types of project, it is possible that both of these elements be fixed (eg, a fixed price contract), or that there be a sales contract with fixed volumes, but with a variable tariff reflecting changes in inflation. In such circumstances, the inherent risks may be easily managed (eg, a private sector power plant).

Contracts for differences, a recent innovation in the power sector (eg, Hinkley Point nuclear power plant in the United Kingdom), provide a similar method for underpinning revenues for project promoters.

The other key consideration in payment formulae may be how much usage, traffic or throughput there will be. On occasion, demand can be relatively predictable – for instance, for scheduled airline traffic through an airport. But on other occasions, it can be most speculative, such as cash toll roads in emerging markets.

Not only are potential traffic volumes a risk, but so is the users' willingness to pay.

Unsurprisingly, the projected traffic forecasts have not been achieved for a long list of private transport infrastructure projects over the past 30 years – for instance, Eurotunnel (United Kingdom/France) and M1/M15 (the Budapest to Vienna toll road).

Notwithstanding the skills of traffic forecasters, it is not an exact science. It also takes time, and this can be a key consideration when project sponsors are preparing the implementation programme. Quite often, alternative structures may be preferable and quicker to implement.

On such occasions, sponsors may propose that payment to the project company be made against measures of availability or performance. This structure is often favoured for highways, railways, metros and even pipelines when throughput is uncertain. There can be a range of possible performance regimes defining the payments to be made and the penalties imposed for less-than-contracted performance, and these will be discussed in later chapters.

However, the risks are somewhat different than for direct user payments. The prime risks will now be whether:

- the project company will perform, or deliver, the service to the standard required without penalty; and
- the payer is creditworthy.

Such risks are often much easier, and quicker, to evaluate than for traffic. As a result, lenders, which are, by nature, risk averse, often prefer project financings based on such availability payment structure.

Lastly, many projects do not generate 100% revenues during the first period of operations after project completion. It can take time to build up revenues. Analysts should be alert to this feature.

(b) Operating cost risks

For many infrastructure projects, the operating costs may be relatively small compared to revenues. Hence, any changes to operating costs will have minimal impact on profitability. However, if there are any key supply components to the project, such as a fuel supply contract in a power project, then financiers will wish to ensure that the supplies of such a key component will be assured for the project life under a predictable price regime.

Financiers may also wish to ensure that spare essential items are kept on site, in the event of a breakdown in the supply chain. To cover this risk, the assets required in which to store such items, the volume and cost of such spare supplies, and their insurance, should be within the original capital investment programme.

A second risk to cover is management failure. It is, indeed, surprising how often project sponsors fail to review closely the ability and experience of project managers. Prudent lenders and investors will insist, through the terms and conditions of the finance that they provide, that if the project starts to fail to perform, they have the right to change the management.

Lastly, performance risks need to be considered. Normally, construction and equipment supply contracts will be underpinned by warranties and liquidated damages for under-performance. Typically, warranties under which the original supplier will repair, at its cost, any defect will be available for three to five years after completion date. After that, suppliers should make a commitment to ensure the ready availability of spare parts, as needed, albeit that any costs associated with repairs will be for the buyer. In anticipation of such event, the unit prices for labour and materials may have been identified under the original supply contract.

3.3 Technical risks

Just because the contractor or equipment supplier has a long history of successful performance should not allow prudent investors and lenders to overlook the possibility of technical failure.

Normally, and as mentioned above, the acquisition of major items of equipment will be supported by warranties for three, possibly five, years. If a technical failure arises within that period, the original supplier will have to repair the item at its cost. If there is a technical failure after the warranty period, then repairs will be for the account of the buyer/project company, in which case the buyer should negotiate at the outset a technical services contract, probably with the original supplier, under which the supplier will agree to repair equipment failure outside the warranty period with payments based on pre-agreed unit prices for labour and materials. The supplier should also ensure the availability of spare parts during the life cycle of the project.

In practice, for items such as turbines, the original suppliers often offer comprehensive service and maintenance contracts for the equipment that they supply, and they monitor the performance of the equipment remotely.

Another feature to be taken into consideration is that after a number of years the performance of a project may deteriorate, even when the project has received regular maintenance. This is common for many types of power project, and financiers need to be aware of this issue. Mitigation measures may be elusive to cover this risk, the only option being to limit long-term financial exposure, if such a possibility exists – for instance, in wind farms, which can become much less efficient due to worn gearing after 10–12 years.

Lastly, there is the risk of the technology itself. Prudent financiers will wish to know whether the technology has been used before and what the experience was like. To mitigate this risk, the project company may seek the advice of consultants, but a conservative approach is advisable, notwithstanding that the promise and prospects for using the latest and most up-to-date technology may *prima facie* seem most attractive. As mentioned in the chapter on governments' options, the underlying principle should be to use proven technologies.

3.4 Environmental and social risks

In recent years project financiers have become much more sensitive and responsive to the need to ensure that the projects that they fund respect the environmental and social regulations of the countries in which they reside.

As infrastructure projects interface directly with the public and often involve investment in major structural assets, these requirements can become even more important. Many such regulations now cover climate change issues as well.

An important feature of such risks is that the evaluation of the impact and the implementation of mitigation measures can take time. In many cases, this process can be a critical path item in the schedule for preparing and achieving financial close. Consequently, project developers should address environmental issues at the earliest possible date, particularly if a comprehensive and transparent public consultation process is required.

Most jurisdictions will have their own national environmental and social framework for assessing projects. However, given that the greater portion of funding infrastructure projects comes from loans, the guiding principles are now often based on the Equator Principles (www.equator-principles.com), which are based on the principles and methodology adopted by the International Finance Corporation (IFC), the private sector arm of the World Bank.

More than 80 major international banks active in infrastructure project finance have signed up to the Equator Principles. This represents around 75% of the banks operating in this sector.

The principles are voluntary guidelines, not regulations. However, if a bank supports a project which is non-compliant with the Equator Principles, it may be most difficult for that bank to syndicate, or share, that loan with other Equator Principles-compliant banks. It is indeed common to find in principles-compliant banks that a pre-requisite to a proposal approval by the credit committee is the confirmation from an independent expert within the bank that the proposal is compliant with the Equator Principles.

Under the Equator Principles, projects are classified as A, B or C projects whereby:

- A are projects with adverse social and environmental impacts;
- B projects include most construction and commercial projects (eg, housing); and
- C projects are refinancings.

Infrastructure projects are likely to be A projects.

The principles apply to projects with a value of $10 million or more, or equivalent in another currrency.

To comply with the principles, the borrower/project company must prepare an acceptable and approved environmental impact assessment for category A and B projects.

In addition, the borrower/project company has to comply with the principles, monitor project progress and report regularly. However, allowances are made for those borrowers/project companies that are inexperienced in such matters.

The principles have primarily covered environmental and social impacts of projects, but climate change issues are increasingly coming into consideration too under the principles.

Nevertheless, and despite the aspirations of the signatories, the principles are not perfect. Some more advanced countries, where environmental laws and regulations are deemed established and compliant with the principles, have 'designated status', which means that, on occasion, when national policies demand that a specific project investment be implemented come what may, the principles can be overlooked. Consequently, the principles are perceived as having no teeth as sanctions are either not available or not applied.

The principles also provide that the recommended analysis include "consideration of feasible environmentally and socially preferable alternatives" (Equator Principles, 2013, Exhibit II, b)). Again, this may, on occasion, be overlooked – and no sanction is available.

Whereas the Equator Principles cover lending banks (and financial advisers to projects since June 2013), there are currently similar initiatives under the UN Principles of Responsible Investment (www.unpri.org) covering environmental, social and governance (ESG) issues for investors and asset managers. The UN programme covers debt raised from the bond markets.

To date, the UN guidelines have garnered over 1,000 signatories. These guidelines may be less prescriptive than the Equator Principles, but there is no doubt that the trend towards more sustainable developments is inevitable. However, the UN guide has yet to embrace fully the environmental and climate change issues associated with ESG principles, other than in a general way.

3.5 Financial risks

The key risk for lenders will be the borrower's ability to service debt.

Likewise, for investors the risk is whether the anticipated profits and rewards will be achieved.

A key measure of such risks, therefore, will be the ratio between debt and equity in the borrower's/project company's corporate structure. If there is too much debt, then there is the possibility that, after operating costs have been accounted for, net revenues may be insufficient to service debt (ie, pay interest, fees and repayments). Similarly, if there is too much equity, then the returns for investors may not be attractive. The result, therefore, will have to be a balance, albeit based upon subjective assessments of uncertainty and risk.

Lenders will assess all the physical risks, particularly capital costs, operating costs and revenues, to identify what may be an acceptable debt-to-equity ratio. Given such an acceptable scenario, lenders will impose on borrowers additional constraints and covenants – for example, escrow and reserve accounts, minimum debt service cover ratios, dividend payment constraints, and security over the project company's assets. Details of such covenants will be described in later chapters under loan terms sheets.

Similarly, if lenders perceive that investors may gain excessive reward or profit for the underlying project risks, or investors obtain significant profits while much of the debt remains outstanding, lenders may either reduce the amount of debt that they will provide, or provide only loans with a shorter repayment period. After all, why should investors reap handsome rewards before lenders, which are risk averse, receive repayments on their loans? To a certain extent, the project early repayment mechanism (PERM) (or 'cash sweep' mechanism) often applied to commercial bank loans in recent years reflects this concern.

A number of other issues need to be noted relating to financial risks.

3.6 Interest rate risks

Commercial banks obtain much of their funding from the short-term money markets, where interest rates change daily, albeit by miniscule amounts. Historically, such banks provided loans to projects where the interest rate was based on a margin over a base rate (eg, 6-month LIBOR (London Interbank Offered Rate)).

However, the project company would usually prefer to receive loans with fixed interest rates, so that future cost flows could be more accurately forecast.

Banks would, therefore, offer to their borrowers a swap arrangement, whereby the variable interest rate was converted into a fixed rate.

Figure 4.2: Interest rate swap

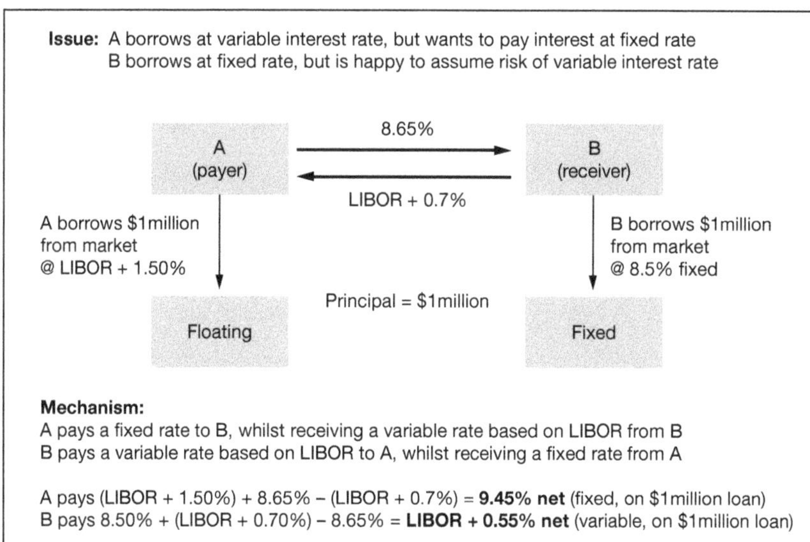

Source: author

A swap is purely an exchange of value agreed between two parties at certain dates in the future. An example of the mechanics of an interest rate swap is given in Figure 4.2. A few caveats should be mentioned, however:

- Inherently, the swap agreement is a separate commercial contract between two parties. It will not appear as a financial obligation on the balance sheet of either party, albeit that there may be comment in the notes to the balance sheet as to the aggregate amount of swaps the company has entered into. It is not the same as a loan agreement, which will be recorded in the borrower's balance sheet. Hence, swap payments are, in effect, contingent liabilities.

- The further into the future the swap agreement is in force, the less flexible it is to renegotiate if circumstances change. This reflects the lower liquidity in the swaps markets for long-term maturities. For example, if the project experiences delays, project completion could be set back one year. This could have an impact for the borrower, which may be easily able to renegotiate the payments dates for a loan, but not the swap. Swap payments may thus have to be made even though the project company is not generating revenues.
- These days, lenders will often offer their borrowers project loans at a fixed interest rate – that is, the lenders are internalising the risk between variable and fixed interest rates. The capital markets, of which the swap market is part, today is large and global, so commercial banks will often act as intermediaries providing fixed rates for borrowers which have variable interest rate loans, and vice versa. But borrowers should always examine carefully the text of the loans offered in this respect.

Figure 4.3: Interest rate swap

Issue: A borrows at variable rate, but wants to pay interest at fixed rate
B borrows at fixed rate, but happy to pay interest at variable rate

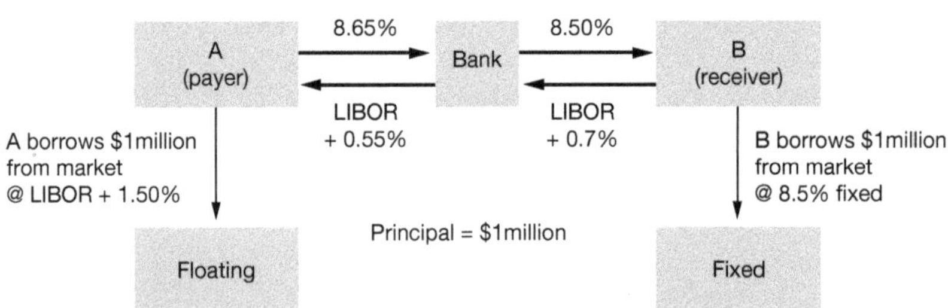

Mechanism:
A pays a fixed rate to B, whilst receiving a variable rate based on LIBOR from B, via bank
B pays a variable rate based on LIBOR to A, whilst receiving a fixed rate from A, via bank

A pays (LIBOR + 1.50%) + 8.65% – (LIBOR + 0.55%) = **9.60% net** (fixed, on $1million loan)
B pays 8.50% + (LIBOR + 0.70%) – 8.50% = **LIBOR + 0.70% net** (variable, on $1million loan)

Bank takes 0.15% + 0.15% = 0.30% fee for the transaction

Source: author

3.7 Currency risks

Currency risk can be a major uncertainty for infrastructure and private, public service projects, particularly in emerging markets.

This comes as no surprise given that much of the costs, both capital and operational, and revenues are generated or paid in local currency, whereas the main and only source of debt and equity could be in hard currency. In such situations, devaluation of the local currency against the hard currency is a likely event within a project life cycle of 20 to 30 years, increasing the financial burden on the borrower/project company. A number of large infrastructure projects have failed for this reason.

Figure 4.4: Currency swap

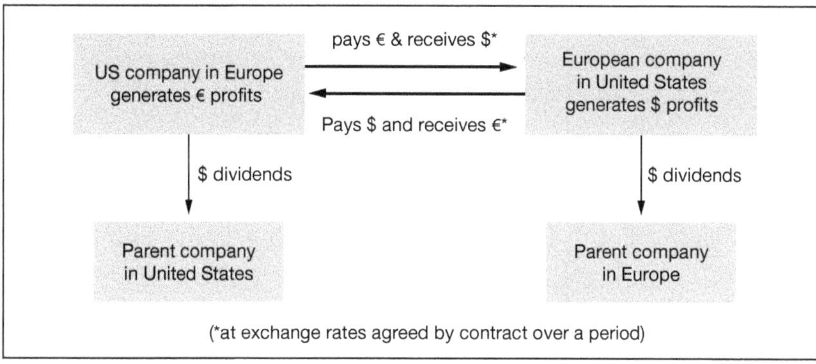

Source: author

Just as interest rate risks can be mitigated by the use of the capital markets, so too can swaps be negotiated to mitigate currency risks. However, the inherent potential mismatch between the swap agreement and the loan debt service profile needs to be carefully managed. A prudent financial manager may use such mechanisms to mitigate a significant portion of the financial risks (eg, up to 70%), but it may be risky to attempt to cover 100% of the perceived risks with such tools. Projects have a habit of never following the predicted path.

It should be mentioned that the derivatives markets can also sometimes be used to fix prices and volumes for commodities. The inherent risks are similar to those linked to interest rate and currency swaps, but invariably the commodities futures market is shorter and 'thinner' (or illiquid), which reflects smaller volumes and values. (In 2016 the Bank for International Settlements reported that the total exposure in the global derivatives markets was around $555 trillion, of which $315 trillion was interest rate swaps.)

3.8 Loan and investor syndication

Both investors and lenders often prefer to have partners in any project financing situation.

For lenders, a structure as in Figure 4.5 is often found. One bank will act as lead bank and manage the loan on behalf of a number of other banks, although each bank carries the credit risk on the borrower in proportion to its participation in the transaction.

However, while lenders prefer to have a partner, there can be too many in big deals. In infrastructure project financing, many lenders will have a minimum threshold deal value (eg, £20 million) below which it is not cost effective for them to undertake the due diligence on the borrower and the underlying project transaction. Likewise, lenders may have a maximum amount that they can lend under their central bank regulations to any one borrower or to any one jurisdiction (ie, they have country limits).

Lead banks are generally happy to manage syndicates with four or five other banks, but some projects exceed this number – for instance, Eurotunnel in 1984 had over 200 banks in the syndicate.

Similarly, investors often prefer to invest in consortia. This is due in great part to the fact that the contractor and operator may be different parties with differing objectives, participations and investment time horizons.

Figure 4.5: Loan syndication

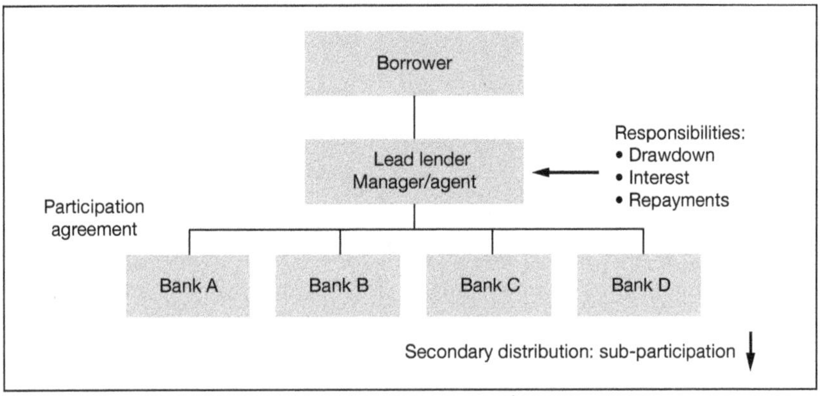

Source: author

3.9 Taxation risks

The project company will be subject to the taxation regime of the jurisdiction in which the project resides. For investors and lenders to any such project, the taxation risks represent the uncertainties of investing and operating in any particular market.

However, in recent times many private infrastructure and public service projects have been so structured as to optimise – or, some might say, minimise or even avoid – tax liabilities for the project company. Multi-layer corporate structures are not uncommon, to the detriment of transparency and, possibly, governance.

Using tax havens for the domicile of investors, pinpointing equity in the funding structure and using the tax-deductible interest payments on subordinated debt are some of the mechanisms commonly encountered in this context.

The G20 countries have expressed a desire to support transparency and good corporate governance in companies, including the avoidance of aggressive tax structures.

Hence, in future investors to infrastructure and public service projects will have to ensure that they are more fully compliant with national tax and public transparency regimes than perhaps they have been to date.

3.10 Legal and political risks

Infrastructure project finance deals are complex. There could be over 40 commercial and financial documents to be negotiated and signed at financial close.

One measure that could minimise this risk is to have common contractual documents. In practice, this is difficult to achieve. Each set of project documents has to be drafted anew.

A second measure is to ensure that there is a clear legal framework, regulation or law for private sector entities undertaking infrastructure and public service investments, such as a PPP concession law. If the intention is to attract foreign capital to such projects, then it advisable that consideration be given to the use of international arbitration to resolve disputes rather than the local courts.

With respect to political risk, the mitigation measures are limited. Apart from insurance, the participation of development banks that enjoy 'preferred creditor status' can alleviate some political risks – for instance, via the use of the A/B loan structure (see the chapter on the sources of financing). It is also in this area that international arbitration has its greatest utility as a risk mitigation tool (see the chapter on the contractual framework).

4. Risk mitigation – the role of insurance

All private projects require insurance, not least against third parties, fire and theft. Lenders will demand this as they take security on the project assets.

It is worth noting, however, that publicly funded projects are often not insured, while multinational company projects are often self-insured. In addition, when an unforeseen event arises:

- one needs to establish a claim where the project is insured, which takes time; and
- with guarantees, the principle is 'pay now and argue later'.

Financiers to private projects, whether providing debt or equity, will expect to see an acceptable, comprehensive insurance package put in place as a condition precedent to funding.

Typically, an infrastructure project will require policies covering the areas highlighted in the table on the next page.

For political risks, the events which have to be covered include:

- physical violence (strikes, riots, war, civil unrest, terrorism, etc);
- commercial environment risks (currency inconvertibility and transfer, economic and political instability); and
- investment environment (expropriation, contractual disputes, legal and regulatory disputes).

The insurance market for infrastructure projects is highly specialised. On

Construction phase	Operations phase
Works/assets policies: • construction all risks • material damage • builders all-risk Operations-related policies: • delay in completion/start-up • advance loss of profit • transportation delay Contractor liabilities: • employer's liability • workmen's compensation • third-party liability	Works/assets policies: • property all risks • material damage • machinery breakdown • engineering and statutory Revenue-related policies: • business interruptions • machinery consequential loss Contractor liabilities: • employer's liability • workmen's compensation • third-party liability

occasion, unusual risks, such as fire in tunnels, have to be covered and very few insurers will be available to provide policies against such risks.

Accordingly, project promoters will often employ an insurance adviser or broker to assemble a comprehensive package. The leaders in the field are Aon, Marsh, and Willis Faber & Dumas, which provide advice and assemble the required insurance package to place with brokers.

In addition, for investors in emerging markets, MIGA of the World Bank provides investment insurance, as well as some of the export credit agencies and national development banks.

5. Concluding remarks – cross-sector financial structures

A comprehensive risk analysis will help to identify which funding structure is the best suited to manage the underlying risks of the project at issue.

For a risky project, the proportion of equity required will be higher than for a less risky venture. Generally speaking, infrastructure and public service-type private projects fall into the latter category.

At the risk of generalising, the proportions shown in the table below often prevail.

Sector	Developed markets Debt/equity	Emerging markets Debt/equity
Commercial property/tourism	50/50	30/70
Industrial projects	70/30	60/40
Infrastructure and power	80/20	70/30
PPPs	85/15	80/20

Further, at the project concept stage the funding structure may be assumed as pure equity and debt. By the time financial close is reached, though, it is not uncommon for two or three layers of subordinate debt or shareholder loans called 'mezzanine capital' to have been imposed by both investors and lenders to maximise their returns and, possibly, minimise tax liabilities.

Sources of finance

1. Introduction

One of the key principles of project financing is to have all the funds needed for a project's implementation committed at the outset – before the two- to three-year construction phase even starts.

A number of steps need to be taken to ensure availability of the funds to the project company at any point during the development of the project. For equity, this could require third-party guarantees to support the shareholder, or third-party security as may be provided by an irrevocable letter of credit (ILOC). For loans, borrowers will normally pay a commitment fee to the lender, calculated as a percentage of the amount of loan not yet used or drawn down, which will commit the lender to allow disbursements to the borrower, when called for, provided that the borrower has complied with normal covenants under the loan.

Unfortunately, examples abound of this basic funding principle being breached.

Another noteworthy characteristic is that in most cash flow-based project financings, lenders insist that equity be used to fund project costs first, and only when that has been used up can debt be disbursed.

2. Equity

2.1 Common features

Equity is risk capital. It has lower priority than debt in the event of bankruptcy.

The four main types of equity that may be used in infrastructure developments are outlined below.

New investment capital: This consists of funds from investors that have an interest either in the project's implementation or in gaining financial reward, or both.

Equity provided by investors sourcing such money from current and future profits of their ongoing business: Whereas the availability from current resources may be assured, there is a risk that, if future profits are not generated from the investor's ongoing business, later injections of equity may not be available – in which case, additional security will be required, as mentioned earlier.

In-kind contributions, such as land and technology, or a political stake: The difficulty is that the value of any in-kind equity contribution is usually manifest only once the project has been completed and has moved into the operations period, generating revenues or providing economic value. Until such time, the in-kind value is notionally worthless.

Accordingly, there is a strong argument to suggest that much, if not all, of the inherent value of in-kind contributions – whether it is the land where the project is sited, the technologies to be employed or a stake taken by a host government for political/social reasons – is best remunerated through some form of licence fee, royalty or tax.

Such a framework may appear to be fairer and more reasonable to all parties. The alternative is to use expert advice; however, the basis for valuing such in-kind contributions could still be speculative, with little justification for the conclusions.

Issue of shares in the project company: To many project developers, this may appear the most attractive option. It is also the most difficult.

It is common for companies throughout the world to raise equity capital through the sale of shares on an exchange (ie, through an initial public offering or IPO). However, the majority, if not all, of those new issues are for companies which already have established a business model and are seeking new capital for expansion and investment. Prospective investors can readily make an assessment of the existing business model and make a judgement as to whether to subscribe to the share offering.

With a project – and even more so with an infrastructure project where the construction period may last two to three years – there is no ongoing business to evaluate, and there will not be one until the end of construction. Accordingly, the risks for potential investors are much higher than for a corporate share issue.

When such offering is attempted, it is common for it to be underwritten by an investment bank, which will buy any shares not sold through the offering. This is to make up for the uncertainty as to whether potential investors will respond to any share offering and whether the full offering will be subscribed; it ensures that the issuer receives the full value of the shares offered.

Such underwriting, taken together with all the preparatory and administrative costs (eg, publishing a prospectus which meets the stock exchange requirements) makes the issue of shares a relatively expensive exercise, particularly if much uncertainty overhangs the issue. Hence, this method for raising equity finance is a rarity for new infrastructure projects.

2.2 Types of shareholder

The main categories of shareholder are:

- construction contractors (which seek to win the construction contracts);
- equipment suppliers (which seek to win supply contracts);
- operators and public service utilities (which seek to win the operations contract);
- project developers and entrepreneurs;
- development banks and agencies (for emerging markets);
- new shareholders (in case of an IPO);
- private equity;

- sovereign wealth funds; and
- offsets.

All the above are potential shareholders in the project company. Development banks and offsets as a source of equity will be discussed in section 3 of this chapter, but comment is required at this juncture in respect of private equity and sovereign wealth funds.

2.3 Private equity – infrastructure funds

Private equity funds originated in North America, when investment banks and boutiques set up investment funds to:

- buy up poorly performing companies;
- turn them around, often by selling off under-performing assets; and
- sell on the company after three to five years, hopefully at a profit (ie, a capital gain over what they bought the original company for).

Such investment activities made some investment bankers billionaires.

In the late 1990s, investment banks, largely led by Macquarie Bank and Babcock & Brown of Australia, identified this mechanism as an appropriate way to attract life insurance companies and pension funds to support infrastructure developments. Twenty years on, Macquarie is still the leader of the pack, but today the private equity funds of many other international investment and commercial banks also focus on supporting infrastructure development. (Babcock & Brown is no longer active in the projects business.)

The mechanism is as shown in Figures 5.1 and 5.2.

Figures 5.1: Private equity fund formation

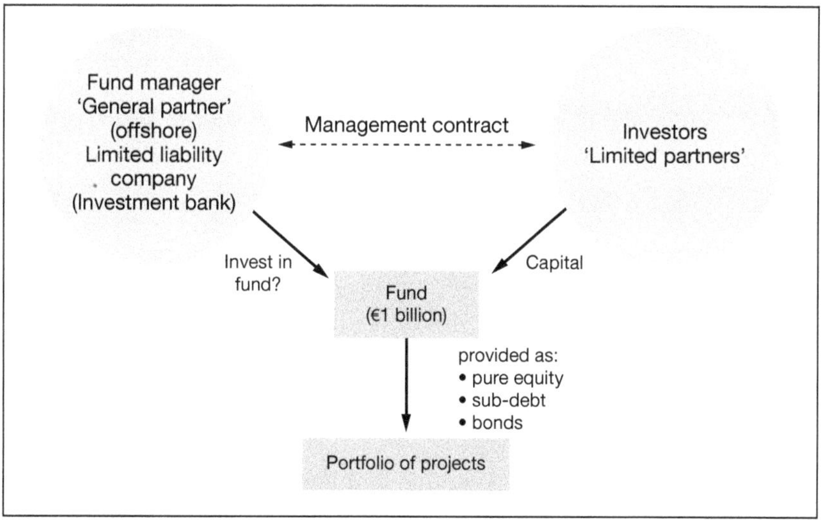

Source: author

Figure 5.2: Private equity fund operations

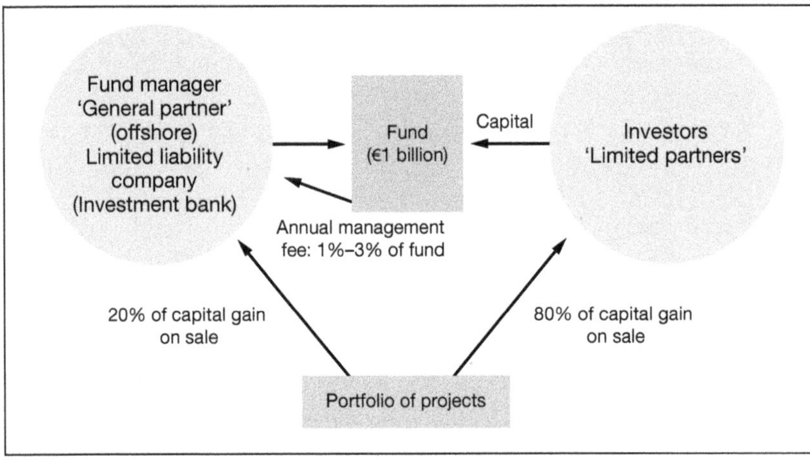

Source: author

Initially, the private equity manager will set up a fund, as a limited liability company, made up of investors called 'limited partners', such as pensions funds, life insurance companies and wealthy individuals. Typically, such fund might have an overall value of £1 billion equivalent, and be set up in a tax haven for taxation optimisation.

The manager may or may not be an investor in the fund, but will have a management contract with the fund investors, for which it will receive an annual fee. Typically, that fee (certainly in the early years of private equity) could be as much as 3% of the fund value. Further, such management contract could be for the full life of the fund, irrespective of whether investors sell their participation to third parties at a future date.

The manager will then use the fund resources to invest in shares, subordinate debt or bonds in infrastructure project companies.

After some years, some of the investments in projects may be sold to other investors. If a capital gain is made, then a portion of that gain, known as the 'carried interest', will go to the manager and the balance to the investors. Such carried interest could be as high as 20%. However, with growing competition between funds in recent years, the managers' fees have been reduced to closer to 1% for the annual fee and 10% for carried interest.

On the plus side, such funds:

- have attracted long-term investors to private infrastructure investments; and
- have provided an opportunity for pension funds and life insurance companies, which seek long-term stable investments, to invest in infrastructure.

However, the involvement of private equity in infrastructure finance can have negative implications too:

- The managers of private equity funds, which control the investment cycle, typically seek to 'churn' (ie, sell) investments made within three to five years – not least so as to realise any carried interest fees from any capital gains arising. However, five years or less is a short period in terms of the life cycle of an infrastructure project. The changing of shareholder investments in infrastructure and public service assets can be destabilising. (Not all funds follow this pattern, though, and it is increasingly frequent for funds to take a much longer perspective.)
- Such funds are often domiciled in tax havens, so issues of transparency, governance, accountability and probity can arise. For infrastructure and public services, this can be a sensitive issue. Some governments (eg, the Victoria State Government in Australia) impose a probity, or 'fit and proper person', test on any shareholders of private project companies responsible for investment and delivery of infrastructure and public services.

2.4 Sovereign wealth funds

Sovereign wealth funds share many of the characteristics of private equity funds. Indeed, many invest in such private equity funds. However, the key difference is that sovereign wealth funds have a political dimension, whether perceived or not.

Figure 5.3: Sovereign wealth funds 2015

Fund country [date of establishment]		Name	Assets established ($ billion 2015)
Norway	[1990]	GPF	890
United Arab Emirates	[1976]	ADIA	770
Saudi Arabia	[N/A]	SAMA	760
China	[1997] [2007] [2000]	SAFE CIC NSSF	570 650 240
China (Hong Kong)	[1993]	HKMA	400
Singapore	[1981] [1974]	GIC Temasek Hldgs	320 180
Kuwait	[1953]	KIA	550
Australia	[2006]	CDPQ	95
Russia	[2008]	Nat Welfare Fund Reserve Fund	80 90
Qatar	[2005]	QIA	260
United States	[N/A]	Alaska Permanent Fund	50

A good example of this arose when in 2006 the UK shipping and container port manager P&O was sold to state-owned DP World of Dubai. P&O had had some container port concessions in the United States, and the US Congress demanded that DP World divest itself of such port concessions, as they were viewed as strategic assets by the US government.

In the United Kingdom, where arguably more private concessions (eg, private finance initiatives or PFI) and privatised public service utilities exist than any other country (estimated as at least 1,000), such sensitivities have not arisen.

Nevertheless, sovereign wealth funds often take a long-term perspective. To date, their asset managers have tended to invest in real estate, banks and the capital markets. However, over the 2013–16 period a number have turned their attention to infrastructure investment, which more closely adheres to their investment objectives in many respects.

During 2012–15 a number of major infrastructure investments in railways and roads (among other things) were announced in emerging markets, particularly in Africa, where sovereign wealth funds have made direct loans to governments under what is known as the 'Angola model' – that is, long-term loans to governments to fund infrastructure, with repayments made via the export of raw materials or commodities such as oil and gas.

2.5 Issues facing investors

(a) Changing profitability over time

Investors will calculate their potential profitability as an internal rate of return (IRR) based on the cash flow projections for the project. With infrastructure projects, particularly if the construction period is long (ie, two to three years), an acceptable IRR may not be achieved for some years (eg, eight to 10 years). This may be too long for investors such as private equity investors.

Hence, if such investors wish to participate in infrastructure projects, hoping to achieve higher returns than the underlying cash flows can generate during the investment period, they must do so with the expectation of being able to sell their participation at a capital gain to make up for the shortfall profit that they would otherwise have generated if they had kept their investment in the venture until such time as an acceptable IRR had been achieved. Selling at a capital gain may, or may not, be possible, and represents a key risk area for investors in infrastructure.

To assess such risk, analysts should undertake profitability (ie, IRR) calculation on cash flow projections for differing periods (eg, five, eight, 10 and 12 years) for infrastructure developments, and compare the results against their expectations for returns, given their investment horizons.

(b) Dividend policy and payment availability

In cash flow project financings, lenders may impose dividend constraints on shareholders in the project company until they can be sure that the project is performing well and able to cover its debt service payments. Hence, there may be constraints on such payments in the early years of operations.

Further, as the project proceeds, if the debt service cover ratio drops below predetermined levels, lenders may limit, or even not allow, dividend payments until the cash flows are restored to health.

Likewise, if during the operations period the project turns out to be more profitable than expected, notional dividends would then be higher than expected. In such circumstances, lenders may require loans to be repaid early rather than dividends paid to shareholders.

In many ways, this latter constraint has a similar impact to the use of the 'cash sweep' mechanism that has become a common loan condition following the imposition of the Basel III requirements (which constrain banks' ability to lend long term by demanding higher capital support for long-term loans). Under a cash sweep mechanism, if a project is generating enough cash to pay dividends after a specified number of years, then the borrower has to repay debt early rather than pay dividends.

(c) ***Currency convertibility and transfer***

For infrastructure projects in emerging markets, where the capital and operating costs and revenues may be in the (weak) domestic currency while equity and long-term debt are provided in hard currency, the inherent currency risk can be high. Not only does that affect debt service, but also dividend payments. The use of insurance and support from development bank mechanisms probably represent the optimal mitigation measures.

(d) ***Inherent capital balance of the project company***

Investors will review the capital structure – that is, the proportion of debt to equity – of the project company. Is it reasonable for the sector and the inherent risks?

(e) ***Availability of funding***

Investors will consider whether all the funding (debt and equity) is fully committed at the outset. A prudent investor will also wish to ensure that standby facilities (both debt and equity) are arranged to cover contingencies.

(f) ***Exit strategy and the secondary market***

Financial investors will consider whether there are potential buyers for their shares, in case they wish to sell at any time, and a secondary market. If the market is limited, then this could constrain how much they will invest.

Likewise, contractor and equipment supplier investors will commonly wish to sell their shares once project completion is achieved. They will wish to go and build or supply another project; that is their prime business. Consequently, they too will review their exit strategy.

(g) ***Partnering***

Many investors will prefer to partner with other investors rather than be sole investors in a project.

(h) ***Political risks***

Political risks cannot be avoided, particularly in emerging markets. Accordingly, the optimal mitigation measures may be to seek support from development banks, arrange appropriate political risk insurance policies, and look to international arbitration to resolve disputes.

(i) ***Taxation***

There have been growing demands by host governments for companies to pay their just dues in tax. For infrastructure and public service projects, which interface with the public, this will be of increasing importance. Consequently, in future the extensive use of tax haven vehicles to channel investments into such projects may become constrained and open to greater scrutiny than hitherto.

(j) ***Financial engineering***

In recent years many investor groups, particularly private equity, have employed what some would argue are aggressive, albeit legal, tax optimisation structures in project companies. One such mechanism commonly employed is for the equity component of the project company to be subscribed primarily as a shareholder loan, or subordinate debt, at a higher-than-normal interest rate – with the balance provided as pure equity, commonly described as 'pinhead equity' as it is often minute in comparison.

The benefit for the investor can be that, in certain tax jurisdictions, interest payments on such shareholder loans or sub-debt are an allowable cost before tax. Hence, in effect such interest payments on such sub-debt are dividend payments before tax.

An example of such a structure was the UK M6 Toll (Midland Expressway) funding for the Birmingham North Relief Road in 2000. The overall capital cost was £832 million, of which £685 million was senior debt, £145.5 million was subordinated debt and £1.5 million was equity. The interest rate on the senior debt was at a margin over base rate of around 7%, whereas the interest rate on the subordinated debt was 12%.

Further extremes of the use of this mechanism can be found in other public service utilities such as Wales & West Utilities, a UK, private equity-owned, wholesale gas distribution monopoly, where the sub-debt portion of the corporate funding carried an interest rate of 21% a year between 2007 and 2010, when the base rate was around 6%, dropping to 15% in 2011–12, by which time the base rate had dropped to an average 1%.

Tax authorities are beginning to be aware of such structures and acting accordingly. In some jurisdictions, such sub-debt interest payments may be allowable if there is a good commercial reason for them to be so (eg, the United Kingdom). Many such sub-debt facilities are, however, primarily structured to minimise taxation, which is a financial issue. Such structure has no impact on the commercial operations of the project company.

3. Debt

3.1 Introduction

Under the category of debt, the main sources are:

- international development banks;
- national development banks;
- export credit agencies (ECAs);
- commercial bank loans;
- bonds;
- Islamic finance; and
- leasing and offsets.

The following section describes the key features of each of these debt sources. However, an exhaustive description is beyond the scope of this chapter.

However, mention should be made first of the role of aid, grants and subsidies or subventions in infrastructure project financing. Such funding falls outside market norms, and will come with its own terms and conditions attached.

For example, in African countries a number of infrastructure projects (particularly for rail) have been announced that are financed by concessionary funding from China. The main rationale for such deals is both to support local economic development, and to provide China with access to commodities. Such Angola model deals do not necessarily follow conventional banking criteria. Similarly, a number of countries provide tax credits to support renewable energy projects.

Such subventions have a role in funding infrastructure developments, but their value has to be assessed individually.

3.2 International development banks

International development banks are commonly referred to as international financial institutions or IFIs.

The main players in this category are:

- the World Bank (and the International Finance Corporation for private sector projects);
- the Asian Development Bank;
- the African Development Bank;
- the European Investment Bank (EIB);
- the European Bank for Reconstruction and Development (EBRD);
- the Inter-American Development Bank;
- the Islamic Development Bank; and
- Corporacion Andina de Fomento (CAF).

Such institutions have governments as their shareholders. They are set up under international law, so their loans can enjoy treaty status. They also enjoy preferred creditor status, which means that, when a member country runs into financial difficulties:

- the IFI has priority access to the borrower's foreign exchange earnings; and

- there should be no impedance of foreign exchange remittances by the borrower.

In effect, IFI loans to governments or state agencies will not be rescheduled, but become due and paid as originally negotiated.

Historically, this principle has held. A number of countries have got into financial difficulties (eg, Argentina, Russia, Peru), but within living memory there has not been a default on an IFI loan. (If, and when, such circumstances arise, the International Monetary Fund should be able to assist in arranging a debt rescheduling programme.)

In general, IFIs provide financing to both public and private sector borrowers, although the World Bank deals only with governments and state agencies. A number of these IFIs (eg, IFC and EBRD) may also provide equity.

In the case of a loan to a government, then such loan will enjoy a sovereign guarantee. That means that, notionally, the loan has received the approval of the host parliament – not least because under the preferred creditor status of the lender, a lien over national assets is implied.

Such security has to be compared with ECA and commercial bank loans, where a government guarantee may be provided by the borrower, but such guarantee is given by, say, the minister of finance, under delegated authority of the host government.

IFIs, as their name suggests, have the prime objective of developing economies, so their funding may be longer term than is available through ECAs or the commercial banking markets. Such loans are usually in hard currency, and borrowers have to comply with strict requirements with respect to procurement of contracts and equipment, as well as environmental standards. As a result, many project sponsors complain that IFI funding can be bureaucratic and tedious to negotiate. IFIs may, however, offer the only source of long-term funding available in some markets.

IFI A/B loans: In the context of infrastructure, particularly privately funded infrastructure such as public-private partnerships (PPPs), the support of IFI funding via what is termed the 'A/B loan mechanism' can be key.

Under this mechanism, which applies to private projects only, the A loan is provided by the IFI, whereas the B loan comes from a commercial bank. Both loans will normally be on similar terms and conditions, and each lender assumes the commercial credit risk of the borrower – that is, the ability of the borrower to service the loans from normal commercial activities. However, in the context of political risks, the commercial lender shares in the preferred creditor status protection that the IFI enjoys.

In addition to such loans, the IFI may also provide equity. In such event, the IFI will usually limit its overall exposure in any one project to, say, 35% of project costs, with the balance provided by commercial bank loans and other equity. However, there can be exceptions to such limits, such as plant expansions.

Furthermore, assuming that any specific project can be shown to have a potentially significant economic impact for the host country, it may be possible to negotiate that the IFI A loan have longer maturity than the B loan, or that the repayment schedule be sculpted to match the cash flow projections of the project more closely.

Another mechanism, common in IFI infrastructure-type financings, is the use of partial risk guarantees, which represents, in effect, a credit enhancement technique to extend maturities of debt and provide some default risk cover. Typically, the IFI will guarantee up to 100% of debt service payments to commercial lenders on a project, subject to a maximum cumulative payout limit of, say, 30% of the loan amount, in event of default. Such a guarantee can incentivise commercial lenders to lend longer term than they might otherwise do, given the capital they have to use to support such debt.

Beside the above, IFIs might also have some political objectives which they hope to achieve, such as:

- 'transition impact' – that is, supporting programmes and projects to promote market economies;
- 'additionality' – that is, a measure as to how much private capital is attracted to a specific deal relative to the amount of IFI financial support; and
- 'integrity' – that is, the promotion of good governance and probity.

To conclude, the IFIs play a crucial role in the promotion of infrastructure development in emerging markets and, in particular, the use of private capital to fund such projects. Each year, the IFIs will review the recipient governments and the projects which are to be supported in each region or country over the following period.

The IFIs may also have available technical assistance funds – that is, grant money to support project preparation and other essential aspects of successful project development, such as the creation of a legal framework to promote PPPs.

It is, therefore, essential, given current constraints imposed by regulators upon private commercial lenders on their ability to lend long term, that governments and agencies seeking to develop infrastructure projects in emerging markets have early contact with the IFIs focused on that region.

Each IFI has its own specific criteria and limits for participating in infrastructure. Furthermore, it is often the case that some of the regional, smaller IFIs are at the vanguard of project development in infrastructure, and may well have easier access to technical assistance funding, with the larger IFIs providing the bulk of funding in the event. Thus, smaller IFIs, such as the Nordic Development Bank, the Black Sea Development Bank and the African Finance Corporation, are very active in their field, while the World Bank, the EIB and the CAF provide the bulk of IFI funding in the regions in which they operate.

3.3 National development banks

Institutions in this category include:

- the Overseas Project Investment Corporation, United States;
- the Japan Bank of International Cooperation, Japan;
- KfW, Germany;
- Proparco, France;

- FMO, Netherlands; and
- Danida, Denmark.

Such banks are usually created under domestic law, are state-owned, and raise the funds they need in the financial markets against a host government guarantee.

Their role is to support exports and the development of their economies, so they have both a national and international business perspective. They can usually provide both equity and debt on what they describe as 'commercial terms'. Further, many are set up as not-for-profit organisations, or at least they are required to maintain a certain level of return on capital.

The sectors that they support include:

- development cooperation;
- environmental protection;
- export finance;
- infrastructure;
- new technologies;
- political risk insurance;
- renewable energy;
- small and medium enterprises; and
- start-up enterprises.

These national development banks often play a key role in supporting their national exporters in their participation in infrastructure developments overseas. The United Kingdom has no national development bank, the closest thing being the Commonwealth Development Corporation, whose equity portfolio was sold to private equity interests (Actis) in 2004, and which today tends to pursue wider developmental goals than direct support for UK exports and UK economic development.

One of the most successful national development banks has been KfW of Germany, which has been a key ingredient in German industrial and manufacturing growth since the end of the Second World War.

3.4 ECAs

Most industrialised countries have their own ECA to support the export of capital goods and services (eg, consultancy contracts).

The main ECAs are:

- CESCE, Spain;
- Coface, France;
- ECGD, United Kingdom;
- EDC, Canada;
- EKF, Denmark;
- EKN, Sweden;
- ERG, Switzerland;
- KfW-IPEX, Germany;
- NCM, Netherlands;

- OKB, Austria;
- OND, Belgium;
- SACE, Italy; and
- US Ex-Im Bank, United States.

These ECAs are usually actual agencies or departments of government.

Some ECAs act as lenders – that is, they provide loans ('credits') directly to exporters or buyers, whereas other ECAs act as guarantors to commercial banks that provide exporters or buyers with loans.

The terms and conditions for such loans (ie, the interest rates and repayment periods) are governed by the OECD Consensus Agreement; so for any particular project opportunity, any export credits offered in support of contractors or equipment suppliers should have similar terms.

Interest rates are fixed for the loan period, payable on the outstanding amount every six months after the first drawdown; the rate will be somewhat lower than commercial interest rates for the borrowers concerned.

Likewise, the repayment period may well be longer than what is available from commercial banks, with repayments based on equal semi-annual instalments. However, on occasion it may be possible to negotiate, particularly for project cash flow financings, for repayments to be made on an annuity basis, which is less onerous to the borrower in the early years of operations.

The credit, or loan, amount available under export credits is limited to 85% of the export value, with possibly another 15% value to cover local costs if the exporter has installation and commissioning responsibilities. In addition, export components from third countries may be allowable for cover under the export credit up to, say, 30% of the value. The balance of funding, therefore, has to come from other sources, such as commercial bank loans or equity.

The security that borrowers have to provide is usually a government or corporate guarantee, although most ECAs will entertain cash flow project financing.

Under the OECD Consensus, countries – and, therefore, borrowers therein – are classified as either Category I or Category II, the former being considered 'richer' and so commanding repayment periods of between five and eight and a half years, whereas the latter, 'poorer' countries can have repayment periods up to 10 years. Renewable energy and nuclear projects can obtain repayment periods up to 18 years (eg, the China/South Korea export of nuclear reactors to the United Arab Emirates).

Given the above, one might expect that ECAs from one country will have identical costs to those from another. This is not always the case, and differences can arise due to the relevant ECA's insurance premium that the exporter has to pay to its ECA to gain access to the concessionary ECA funding.

Figure 5.4 represents a typical export credit facility for a large value contract (ie, greater than, say, $10 million) known as a 'buyer credit':

- The buyer considers buying some equipment from a seller from country A.
- The seller offers a price (eg, 100).
- The buyer requests that the seller offer a funding package to support the contract.

Figure 5.4: Buyer credit (ECA as lender) (Large value: >$10 million)

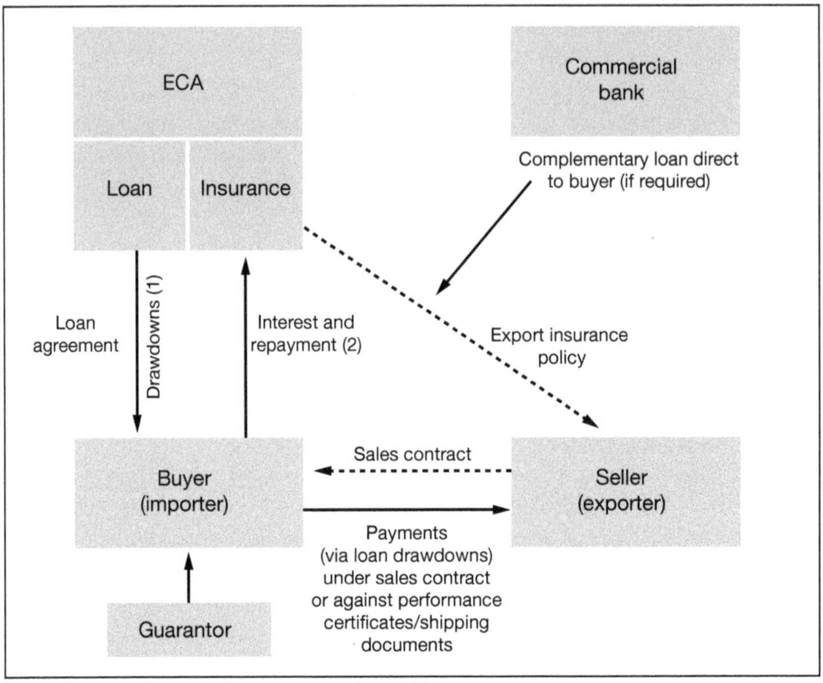

Source: author

- The seller seeks the support of its national ECA, which in this case is a direct funder or lender.
- The ECA undertakes a credit assessment of the buyer (and, if necessary, asks for additional security or guarantee), and confirms support for the seller's export contract. The ECA charges the seller an export credit insurance premium, which is a percentage (say, 3%) of the contract value.
- The seller then adjusts its price to 103 to include the insurance fee in the price of its sales contract, and offers the buyer an export credit loan.
- The buyer wishes to receive a competitive quote from a seller in country B. The price for the equipment without credit support is, again, 100.
- The buyer requests a funding package, and the seller in country B consults its national ECA.
- Country B's ECA agrees to support the sales contract, and the seller includes the cost of the insurance premium in its offer, plus an export credit loan.
- However, on this occasion the export credit premium from country B is 5%, as country B has limited capacity available for additional credit exposure to the buyer's country.
- The contract is awarded to the seller from country A, whose sales price is 103, against 105 from country B.

These differences in export credit premiums can make all the difference between choices of source of supply of equipment. The premiums change from year to year, and many ECAs keep their assessments, which include not only credit but also political considerations, confidential.

If the seller now wishes to offer a 100% funding package, then additional finance – often termed a 'complementary loan' – will be sought from commercial banks, or buyer equity to fund the balance.

The contract can now be signed and the funding put in place. As the seller ships goods to the buyer, or when contractual performance milestones are achieved, the buyer makes payments to the seller, drawing down on the export credit facility, commercial bank loan or the buyer's own equity resources.

When the export contract has been fully completed, the seller will have received full payment for the exported goods, and the buyer will have created an export credit and/or commercial bank loan obligation, on which interest and repayment will have to be paid over future periods to the ECA and any other lenders. For cash flow project financing deals, interest on loans and export credit may well be rolled up or capitalised.

Figure 5.5: Buyer credit (ECA as guarantor) (Large value: >$10 million)

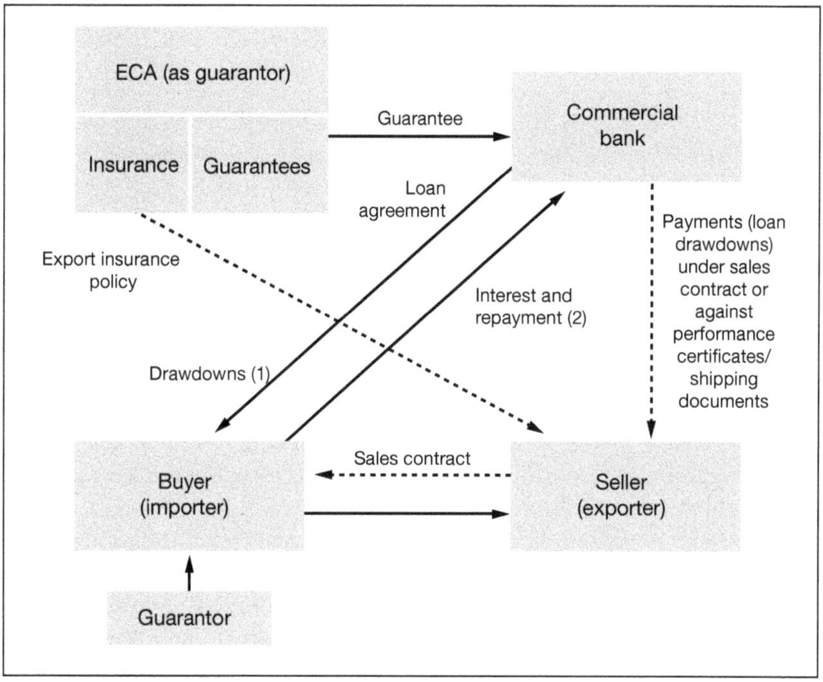

Source: author

In Figure 5.5, the buyer credit mechanism is shown for cases where the ECA is a guarantor rather than a lender. The procedure is identical, in effect, to the buyer receiving a loan from a commercial bank rather than an ECA.

However, in the event that the buyer defaults on the ECA loan, for the bank there is the additional security of the guarantee from the ECA, which is usually a governmental institution. On occasion, depending on the final funding structure of the deal, the guarantee that the commercial bank receives might not cover 100% of both political and commercial risk, and some risk-sharing with the ECA takes place. As always, there are small variations between ECAs.

Figure 5.6: Supplier credit (ECA as guarantor) Small value (<$10 million)

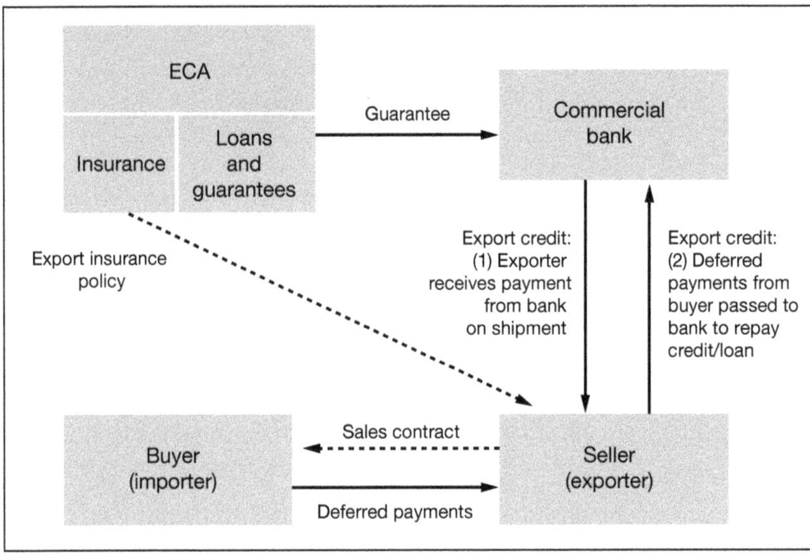

Source: author

Figure 5.6 shows the basic structure for a lower value deal (ie, below $10 million), known as a 'supplier credit'. In effect, the ECA credit is offered on a deferred payment basis. The documentation and administration is simpler, and it is quicker to negotiate and implement.

Similarly, Figure 5.7 shows the framework for a line of credit. Such arrangements may be set up for specific markets in any country. The intermediary in the importing country could be a creditworthy bank which on-lends, in effect, to small and medium enterprises. Review of the websites of many ECAs will identify those banks for which the incumbent ECA has already set up lines of credit, which can be readily accessed by smaller exporters without having to negotiate deal-by-deal arrangements. Similar lines of credit may be set up for large projects, where there could be supplies from a number of sources and countries.

ECAs can play a key role in infrastructure projects in many markets. Clearly, for projects like roads, bridges or tunnels, which are primarily concrete and some steel, the opportunities for employing ECA finance may be limited, but in other infrastructure sectors, such as power, they can make a significant contribution.

Lastly, ECA finance requires efficient administration and timely payments. All

Figure 5.7: Line of credit (ECA as guarantor) Supply package (eg, a series of small energy efficiency projects)

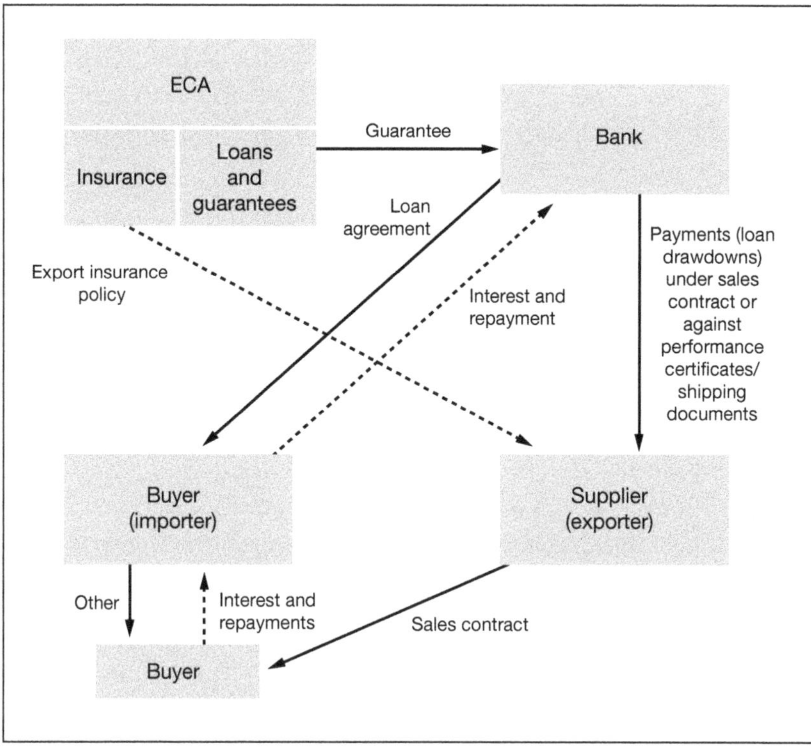

Source: author

the big international banks – not just those national banks of the exporting countries – are well versed in the individual requirements of the major ECAs, and the choice of supporting banks for deals which include ECA funding can be critical. Ideally, the bank should be active in both the seller and buyer markets.

3.5 Commercial bank loans

Commercial bank loans are the primary type of debt for infrastructure projects. They are more flexible than other debt sources, although the repayment periods available may be shorter than for IFI or ECA loans. The market is also competitive, as not only are commercial banks lenders, but they may also wish to play a role as arranger and coordinator for other sources of funding.

Once the need for a private infrastructure project has been determined, the developer, as represented by a project company, will wish to identify and appoint a lead bank to help assemble the funding package. Potential lenders may then be asked, either by the developer or the lead bank, to present outline term sheets, which should summarise the terms and conditions upon which lenders will provide loans. A more detailed term sheet may follow.

A detailed term sheet will consider the following key features:

- Project – the term sheet will describe the project and costs for which the loan is to be used;
- Borrower – the term sheet will identify the project company as borrower;
- Shareholders and sponsors – the term sheet will identify the key project shareholders and sponsors;
- Co-lenders – the term sheet will identify other lenders which intend to participate in the loan;
- Amount and currency – the term sheet will describe the value and currency of the loan;
- Availability period – the term sheet will specify the period for which the loan will be available;
- Interest rate – the term sheet will specify:
  - whether the interest rate is fixed or variable;
  - the base rate (eg, 6-month LIBOR);
  - the interest rate margins over base rate;
  - the payment period for interest (eg, every six months, in arrears);
  - whether the interest is capitalised (ie, calculated, but not paid, so added to the outstanding amount of the loan);
  - whether, once the project has been completed and moves into operations, interest and repayment amounts will be synchronised to occur on the same date so as to minimise loan administration, as if often the case;
- Commitment fee – the term sheet will specify the percentage payable per annum on the unused amount in advance (or in arrears); note, however, that by paying this fee, the lender cannot refuse drawdown by the borrower if the borrower has given due notice and met all the conditions precedent to drawdowns;
- Front-end fee (often combined with the administration fee) – the term sheet will specify the fee paid on loan signature (ie, at financial close) to cover the fees due to the lender and the advisers to cover negotiation costs and ongoing loan administration;
- Prepayment amounts and fees – the term sheet will explain what happens:
  - if the borrower wishes to prepay the loan – then there will be minimum amounts of the loan (eg, $1 million) which can be repaid at any time;
  - if prepayment arises – then there will be a prepayment fee due to the lender, usually expressed as a percentage of the loan amount, for arranging such prepayment. If any prepayment requires unwinding of swap arrangements (eg, interest rate swaps), then the costs for the borrower can be significant;
- Repayment schedule – the term sheet will describe:
  - when repayments start (usually six months after project completion);
  - the frequency and amount of the repayments (usually paid in equal, semi-annual instalments);
  - whether the repayments are on annuity basis (which is often the case in cash flow financings);

- Lender's security – the term sheet will specify:
  - whether a lien exists over the project company assets and land;
  - how any insurance payments arising are assigned;
  - how the project company's movable assets are assigned;
  - whether there is a pledge of the project company bank accounts;
  - whether there is a pledge of the project company shares;
  - any requirement for the project company to set up the following reserve accounts:
    - debt service reserve account (with the next debt service payment due);
    - maintenance reserve account (an amount to cover future major maintenance events);
    - insurance premium reserve account (the next insurance premium due);
- Credit support – the term sheet will provide:
  - an agreement with the project sponsors to provide equity;
  - performance guarantees from the shareholders (eg, completion);
- Project agreements – the term sheet will describe the assignment of (as applicable):
  - licences and permits;
  - construction contract with [x];
  - operations and maintenance contract with [y];
  - supply contract with [z];
  - sales contract with [xx], for the purchase of [yy] (volume) at a price of [zz];
- Conditions precedent to loan effectiveness – the term sheet will describe:
  - the insurance policies agreed and in place;
  - the acceptable environment impact assessment;
- Conditions precedent to drawdowns – the term sheet will describe the covenants imposed to allow drawdowns, such as certification of invoices, satisfactory performance, etc;
- Accounting standards – the term sheet will specify which accounting standards are used (International Accounting Standards or Generally Accepted Accounting Principles);
- Dividends – the term sheet will specify the requirements to pay dividends (eg, no dividends before [date] or unless the debt service cover ratio is higher than [x]);
- Indebtedness and expenditures – the term sheet will list the covenants by the borrower, such as:
  - maximum annual expenditure allowable;
  - maximum annual lease payments allowable;
  - maximum short-term debt allowable;
  - maximum subordinated debt allowable;
  - maximum annual hedging transactions allowable;
  - negative pledge (ie, if the borrower wishes to raise additional debt, it has to ask the lender's approval first);

- Financial covenants by the borrower – the term sheet will specify:
  - the minimum debt service cover ratio to be maintained;
  - the debt service cover ratio which triggers early loan repayment rather than payment of dividends (ie, cash sweep);
  - the debt service cover ratio which triggers the lender's step-in rights;
  - the debt service cover ratio which triggers default;
  - the percentage of cash sweep after [x] years; and
- Additional covenants – the term sheet will provide additional covenants relating to events and conditions which can give rise to suspension of the loan or termination.

It is also worth noting that some national banking regulators may impose limits or provisioning requirements in respect of lending operations on certain less creditworthy borrowers and/or countries. Such loans will be more expensive for the borrower than might otherwise have been the case.

3.6 Bond issues

Bonds as debt instruments must first be differentiated from performance or surety bonds, which are insurance products.

Secondly, bonds are tradable instruments. Bond certificates are issued with a face value, say $100 each, and can be traded on stock exchanges, just like stocks and shares. Such bonds attract an interest rate, like interest on a loan. If the interest rate for a specific bond, given its risk and perceived creditworthiness of the issuer (ie, the borrower) is higher than what the market might normally expect for such risk, then the face value might rise to $105, and vice versa.

Historically, governments have used the bond markets to finance their budgets. There is a wide variety of bonds available, both short and long term, and in a wide range of currencies. According to statistics from the Bank for International Settlements, the worldwide bond market amounts to $80 trillion, of which the US municipal/government and corporate bond market amounts to around $30 trillion.

Furthermore, some bonds have very long maturities – for instance, the AAA-rated $750 million 100-year bond issue by the Massachusetts Institute of Technology (MIT) at 5.6% issued in May 2011, when 30-year US government bonds were at around 5%. The MIT issue was four times over-subscribed when brought to market. Similarly, 100-year 'green' bonds are now being promoted in the United States in support of renewable energy and energy efficiency programmes.

The exchange chosen to sell the bonds that a company/borrower intends to issue will lay down strict requirements as to the sales procedure to be adopted. A prospectus will have to be prepared, usually with the help of an investment bank, and the issue normally has to be underwritten, again by an investment bank, to ensure that on issue the full amount of funding is raised (see Figure 5.8). The bond will be sold typically to institutional investors – that is, pension funds and life insurance companies – and the trustee/fiscal agent will undertake the administration issues of the bond.

Figure 5.8: Bond issue

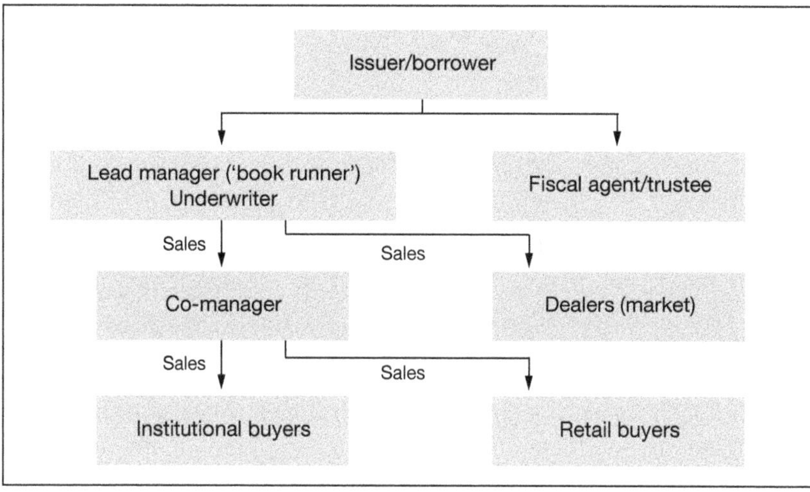

Source: author

The numerous costs and expenses with fixed values incurred in the process make a bond issue expensive. Hence, bond issues for amounts of less than $100 million equivalent may not be cost-effective when compared with loan finance.

On occasion, off-market, private placements may be possible, such as Rule 144a-type bonds in the United States where certain qualified institutional investors are allowed to invest in such bonds. Similarly, issuers which are new to the bond markets or have not an established bond market profile may find this 144a route preferable to gain access to the market.

One of the main drawbacks of using bonds for projects, particularly infrastructure projects when the construction period may be two to three years, is that, at issue date, all the funding from a bond becomes available for use by the issuer. By contrast, the project for which the bond issue may be intended has costs spread over an extended period. Accordingly, with a bond issue any surplus funds not used have to be placed on deposit in a bank, where deposit rates may be low, until such time as it is required to cover costs. Consequently, bond funding during construction can be financially inefficient. Loans are more flexible and cost-effective.

Bonds, which quite often are available for longer periods than loans, are more effectively employed to refinance loan-type debt once a project has reached completion.

Thus, given that project risks may well be perceived as having diminished once project completion has been achieved, it may be possible to refinance a loan of, say $100 million, with a bond issue of $105 million, thereby making a windfall profit for the project company. However, particularly for PPP concessions, the usual principle adopted is for any such windfall profit to be shared, usually 50/50, with the host government concession grantor.

The issue arises, therefore, of whether bond investors might commit at the outset of construction to refinance bank loans on project completion. Thus, in 2013 Dutch pension fund APG committed at the outset of the €250 million N33 PPP Highway project in the Netherlands in 2013 to buy out (ie, refinance) 70% of projects loans on completion. However, that is a problem which to date remains largely unresolved.

Another issue arising from the use of bond funding for infrastructure and public service projects is that the identity and location of the investors can be quite diffuse. Typically, bond investor groups or individuals are domiciled in tax havens, which raises issues of transparency, among others. For public services in some jurisdictions, this can be a sensitive issue.

Following on from this, another problem can arise in the event of the rescheduling of the financing of a project – for example, if significant delays arise and bonds are one of the sources of finance. For bank loans, should such a scenario arise, meetings can be set up with the lenders within days and hopefully rescheduled debt agreed shortly thereafter. (Note that when such situations arise, usually the lenders are at a disadvantage to the borrower as the most obvious way for lenders to ensure that they have their loans repaid is to support remedies to restore operations, production and cash flows as soon as possible.)

With bonds, should rescheduling be required, the first step is to identify the bondholders, whose identity and location may be obscure, notwithstanding the list of bondholders held by the trustee. Secondly, bondholders have to be informed as to the default event. Thirdly, proposals for a remedy have to be put to them. Lastly, an agreement has to be reached on the terms and conditions for the remedy. The process can take months, if not years, and the fees for lawyers and advisers (typically, an investment bank) to support the process can be high. Accordingly, such a scenario is to be avoided if at all possible.

For many years, investors in bonds have enjoyed the analytical support of the ratings agencies Standard & Poor's (S&P), Fitch and Moody's. For a fee paid by the issuer, these agencies will analyse the creditworthiness of issuers and evaluate their business prospects, providing as a result a rating (see Figure 5.9, which represents a guide). The agencies do not use precisely the same nomenclature and assessment criteria when providing an assessment, but the ultimate aim for an issuer is to be classified as 'AAA'.

The key measure provided in Figure 5.9 is to be 'investment grade' – that is, BBB- and above on the S&P scale. With this status, issuers will be able to obtain longer maturity bonds at lower interest rates than for a rating in the 'sub-investment', or 'junk bond', section. Indeed, some trustees of pension funds and life insurance investment managers will buy, or invest, only in investment grade bonds, so the division has some impact for issuers.

In addition, regulators to private sector, public service utilities may require such utilities to maintain an investment grade rating under their licence.

However, ratings can change. A prime example of that was Enron, which for many years was considered the blue-chip company in the US energy market with an AAA rating. Then corporate mismanagement came to light and the rating dropped to junk (ie, sub-investment) status within a few short days. As many pension fund investors could invest only in investment grade paper, they had to sell Enron bonds

Figure 5.9: Bond issues – ratings

S&P Fitch	Moody's	Comments
AAA	Aaa (Prime 1)	Best quality; capacity to pay interest and principal very strong
AA+, AA, AA-	Aa1, Aa2, Aa3 (Prime 1)	Very strong capacity for repayment
A+, A, A-	A1, A2, A3 (Prime 2)	Strong capacity for repayment
BBB+, BBB, BBB-	Baa1, Baa2, Baa3 (Prime 3)	Moderate protection of interest and principal speculative grade
BB+, BB, BB- B+, B, B-	Ba1, Ba2, Ba3 B1, B2, B3	Highly vulnerable to adverse business conditions Identifiable vulnerability to default
CCC+, CCC, CCC- CC SD, D	Caa Ca	Highly speculative; often in default Default quite possible

S&P short-term ratings:	A-1+ = AAA to A+	B = BB+ to B-
	A-1 = A+ to A-	C = CCC+ to cc
	A-2 = A- to BBB	D = SD to D
	A-3 = BBB- to BB+	

Source: author

immediately. The market was flooded with these bonds, and Enron became insolvent.

In the context of infrastructure projects, and indeed for any project, the main difficulty for the ratings agencies is that they are evaluating a new, as yet to be established, enterprise, whereas many of their normal ratings activities are for corporate or sovereign entities which have ongoing businesses. Hence, it is quite common for a prospective project bond to be given junk status. Consequently, access to the very longest debt via bonds is limited and the interest rates available are higher.

One way to overcome this issue for projects is to use bond 'wraps'. Bond wraps started out in the US municipal bond market, where smaller, but well-managed and creditworthy, utilities were seeking to raise debt via the bond markets. (The US state governments and municipalities rely on budgetary and fiscal receipts for funding public services, plus bond issues raised in the markets.)

However, due to the smaller amounts of many municipal issues and also the lack of knowledge amongst investors as to who or what the issuers were, such municipalities were sometimes shut out of the market, or, if they were able to issue a bond, it was given junk status.

Some US AAA-rated insurance companies, such as AIG, AMBAC and FCIA, spotted an opportunity to offer such issues credit support, or enhancement, whereby for a fee the insurance company became the prime obligor for issues by such utilities.

Furthermore, such 'wrappers' often collected a number of smaller municipal bonds into a portfolio, which was more attractive to the market. Through this mechanism, the insurance companies became known as 'monoline insurers', and many US municipalities benefited from their support.

Later, these same insurance companies assessed and successfully 'wrapped' project bonds, not only for US project issuers, but for other national projects too, such as UK PFI hospitals. Unfortunately, however, these insurance companies went on to wrap sub-prime mortgage bonds in the early–mid 2000s, so when the financial crisis hit, they went down with sub-prime businesses and largely disappeared.

However, the concept of wrapping project bonds has value and has not entirely disappeared. In the past five years a new such wrapper, assured guaranty, has resurrected the concept with some success.

I would like to make three final comments:

- Investors in bonds tend to prefer bonds for which there is a secondary market – that is, where there are plenty of buyers – in case the investor wishes to sell. Project bonds, however, are often quite specific and not as widely held as for large multinational companies or government issuers. The market for project bonds may be too illiquid for some investors.
- Project bonds over the years have performed well, in spite of the vagaries of the world's financial markets. There have been few defaults. Each year Moody's publishes a review of project bonds' performance, which backs up this claim.
- Bond investors, not least due to investor and public demand, have increasingly been attracted to funding renewable energy and green projects. To date, a number of investor funds have promoted green bond issues, where the proceeds of the issue are to be used solely for green applications. However, to date no internationally recognised, green rating system has been developed to assure financiers that the funds raised will be used for green purposes.

Figure 5.10: EIB project bond credit enhancement. Option: mezzanine loan (funding interest during construction)

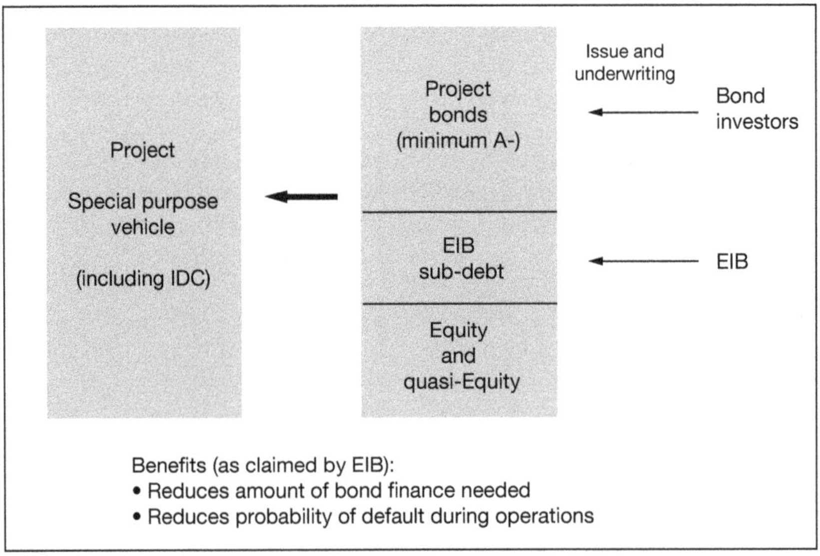

Source: author

In conclusion, it is generally accepted that, as a source of debt for infrastructure investment, bond funding, supported by pension funds and life insurance investors, is the ideal source of long-term debt. The issue as to how to lock in such funding at project outset remains elusive, nevertheless.

The EIB has attempted to bridge this issue through its Project Bond Credit Enhancement scheme (see Figure 5.10), developed in 2013–14. In effect, the EIB provides a mezzanine, or subordinated, loan to cover the interest payments during construction to service investor interest payments.

Alternatively, the EIB, which is AAA-rated, guarantees a sub-debt facility funded by bond investors during the construction period. The first such application of this mechanism was the A11 PPP highway project, which reached financial close in early 2014. However, to date this tool has not been widely used.

3.7 Islamic finance

In recent years, the availability of Islamic finance, particularly in Islamic countries and cultures, has provided an additional source of funding for projects.

Some of the key features of Islamic finance are as follows:

- Islamic finance, or facilities, must comply with the principles of the *Sharia*.
- *Sharia* is Islamic canon law derived from:
  - the *Qu'ran*;
  - the *Hadith* (sayings of the Prophet Muhammad); and
  - the *Sunnah* (ie, the practices and traditions of the Prophet Muhammad).
- Hence, for an Islamic facility to be acceptable, it has to receive approval by an Islamic scholar, as well as all the normal credit hurdles of the financing institution. In the early days, when Islamic funding was applied to projects, some inconsistencies arose between the interpretations of *Sharia* law in respect of projects or funding opportunities in one country compared to others. Today, there are more precedents and consistency in such approvals.
- Uncertainty (*gharar*) in a contract is prohibited. Any risks, gains or losses must be shared between the two parties to such contract, so pre-determined profit is not allowed. Accordingly, speculative financing instruments, such as swaps, are prohibited.
- An Islamic facility must be free from interest (*riba*). Hence, the underlying structure is akin to a lease in conventional financing.
- An Islamic facility must be "for the benefit of society", and certain sectors of business activity are prohibited (eg, anything to do with pork, and alcohol).

Overall, the key difference between Islamic finance and conventional funding is that, under the Islamic facility, the financiers take physical security (ie, ownership) over a project's assets, whereas for conventional funding the focus of financiers is on the cash flows that the project is to produce, albeit they also take a lien over the project's assets.

In the sequence of diagrams comprising Figure 5.11, the procedure for the funding of a project with Islamic finance is shown in four steps:

- Step1: Islamic financiers establish an Islamic special purpose vehicle (SPV) to undertake the project, and appoint a facility agent.
- Step 2 (*Istisna'a* – equivalent to construction financing): the developer (equivalent to the project company shareholders in conventional terms) agrees to construct the project to a specification agreed with the facility agent. As the project is built, the developer receives milestone payments from the Islamic SPV for work completed. Such payments are in many ways equivalent to loan advances under conventional funding. Meanwhile, the Islamic SPV retains ownership of the project assets.
- Step 3 (*Ijara* – post-completion): the developer contracts with the Islamic SPV for use of the assets, and agrees to operate and maintain the assets for a given period. For this, the developer makes payments to the Islamic SPV, similar to lease payments, notionally covering debt service, conventional costs and profit.
- Step 4: under the agreement between the developer and the Islamic SPV, at the termination of the lease the developer will purchase the assets for an agreed amount (called 'termination fee'), usually a token amount.

As seen above, Islamic financiers view risk and security differently from conventional financiers. As a consequence, to execute a project financing with both types of funding requires additional and carefully drafted legal documents. This means that such deals take longer to prepare and the legal costs are higher. It is not surprising, therefore, that to date very few infrastructure project financings have included an Islamic tranche.

Accordingly, there is much to be said for using either 100% Islamic funding for a project, or not at all. However, political and cultural circumstances may not allow that in specific cases.

Historically, Islamic funding has been more commonly found in the financing of real estate assets, equipment and financial institutions, where physical security over assets can be more clearly achieved. Certain types of infrastructure project component, such as vehicles or rolling stock, may be more suitable for such facilities, whereas other fixed construction assets may not.

3.8 Leasing

Leasing as a source of funding in infrastructure projects is often dismissed as inconsequential. However, when one notes that much of the rolling stock and engines for Western European railways are leased vehicles, primarily from financial institution lessors, it becomes clear that leasing can play a significant role.

The key features of leasing are as follows:

- Leasing is a tax-driven financing mechanism – regimes can change with time; and
- Leasing needs lessors which are wishing to reduce their tax liabilities by owning assets on which they can claim capital allowances/depreciation.

The different categories of lease are outlined below.

Figure 5.11: Islamic facility – typical project funding structures

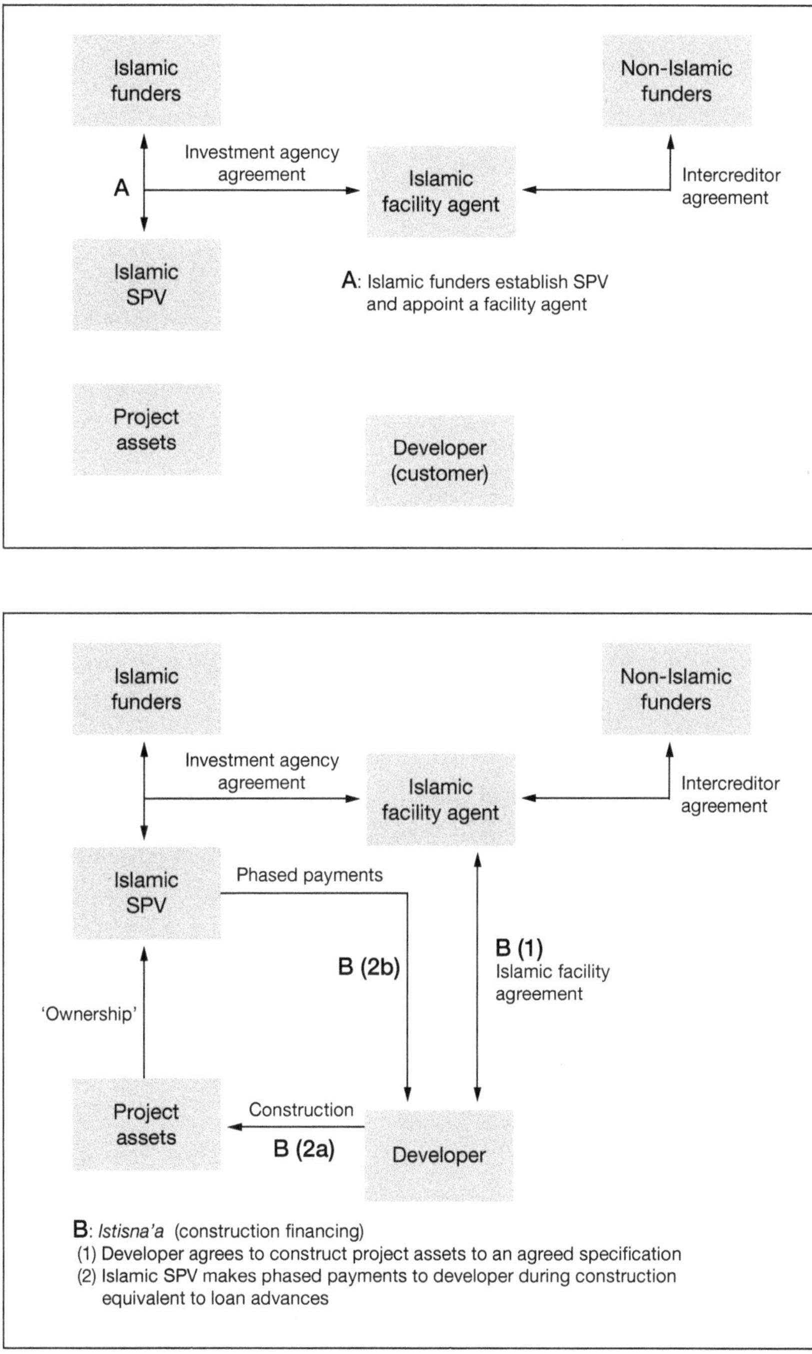

Source: author

Figure 5.11 *continued*

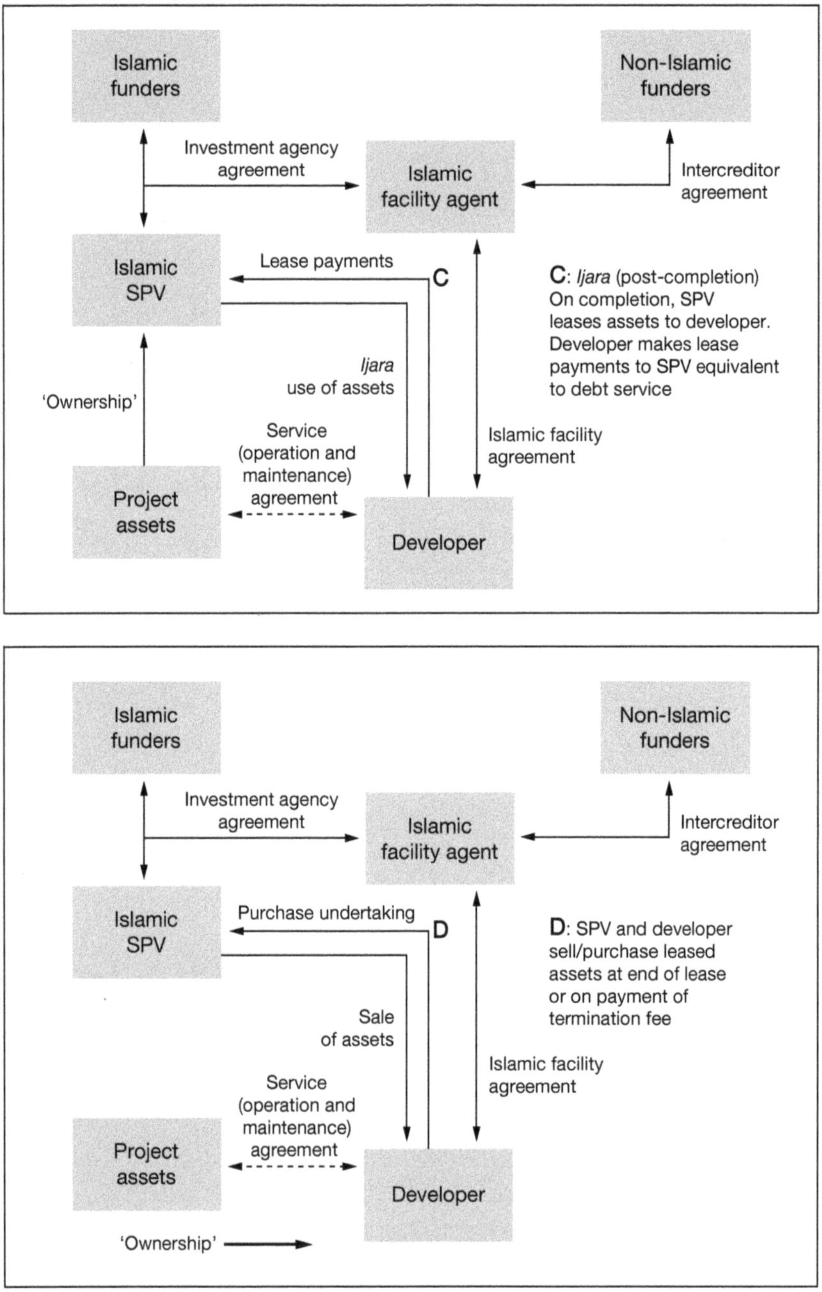

Source: author

Hire purchase:

- Hire purchase applies to small value assets, where the buyer acquires the assets and pays for them on deferred terms.
- The buyer is treated as 'owner' for tax purposes.
- Usually, a down payment of up to 30% of the value of the assets may be required.

Operating lease:

- These are short-term arrangements (eg, for cars or short-term airline operations). Ownership stays with the lessor for tax purposes, although the rentals are revenues for the lessor.
- The lessor has ultimate responsibility for maintenance and obsolescence, although at the end of the lease, the lessee has responsibility to return the assets in the same condition as at the outset.
- A 'wet lease' is when the lessor provides a crew to operate the asset on behalf of the lessee.

Finance lease:

- This is for longer-term rentals (eg, trains, commercial aircraft).
- The lessee does not take ownership of the assets, but claims the economic benefits of ownership.
- If the present value of the lease payments is over 90% of the fair market value of the assets, then it is a finance lease.
- For the lessor, the rental payments are a revenue item covering the costs of purchase of the assets.
- The lessee carries responsibility for operating and maintaining the asset. Further, if the lessee has the right to purchase the asset at the end of the lease for a minimal residual value (eg, 0%–5% of the cost), then the lessee can claim capital allowances against tax.

3.9 Offsets

A brief mention must be made of offsets.

Offsets are an unregulated finance source. They are associated with natural resource (oil, gas or mining), telecommunications and defence contracts between private companies and suppliers, and governments.

As part of the contract, there will be an obligation (an offset) for the private company to invest in national projects up to a value – say, 50% of the contract value – within a given period. Depending on the type of project on which the private company invests as part of the offset obligation, a multiple may be applied. The obligation may be met by equity investment, debt, or both.

For example, let us assume that a multinational – following the award of a mining or telecommunications contract with a government – has a $50 million offset obligation to satisfy. The company finds an industrial project in which to invest $15 million (part equity, part debt). The company is satisfied with the business prospects of the investment.

The host government reviews the potential investment and accepts it as part of the offset. Accordingly, the offset balance to be met drops to $35 million.

The multinational company then finds a second project: a private water treatment plant. The investment this time is only $10 million. However, given the contribution of the project to the economy as a whole, the government is prepared to apply a multiple of five to the investment, which means that the investment valued at $10 million by the company is valued by the government at $50 million in offset terms.

Each government has its own regime, terms and conditions for such offset schemes, some more transparent than others. Notwithstanding the unregulated nature of offsets, the fact is that they exist and in some regions the amounts of money involved are significant. Also, given that many such offsets are linked to the export of commodities, associated offset projects are frequently infrastructure projects (eg, roads, railways).

However, for some, including most IFIs, offsets' unregulated nature and lack of transparency render them unacceptable as a component of infrastructure financing and public service funding.

3.10 Mezzanine capital

Mezzanine capital, as is implied, is a mix of traditional equity and debt. Preference shares, subordinate loans and shareholder loans are all common forms of mezzanine capital.

The rationale for mezzanine capital is usually to optimise risk management, including the impact on the balance sheet of any shareholder's parent company by the provision of debt rather than equity, and for taxation efficiency.

As usual, care should be taken to review closely the terms and conditions of such finance.

Quantitative analysis

Cash flow models and the projections that they generate form the basis of the evaluation of project financing deals.

That said:

- cash flow models are purely a tool for decision-making;
- complexity is the scourge of simplicity;
- it takes time to gain confidence in a cash flow model's capability; and
- the model's integrity should be checked by a third party before use.

A typical cash flow projection is shown in Figure 6.1.

Figure 6.1: Typical project cash flows

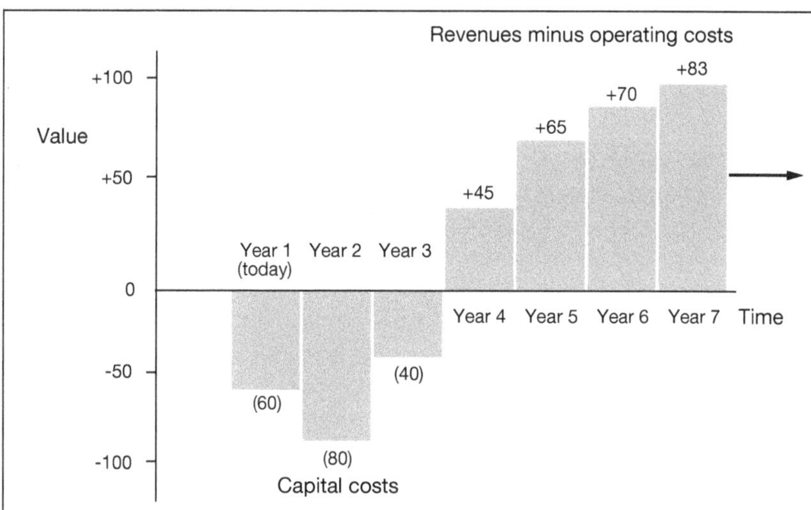

Source: author

1. Measures used by developers and investors

1.1 Payback period

Historically, developers and investors in projects used the payback period as the prime measure of the profitability of any proposed investment project.

For a total capital investment of 180 over three years (see Figure 6.1), the 'payback period', expressed in years, is defined as the date when the aggregate of revenues less operating costs exceeds capital costs (ie, Year 6).

Although this formula takes no account of the time value of money and financing cost, entrepreneurs still use it today.

1.2 Present values and internal rates of return

The common measure used by investors today is internal rates of return (IRR). Mathematically, this measure is based on present value (PV), which is the value today of revenues and costs in the future. To arrive at this figure, one simply applies a compound interest formula, working backwards. The PV of a future value, whether positive (eg, revenue) or negative (cost) can be expressed as:

$$PV = FV / (1 + r)^n$$

where: FV = future value

r = discount rate (%)

n = number of periods or years.

Normal investment analysis will use the opportunity cost of capital as the discount rate.

However, PV measures are not themselves particularly useful to the analyst unless a comparison is being made between two investment opportunities, or cash flows of equal extent over time. In addition, any quote of a PV should also attach the value of the discount rate used to arrive at the PV figure; in practice, that is not always the case.

The underlying mechanism, however, has utility in that the IRR of a particular cash flow projection is defined as the discount rate that must be used so that the PV of the revenue stream equals the PV of the cost stream; in other words, the overall PV, known as the 'net present value' (NPV), is zero.

Figure 6.2 shows a cash flow projection where the PV figures use a discount rate of 10%. This results in an NPV at a discount rate of 10% of 6, derived from the PV of capital costs (166) and for revenues less operating costs (172). The individual PV values for each period are also shown.

If an IRR evaluation is carried out on this cash flow (see Figure 6.3), the IRR comes out at 11%, as expected.

This IRR is often known as the 'project IRR'.

The 'economic IRR', often used by governments in resource planning, includes subjective values for economic costs and benefits, and dis-benefits, in the calculation.

Last but not least, the 'equity IRR' is the key criterion for investors; it is a measure of the equity subscribed (or injected) into a project, compared against the dividend stream as the notional revenues (see Figure 6.4). The result in this case shows an equity IRR of 18%, much higher than the project IRR of 11%.

Figure 6.2: Project rate of return

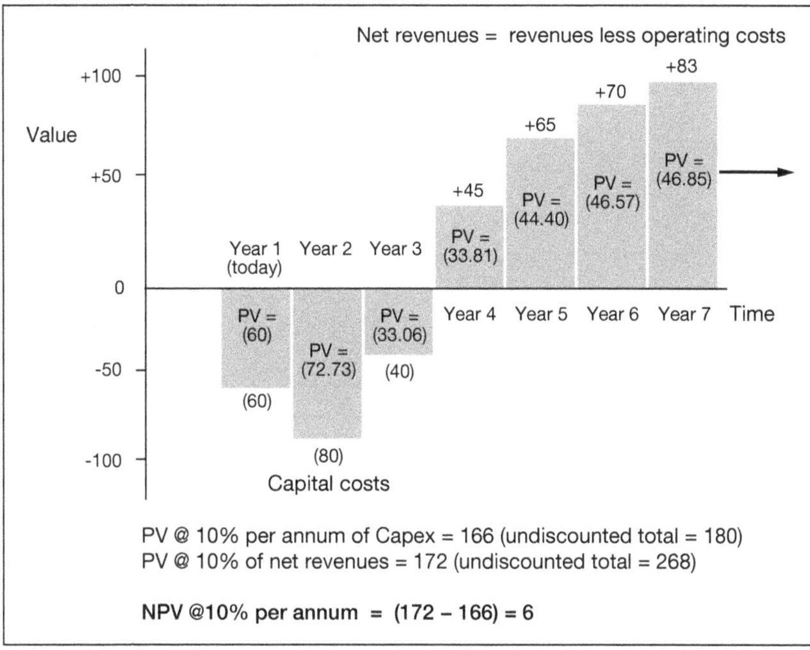

Source: author

Figure 6.3: Project rate of return

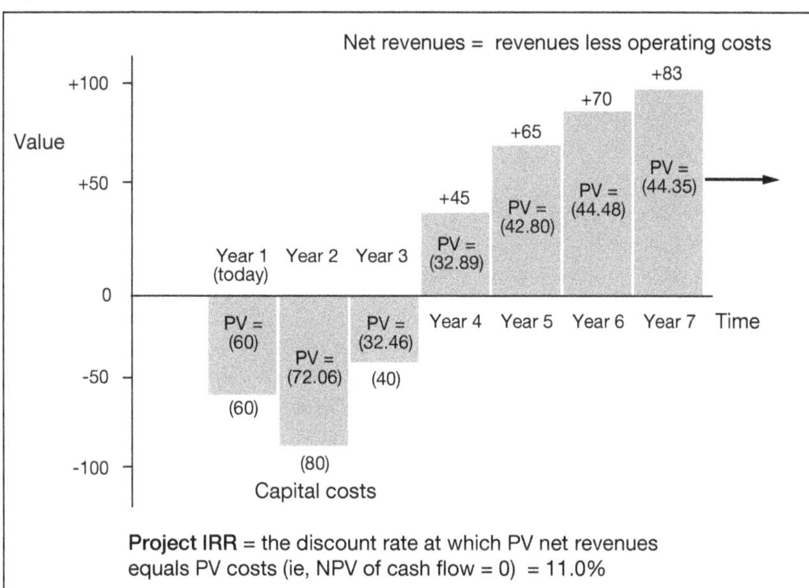

Source: author

Figure 6.4: Equity (shareholders) rate of return

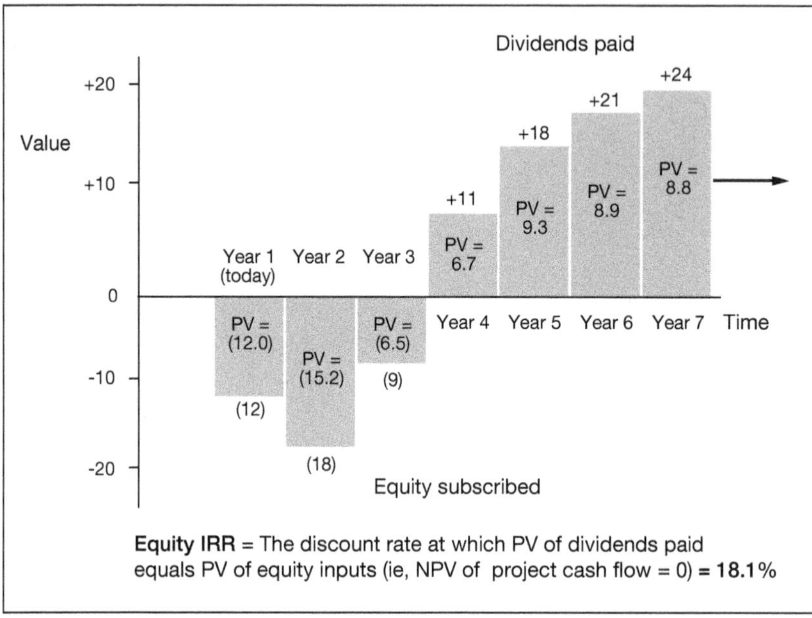

Source: author

This comes as no surprise as, just as for the project IRR, the equity IRR is calculated before funding. If funding is taken into account – for example, at a debt/equity ratio of 80/20 – and given that the cost of debt is low compared to equity, then the investors benefit from the leveraging up of the costs with cheap debt.

Other noteworthy issues include the following:

- Different analysts use different definitions for IRRs, particularly with respect to the data items included in the calculations;
- IRR calculations will change depending on the extent of the period for which the calculations are undertaken. For example, in Figure 6.4, if the project were terminated after Year 6, the equity IRR result would have been very much lower. Hence, if two competing investments are being compared, they must be evaluated over the same time horizon; and
- Local law may dictate in some projects that all surplus cash after debt service and tax cannot be paid out as dividends, and a reserve must be kept by the project company. This money belongs to the shareholders and may generate interest in a deposit account in a bank, but it is not returned to shareholders until the end of the project's life. The value of such money at that date may then be included in the projections, although in PV terms its value could be minute.

2. Measures used by lenders

2.1 Debt service cover ratio

Lenders will calculate the debt service cover ratio (DSCR), which represents the ability of the cash flows to cover debt service payments, for each period in the cash flow projections.

The ratio is made up from:

$$\text{DSCR} = \frac{\text{Free cash flow}}{\text{Fixed charges}}$$

Free cash flow represents:
- project revenues;
- less operating and maintenance costs;
- (plus depreciation – see comment below);
- (plus any cash balances from the previous period – see comment below);
- less increase in working capital;
- less incremental capital expenditures;
- less tax.

Fixed charges represent:
- loan interest paid;
- plus loan repayment;
- plus loan fees;
- plus mandatory payments (eg, lease payments).

As is often the case, there are variations to this ratio, so analysts should take care to understand the data used, in particular:
- depreciation – often the data for any financial cash flow projection has been originally generated by an engineering consultant who may have included depreciation as a cash cost. It is not a cash item. Depreciation is an allowance by the tax authorities for owners to put an agreed amount (depreciation) as a cost before tax to reflect the fact that the assets of production will have to be replaced in the future. Hence, if depreciation has been included as a cost, it has to be taken out of the free cash flow figure; and
- cash balances from previous period – some analysts allow any surplus cash which has not been paid out as dividends to shareholders in previous periods but which resides in the project company's accounts to be included as part of free cash flow. Some (arguably more prudent) analysts do not allow this inclusion.

Overall, the result of this ratio is that it must be greater than 1.0 for the project company to remain afloat. Indeed, given the uncertainty of cash flow projections, lenders will usually require this ratio to be maintained at a level of 1.20, or even higher for more risky ventures.

2.2 Interest cover ratio

This ratio is the same as for the DSCR, except that it includes only interest payments as the denominator.

Not surprisingly, the ratio will be much higher than the DSCR, typically 3.0–4.0 or higher. To the analyst in infrastructure projects, such a ratio has limited utility, though.

2.3 Coverage ratios

The loan life cover ratio (LLCR) and the project life cover ratio (PLCR) are, in effect, very similar. They both take a 'look forward' perspective: one to the maturity of a loan, the other to the end of the project's life.

The ratios are calculated, in the context of the cash flows for the loan life or period, or the project's life, as follows:

$$= \frac{\text{Current value and PV of future free cash flow (or CFADS*)}}{\text{Book value** of outstanding debt}}$$

* CFADS = cash flow available for debt service
** Book value = as stated in the accounts

This formula has a number of variations, depending on the answers to these questions:

- What discount rate should be used for the PV calculations? Normally, the weighted average cost of capital is used, but some practitioners may choose the cost of debt.
- Should the book value or market value of the debt be assumed?
- Does one include amounts held in debt service reserve accounts as part of the cash flow values?

For an infrastructure or public service asset investment project, the utility of this ratio is questionable. In such projects, once construction is completed, the cash flow stream will usually remain consistent at a given level, possibly with some growth due to inflation or increased demand. Then suddenly, after many years, the assets need renewing, or are rehabilitated or even terminated, so cash flow falls to zero. In other words, the LLCR would steadily increase over the years, then collapse.

Where this ratio is useful is for those projects which have a diminishing cash flow, as in natural resources, oil, gas or mining developments.

A typical and simplistic cash flow profile for such a project is shown in Figure 6.5. The cash flow projection, post-completion, is generated by probability forecasts as to how much of the commodity can be produced from the ground.

Estimates and projections of production will usually be provided by a geologist on the basis of probabilities of recovery, with P100 meaning than the confidence of recovery is 100%. Then:

- P90 means that the confidence of recovery is over 90%;
- P50 means that the confidence of recovery is over 50%; and
- P10 means that the confidence of recovery is over 10%.

Figure 6.5: LLCRs Oil and gas – exploration and development

Issue: limited project life or reserves

Project cash flows generated from probability forecasts:
- 1P or P90 = proven (>90% confidence of recovery)
- 2P or P50 = proven + probable (>50% confidence of recovery)
- 3P or P10 = proven + probable + possible (>10% confidence of recovery)

Risk mitigation: single asset or portfolio approach often adopted

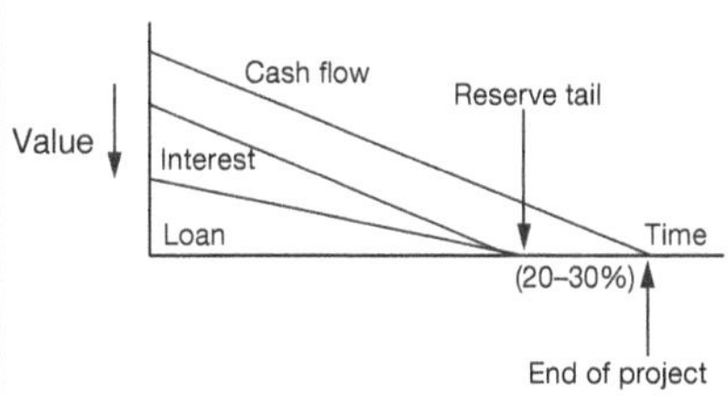

Typical target criteria: LLCR

For instance: for P90: LLCR > 1.5
for P50: LLCR > 1.7

or in any period of the cash flow:
maximum outstanding debt
$= \dfrac{\text{PV P90 CFADS over loan life}}{1.5}$

Issues for consideration:
- Is the discount rate the cost of debt?
- Is DSRA included in CFADS?
- Is outstanding debt discounted?

- PLCR: CFADS over project period

(CFADS = cash flow available for debt service)
(DSRA = debt service reserve account)

Source: author

The P90 data is often taken as the base case for lenders – that is, the cash flow underpinning P90 will have a slightly higher value than the P100 case.

Against this, one can project the debt service profile (see Figure 6.5). Obviously, lenders will wish to ensure that their loans are repaid in full well in advance of the date when the cash flow diminishes to zero. The how and when is very much left to the credit judgement of the lender, but usually the period between the final debt service payment and the end of the project (known as 'the reserve tail') is taken as around one-third of the overall life of the project cash flow.

Another way that lenders approach this ratio is to require throughout the project's life that the LLCR be kept above a certain level, otherwise the loan has to be repaid early.

For example, lenders to such projects will continuously monitor project progress, period by period (or year by year), and may require that the LLCR be, say, above 1.5 for P90 projections and above 1.7 for P50 projections at all times.

For P90, this can be interpreted in any one period (or year) as:

$$\text{the maximum outstanding debt} = \frac{\text{PV @ P90 of CFADS}}{1.5}$$

In the event that the actual debt outstanding at any time in the project's life, as it progresses, exceeds this calculated maximum, then early loan repayments are demanded.

In summary, investors calculate the equity IRR over different time horizons; lenders calculate DSCRs and review the risks or uncertainty to cash flow projections.

3. Cash flow model – practical comments

A cash flow model is an analytical tool and no more than an aid to decision-making. Presentation may represent 40% of the output. Keep the model simple!

The question arises as to the number of time periods that cash flow projections should cover, and the length of each period (eg, one month, six months or one year). The key issue is: what is the cash flow to be used for?

If the model is to be used for decision-making, annual or semi-annual periods will usually suffice. If the projections are to be used for budgeting purposes, then more closely defined figures may be needed – for instance, during the construction period. In this context, the issue of presentation should be kept in mind: will the projections fit the printed page easily?

Cash flow projections are made up from capital costs, revenues, operating and maintenance costs, funding (equity and debt) and tax. Usually, the first three items are provided by engineers, who may, or may not, have made their own assumptions about inflation, currency exchange rates and growth patterns. Furthermore, most financial analysts these days use MS Excel.

Hence, there is some benefit, if time allows (and not least to build up confidence that the model is manipulating data in the manner expected), in building the model through a number of separate worksheets which can be checked step by step using the analysts' own assumptions. Typically, the individual worksheets might cover:

- model assumptions, such as overall costs, unit prices and tariffs for revenues, inflation rates, exchange rates, tax assumptions, etc;
- capital costs (over the construction period only);
- operations and maintenance costs;
- revenues;
- use of funds (drawdowns, debt service and dividends);
- profit and loss account (for calculating tax);
- cash flow statement (from which equity IRR and DSCRs are calculated); and
- balance sheet of project company.

These considerations raise a number of issues in turn. For instance, is a balance sheet necessary? (Note that analysts can spend hours trying to get assets and liabilities to balance.) A balance sheet is only a photograph of the financial status of a company on a particular day. What the status may be on the day before or after might be quite different.

A balance sheet is useful, nevertheless, to estimate the working capital, the financing needed on a short-term basis to fund day-to-day business. However, such figure might be available by other means.

A review of similar projects or companies in the same business sector gives a guide as to how much working capital is needed. That can then be related to a percentage of revenues or operating costs, which may be a much simpler solution to the problem.

Furthermore, during the construction period, a balance sheet has little meaning as no business has been created: the project company has yet to commence operations.

Here are some useful model checks:

- Has inflation been included in the model cash flows? Inflation always exists.
- Is there a growth pattern to revenues and operating costs? Does the data seem credible?
- Has project insurance been included as an operating cost item?
- Is there an allowance in the schedule of revenues and operating costs for a major maintenance event after a few years?
- Has working capital been included?
- Has the impact of currency fluctuation been taken into account?
- Do all the funds used (debt and equity) cover 100% of capital costs?
- Are loans repaid on an equal semi-annual installment basis or as an annuity? (Note that the MS Excel PMT function calculates loan repayments as an annuity.)
- Are the total loans drawn down (ie, used) equal to the loans repaid?
- Is interest capitalised (ie, rolled up)? If so, is the total amount of interest due added to the loan to be repaid?
- Are 100% of cash surpluses paid out as dividends? If not, is interest generated on the surpluses not paid out?
- Are cash flow deficits in any period funded by an overdraft? If so, at what cost?

4. Cash flow model – an example

Figures 6.6 and 6.7 show simplified cash flow projections for a toll-road project. Figure 6.6 contains errors; Figure 6.7 contains corrections. (The author has made best efforts to ensure consistency in the model, but recognises that it is not perfect.)

The structure of the cash flow is obvious. The main errors in Figure 6.6 are that:

- inflation has not been allowed for;
- the loan repayment schedules are wrong; and
- capitalised interest is not repaid with the loan principal to which it applies.

The cells in the right-hand column, however, help to check the calculations.

Figure 6.8 shows the results. From this, one can see that the DSCR (derived from post-tax operating cash flow/total debt service) has a minimum value of 1.22 in the first year of operations, rising to 1.44 and above thereafter, which is quite healthy.

Figure 6.6: Toll-road project

Year	1	2	3	4	5	6	7	8	9	10	11	12	13	14	15	16	TOTALS
Number of vehicles (per day)	0	0	0	0	37,800	42,750	44,330	45,830	44,290	45,210	42,990	44.680	44,650	44,620	44,590	44,570	
Toll fee per vehicle (€)	0	0	0	0	5.00	5.00	5.00	5.00	5.00	5.00	5.00	5.00	5.00	5.00	5.00	5.00	
Revenues	–	–	–	–	69	78	81	84	81	83	78	82	81	81	81	81	
Operation and maintenance costs	–	–	–	–	10	10	10	10	10	10	10	10	13	10	10	10	
Operating cash flow	0	0	0	0	59	68	71	74	71	73	68	72	68	71	71	71	
Less: working capital	0	0	0	0	1	0	0	0	0	0	0	0	0	0	0	0	
adjusted for taxation	–	–	–	–	14	16	17	18	19	20	16	17	19	17	19	19	
Post-tax operating cash flow	0	0	0	0	44	52	54	54	52	53	52	55	49	54	52	52	
Capital costs:	12	60	140	28	–	–	–	–	–	–	–	–	–	–	–		240
Paid for by:																	
Equity capital	12	12	28	6													58
Debt drawn down	–	50	112	22													184
Total funding	[12]	[62]	[140]	[28]													[242]
Debt service:																	
Interest paid	0	0	0	0	14	12	11	10	8	6	5	3	2	1	0	0	
Fees	–	2	0	0	0	0	0	0	0	0	0	0	0	0	0	0	
Capital interest	0	2	6	8													16
Debt repayment	0	0	0	0	20	20	20	20	20	20	12	12	12	12	0	0	168
Total debt service	0	2	0	0	34	32	31	30	28	26	17	15	14	13	0	0	
Cash available for dividends	0	0	0	0	10	20	23	24	24	27	35	40	35	41	52	52	

Notes: Loan 1 = €80 million; repayment = 8 years from completion @ 7%
Loan 2 = €120 million; repayment = 10 years from completion @ 7%

Figure 6.7: Toll-road project

Year	1	2	3	4	5	6	7	8	9	10	11	12	13	14	15	16	TOTALS
Number of vehicles (per day)	0	0	0	0	37,800	42,750	44,330	45,830	44,290	45,210	42,990	44.680	44,650	44,620	44,590	44,570	
Toll fee per vehicle (€)	0	0	0	0	5.00	5.00	5.50	5.50	6.00	6.00	6.50	6.50	6.75	7.00	7.25	7.50	
Revenues	–	–	–	–	69	78	89	92	97	99	102	106	110	114	118	122	
Operations and maintenance costs	–	–	–	–	10	11	13	14	15	15	15	15	20	15	15	16	
Operating cash flow	0	0	0	0	59	67	76	78	82	84	87	91	90	99	103	106	
Less: Working capital adjusted	0	0	0	0	1	0	0	0	1	0	0	0	0	1	0	0	
after taxation	–	–	–	–	14	18	22	24	25	27	28	30	32	34	35	37	
Post–tax operating cash flow	0	0	0	0	44	49	54	54	56	57	59	61	58	64	68	69	
Capital costs:	12	60	140	28	–	–	–	–	–	–	–	–	–	–	–		240
Paid for by:																	
Equity capital	12	12	28	6													58
Debt drawn down	–	50	112	22													184
Total funding	[12]	[62]	[140]	[28]													[242]
Debt service:																0	
Interest paid	0	0	0	0	14	12	11	10	8	6	5	3	2	1	0		
Fees	–	2	0	0	0	0	0	0	0	0	0	0	0	0	0	0	
Capital interests	0	2	6	8													16
Debt repayment	0	0	0	0	22	22	22	22	22	22	22	22	12	12	0	0	200
Total debt service	0	2	0	0	36	34	33	32	30	28	27	25	14	13	0	0	
Cash available for dividends	0	0	0	0	8	15	21	22	26	29	32	36	44	51	68	69	

Notes: Loan 1 = €80mn; repayment = 8 years from completion @ 7%
Loan 2 = €120mn; repayment = 10 years from completion @ 7%

Figure 6.8: Toll-road project – Cash flow results

Year	5	6	7	8	9	10	11	12	13	14	15	16
Interest cover ratio	3.14	4.08	4.90	5.40	6.95	9.50	11.8	20.3	29	64	–	–
DSCR	1.22	1.44	1.64	1.68	1.87	2.04	2.19	2.44	4.14	4.92	–	–

IRR:
Yr 1–7 = <0%
Yr 1–8 = 3.0%
Yr 1–10 = 14.3%
Yr 1–12 = 19.9%
Yr 1–16 = 25.7%

For the equity IRR value, if one assumes that investors might seek a return of, say, 15%, they will only achieve that by staying with the project until Year 11–12. That result is typical for an infrastructure investment.

If investors wish to achieve that rate of return, but at an earlier time horizon, then they must be prepared to take the risk that they can sell their equity to a third party at the earlier date and make a capital gain to cover the balance. That may, or may not, be possible.

Figure 6.9 shows some sensitivity tests:

- A 20% cost overrun drops the DSCR to 1.06. Lenders will demand, therefore, that the project be built by a competent contractor under a fixed price turnkey contract.
- If cash tolls are 10% less than forecast, the DSCR drops to 1.04; at 20% less than forecast, the DSCR drops to below 1.0. This demonstrates the uncertain nature of traffic forecasts for highways. Lenders may fund such a project only against 'availability' payments, transferring the traffic risk to a third party such as the government.
- Unsurprisingly, a 20% increase in operating costs, which are small compared to revenues for a highway project, or an increase of 2% in interest rates has minimal impact on the DSCR.

Figure 6.9: Toll-road project – Sensitivity tests – DSCR

Case	Minimum DSCR
Base case	1.22
20% cost over-run	1.06
Revenues 10% less than forecast	1.04
Revenues 20% less than forecast	? (<1.0)
20% increase in operating costs	1.16
Increase interest rate by 2%	1.18

By undertaking such sensitivity tests on the base case as part of their due diligence, lenders will identify the key risks which might affect debt service, and take steps to mitigate those risks accordingly.

The contractual framework

The private financing of infrastructure follows primarily the three basic frameworks shown in Figures 2.4, 2.6 and 2.7 in the chapter on financial structures. Many similarities exist between these frameworks. In summary:

- Figure 2.4 represents a stand-alone infrastructure operating in a competitive market (eg, a private power station supplying power to a pool), where demand is uncertain;
- Figure 2.6 represents an infrastructure development, where a private company is awarded a franchise or concession to deliver a public service over a fixed period of years, and the customers who use that service pay the private concessionaire (eg, a cash toll road); and
- Figure 2.7 represents an infrastructure development, where a private company is awarded a franchise or concession to deliver a public service over a fixed period of years. Payments are made to the concessionaire, either by the concession grantor or its agent, against performance measures of the service delivered (eg, a public-private partnership (PPP) highway with availability payments).

The final contractual framework for such deals can be complex and have multiple components.

It is not possible within this book to provide draft contractual documents. In any event, individual project finance lawyers have their own styles. However, it is possible to highlight the key issues.

1. Corporate identities and issues

All the contracts that together form the project finance framework share a specific aim, which is to identify the participants' capabilities and responsibilities clearly. Accordingly, each contract should answer the following questions:

- Have the participants the experience and track record to a recognised standard for undertaking such a project?
- Have they the in-depth technical resources available to support the project?
- Have they experience with the underlying technology?
- Are they financially creditworthy? (Participants may be asked to produce recent accounts to establish any claim in this respect.)
- Has the participant allocated qualified staff to perform on the project? (It is advisable to review the CV of the leading executive.)

Even when the questions above are answered satisfactorily, the corporate identity of the participants may remain obscure – and this even if internationally known names are linked to the project.

This is because the project company, or PPP concessionaire, will typically be set up as a single purpose, limited liability company whose shareholders or partners are subsidiaries of major multinational contractors, operators, utilities and investment funds, and these shareholders may be domiciled in a tax haven.

Governments, as grantors of concessions or licences to private entities for infrastructure and public service developments, will wish to ensure that the projects are successful, as will lenders, which will wish to ensure that their loans are repaid.

Hence, both will want to know that any limited liability or shell companies, so set up in support of an infrastructure or PPP development, can meet their commercial obligations. To achieve this, governments and lenders will require, as a component of the conditions precedent to the transaction, that parent company guarantees or equivalent be put in place to support subsidiaries.

A second issue arising from the project company set-up concerns corporate tax. Increasingly, governments are examining closely the mechanisms used by multinationals to avoid (although some see it as optimise) corporate taxation. The use of 'pinpoint' equity, subordinate debt and shareholder loans to represent equity, with higher-than-market rates of interest, are common in many jurisdictions (eg, UK project finance initiative (PFI) projects).

Similarly, multi-layered corporate structures in privately owned, public service utilities are another common feature in the sector – for instance, there are 10 corporate layers between the licensed company for Heathrow Airport and the owning shareholders, giving rise to opportunities to extract consultancy fees to optimise overall taxation.

It is not only on the equity side of the corporate structure that such mechanisms prevail. Quite often, supporting project bond issues may be raised via a tax haven (eg, the Cayman Islands) to minimise withholding taxes and to lower the cost of debt to the project company or concessionaire. However, this introduces issues of disclosure and transparency for public service entities.

It is to be expected, however, that with the growing use of private capital to support infrastructure developments, greater scrutiny and transparency than hitherto will be demanded by governments and the public alike, as the ultimate beneficiaries and payers of such investments.

2. Key project documents

2.1 Common terms agreement

Given the number of inter-locking contracts to be negotiated and put in place, it is sensible to agree the definitions of key terms and conditions at the outset. Whereas many stand-alone project financings, as seen in Figure 2.4, will use an established legal base for all contracts (eg, English law), this may not be the case with PPPs, which are, in effect, licences awarded to local entities to deliver a public service in any one country. It is usual for such contracts to be based on local law, but with the proviso that if any dispute arises as to the meaning of terms and definitions, a specified international law is referenced.

2.2 Implementation agreement

The period between the award of a contract to a private company or concessionaire and the date when all outstanding matters have been negotiated and agreed can be protracted. To ensure that the parties follow the same agenda during this long period, an implementation agreement is put in place to represent the intentions of the contracting parties and the principal terms and conditions upon which both parties are hoping to agree to reach financial close.

2.3 Direct agreement

This optional agreement is between the two main parties to a project-financed deal (eg, a PPP concession grantor and concessionaire, and the lenders). It:

- acknowledges the lenders' rights of security over the project assets (which may not be normally allowed under the host country's legislation);
- describes the obligations of the contracted parties relating to notices of default;
- recognises the step-in rights of the lenders in specified circumstances;
- lists the rights and procedures of the receiver, in the event of liquidation; and
- identifies the terms and conditions under which lenders may transfer borrowers' rights if project assets are sold.

Such an agreement may be useful when the underlying documentation to the proposed transaction is complex, which would require an extended period for preparation and negotiation. A direct agreement, negotiated and agreed at the outset of the process, can establish some key principles of the relationship between the contracting parties.

2.4 PPP concession agreement

PPP concession agreements can be lengthy and complex. The agreement for the 2003 London Underground PPP was over 3,000 pages long. If a problem arose and reference to the agreement was required, assistance from a lawyer as to which clause to review might be needed!

Typically, the clauses of a PPP concession agreement will cover the aspects outlined below.

Definitions and interpretations: This lists the defined terms used in the contract and specifies various aspects such as the formulas to be used to calculate the base rate values referred to in the contract.

Concession: This describes and specifies the services to be delivered and what assets have to be built to deliver such services against an agreed schedule (placed in an appendix).

Concession period: The length of the concession consists of a defined construction period, plus operations. Typically, this might be 20 to 30 years overall. It should be at least as long as the final maturity date of the debt used to fund the project. (Final handover of assets at the end of concession, back to the state, can be complicated if loans are still outstanding at that date.)

Payment regime: This clause explains whether the concessionaire is to be paid by the users of the assets or against some performance measures (eg, availability payments). Usually, under the latter mechanism, payments will be made monthly, with adjustments for inflation, currency, etc. The actual calculation mechanism for payments will be attached as an appendix to the agreement. Further details of such payments will be described in later chapters of this book under the relevant sectors.

Effectiveness: This covers the documents, approvals, permits, licences, insurance policies, representations and warranties which have to be in place for the concession agreement to become effective.

Law and authorisation: This clause lists the legal regulations that a private company must satisfy to deliver a public service.

Access to land and utilities: This highlights who is responsible for the provision of these essential services and items, as well as the associated responsibilities and liabilities.

Independent engineer: This describes the role of the independent engineer. Details may be provided in an appendix.

Specification, design and performance of the construction works: This covers the works to be completed by the concessionaire. Performance guarantees may also constitute part of this clause.

Modifications to the design: This describes how modifications can be agreed between the parties, and, if allowed, who pays, what the responsibilities and liabilities of the parties are post-modification, and how any benefits may be distributed. Lenders will usually expect to be consulted with a right of refusal. However, provided that the overall risk to the borrower's ability to service debt has not risen, approval will normally be forthcoming.

Subcontracts: This describes how major subcontracts can be awarded. Lenders' approval is also frequently required.

Information, rights of access and documents: This clause covers the availability and legal status of these items.

Completion, certification and start of operations: This describes how these milestones are achieved and recorded.

Obligations relating to public services delivered: This comments on the standards and quality of service required of the concessionaire. In some jurisdictions, a probity (ie, 'fit-and-proper person') test may be imposed on any private company or concessionaire wishing to deliver public services.

Employees: This covers the rights and obligations of the concessionaire to its employees, particularly those who might have transferred to employment with the PPP concessionaire from the host government agencies which would otherwise have built and/or operated such a project.

Benchmarking of operations and maintenance costs: As PPP concessions are very long term, there may be a call to benchmark costs at certain points during the concession to confirm that value for money is being achieved. If necessary, adjustments may then be negotiated to unit prices (eg, labour and materials) which make up the bulk of fees to the concessionaire during the operations period. Such mechanism needs to be described in the agreement.

Materials and workmanship of the works: The underlying principle of PPP concessions is that the assets revert to state ownership at the end of the concession period in the same state as they were built. This raises some issues, which need to be addressed in the agreement, as to the expenditures on repair and maintenance that might arise in the latter years of the concession and the approvals required.

Safety: This describes any public safety issues which are the responsibility of the concessionaire.

Records: This lists the records that the concessionaire has to keep relating to performance, among other things.

Taxes: This describes what taxes might apply and who is responsible for paying or collecting such taxes (eg, VAT).

Insurance: This specifies who is responsible for arranging and paying for project insurance and the policies to be adopted.

Financial reporting and model: This specifies which financial reports and records the concessionaire must keep, and their availability. Reference might also be made to the computer model that all parties to the agreement should use when determining budgets and negotiating adjustments to tariffs, etc.

Maintenance fund: Many infrastructure projects, after a number of years, have to be closed for a major maintenance event. Not only may the costs be significant, but closure will also affect the concessionaire's revenues (for meeting costs and paying debt services and dividends). The creation and management of such fund, if required, needs describing in this clause.

Change in law: Should a change in law arise (excluding taxation) which affects the concessionaire's profitability and business, then the underlying principle under PPP concessions is that adjustments to the revenues of the concessionaire may be allowable to compensate for the changes arisen.

Refinancing: Given that the inherent project risks may decrease following project completion, many PPP concessions are refinanced with cheaper and/or longer-term debt finance not long after completion is achieved. On occasion, this may result in a windfall profit, as more funding may be raised via the refinancing by the concessionaire than was available at the start of construction. The concession agreement, therefore, should describe how any such profits may be split between the concessionaire and concession grantor (ie, government). However, practitioners should take care to ensure that any such clause does not affect the on/off balance sheet status of the concession for the government.

Expiry of the concession: As mentioned above, at the end of the concession the assets are handed back to the state. This is a complex handover that requires additional description as to any performance warranties, guarantees or other obligations and liabilities at this point, as well as a description of the transfer of operating manuals, designs, etc.

This raises a further question as to the point of agreeing on a final expiry date for a PPP concession, which is, say, 30 years from the outset. If a concessionaire has been providing a satisfactory service throughout those 30 years, why not let it continue? After all, the state counterpart may not have readily available staff and resources to take back the assets and operate the service. Further, if the concessionaire has not provided a satisfactory service, perhaps the concession should have been terminated earlier?

There has been no clear conclusion to this conundrum. Some argue, with good reason, that indefinite PPP concessions are tantamount to privatisation. This is true. Thus, the optimal way forward might be to allow the PPP concessionaire to continue to operate the assets post-expiry date, but only after a negotiation over the fees to be paid thereafter.

Force majeure (ie, unforeseen events): This clause describes what constitutes events of *force majeure*. Typically, such events:

- will be beyond the reasonable control of the party;
- could not have been avoided with the exercise of reasonable care; and
- render the affected party unable to perform all or part of its obligations under the agreement.

Typical *force majeure* events include earthquakes, floods, epidemic, cyclones, air crash, explosion, acts of war, terrorism and radioactive incidents.

Exclusions will be strikes on site, shortage of labour, materials failure, lack of utilities, equipment delay or wear and tear, and contractual non-payment.

Force majeure is generally seen as a 'neutral' event – that is, any losses or gains arising should be shared equally. The concessionaire (or contractor, if the event occurs during construction) should be able to claim extra time and tariffs adjusted accordingly. Likewise, if extra works need to be undertaken as a result of such event, then additional payment by the concessionaire (or contractor) could be claimed.

Usually, if a *force majeure* event lasts for longer than 90 or 180 days without remedy, then the agreement moves into termination.

The concession agreement must also describe:

- how notices are presented by the parties when such an event arises;
- how remedies are agreed; and
- who is responsible for implementing remedies.

Termination: A description is required covering:

- how notices of an event of termination are presented;
- the mechanism to be used to approve any remedies;
- the limitations which apply to any remedies;
- the rights of the host government to operate the project if the concessionaire defaults (note that lenders may have security over the project assets); and
- the rights of the host government to terminate the concession at any time, given due notice, if it purchases the concession for a value of [x] ('x' being calculated from the value of the outstanding debt plus the invested equity, plus the present value of the lost profit opportunity of the investors).

Under this clause, there will usually be two additional and important features. Firstly, lenders will enjoy step-in rights under the terms and conditions of their loans. After all, lenders will usually have established security over the project's assets until such time as their loans are fully repaid.

Such step-in rights will allow lenders to intervene in a project prior to an event of default when, for example, the debt service cover ratio drops to a dangerously low level, defined in the loan agreements, which threatens the ability of the borrower to service debt. Such step-in rights allow lenders to impose their own solutions to problems arising (eg, replace management).

Secondly, in the event of termination, for whatever reason and including concessionaire default, lenders will require the host government to pay out all outstanding debt before the host government can take back and operate the assets.

Governments often find this condition difficult to accept. However, they need to remember that a key component of lenders' security in these types of financing is security over the project assets for as long as their loans are outstanding.

It should also be said that, if a cause for termination arises, termination is the last resort for both parties. Not only does the concessionaire lose its contract, but then the government grantor and any lenders, which might have outstanding loans, will have to find a replacement if they wish to continue delivering the underlying public service. That takes time and money.

Termination is thus an event to be avoided if at all possible, but it represents to the concessionaire the ultimate threat. In fact, there have been very few PPP-type concessions anywhere in recent years, which the author is aware of as having been terminated for concessionaire failure.

Governing law: As PPP concessions are public services in a specific jurisdiction, it is only reasonable – indeed, it may be a legal requirement – that the governing law for the agreement be local law. In which case, to the extent that there may be non-local investors, lenders, contractors and operators associated with the concession, in the event of a dispute about interpretation, reference may be made to an established international law base.

Dispute resolution: Usually, there will be dispute resolution procedures described at three levels:

- day-to-day managerial disputes, which can be handled locally;
- more difficult disputes, which are referred to independent expert opinion or disputes panels made up of both parties, plus some experts; and
- arbitration.

Given that one party to a dispute for a PPP concession will be a government or government agency (unlike most international arbitration disputes, which involve two private parties), it is normal for such disputes to be brought to a tribunal under the procedures of either the UN Commission on International Trade Law (better known as UNCITRAL) or the World Bank's International Centre for Settlement of Investment Disputes (ICSID). The London Courts of International Arbitration and the International Chambers of Commerce provide alternatives.

The option of taking disputes to court is not usually attractive as it is slow, public and the impartiality of the court cannot be guaranteed when making claims against a host government.

The preferred arbitration process is that governed by the Convention of New York, set up by the United Nations in 1958–59. Governments that have both signed and ratified the convention agree:

- to use the procedures to choose arbitrators and set up tribunals;
- to follow the procedures for the presentation of evidence and conduct of the tribunal;
- to abide by the arbitrators' decisions, unless some material evidence has been omitted in the tribunal hearing; and
- to pay whatever compensation is deemed appropriate by the arbitrators (ie, governments cannot claim sovereign immunity).

Most governments have signed up to and ratified the convention (see www.newyorkconvention.org), albeit some with the proviso that if there is a dispute between the host government and a national claimant, then national arbitration procedures will be adopted.

A number of project-related disputes have now been resolved through this mechanism. It provides foreign investors and participants in PPP concessions some degree of political risk cover. Reports of such disputes and the tribunal decisions can be found on the ICSID website.

Sovereign immunity: For the above arbitration clause to be effective, a sovereign immunity clause must also be included in the agreement. In other words, should a government be taken to arbitration to resolve a dispute under such agreement, and the tribunal's decision goes against that government, then the government cannot under the New York Convention claim sovereign immunity and refuse to pay the counterparty the compensation as determined by the tribunal. On occasion, such refusal has, in fact, arisen, but the immediate impact on the recalcitrant government's international trade has been dire, such that it paid up the fine within a few short weeks or months to restore its international reputation.

Assignment: There will be clauses to restrict assignment of the agreement without approval of the other party and, most probably, lenders.

Other issues: Lastly, there may be additional clauses on items such as confidentiality, conflicts of interest, language, signatories, waivers, indemnities, know-how and intellectual property.

The final document may well be 100, sometimes 300, pages long.

2.5 Construction contract

(a) General aspects

The engineering, procurement and construction (EPC) contract is a key component of the project finance framework. This contract also arguably covers the period of highest risk in any project. Hence, governments and financiers need to be conversant with the key issues.

On occasion, the EPC contract terms and conditions may be incorporated into a PPP concession agreement if a contractor is a significant shareholder in the concession company and takes responsibility for constructing the project. Alternatively, the EPC contract can be a stand-alone contract with the concessionaire.

In the latter case, there is contractual separation between the concessionaire and the EPC contractor. This will allow competitive tendering to take place, ensuring value for money. In the former case, where a shareholder in the concession company is the EPC contractor (not an uncommon situation), there is the possibility that the EPC contract may be over-priced – that is, the EPC contractor is, in effect, taking its dividends out of the project through the profits on the EPC contract.

Such circumstances arose with the Eurotunnel project and with the Metronet consortium in the London Underground PPP, contributing to the ultimate financial collapse of these projects.

It is important, therefore, that the prices for the construction activities be competitive, and that, where a bidding EPC contractor is also a shareholder in the project company, negotiations be undertaken at arm's length.

This problem is widespread in infrastructure projects, as contractors take a shareholding in the concessions in order to gain priority access to construction or equipment supply contracts. It is therefore important to take steps to minimise the risk to the value for money. One measure is to ask an independent, third-party expert to provide opinions as to the market prices for such contracts.

(b) Specific clauses

The key requirements are for the EPC contract to be completed:

- to the agreed schedule;
- to the agreed price; and
- to the agreed specification.

Ideally, such contract should be 'turnkey' – that is, the contractor not only builds the project, but also hands it over to the buyer on completion ready to use.

The EPC contract will include items clauses covering the specific aspects outlined below.

Definitions: This will specify some defined terms, while the description of the 'works' may be in an appendix.

Start and completion dates: This clause specifies these key dates.

Completion: This clause provides a definition of the tests to be undertaken to confirm that the project has been built to specification. It also specifies the arrangements and documents to be exchanged on the handover of works to the project company, as well as drawings and manuals.

Extensions to completion: This specifies the circumstances allowable and describes the impact on tariffs/revenues.

Certification procedures: This explains the role of the concessionaire/project company's engineer.

Delays to completion: This clarifies when and how the contract can be terminated without payment (beyond [x] days) if delays arise that are due to the contractor.

Early completion: This specifies whether the EPC contractor receives a bonus (as the project is available for use earlier) upon an early completion.

Performance warranties and liquidated damages (eg, for late completion): This clause describes the warranty period during which the contractor will have to remedy any defects, should they arise, at its own cost and expense, and also the penalties for late completion, usually 10%–20% of the contract value, with an agreed maximum.

Transfer of title to assets: This clause specifies that the asset title will transfer from the EPC contractor to the project company upon certification of completion.

Contract price: This clause covers the payment terms (ideally, fixed), any milestone payments, and invoicing and verification.

Payment and performance bonds: Where relevant, this clause will specify whether advance payments need to be supported by an irrevocable letter of credit or other form of support.

Price variations: This will specify what price variations are allowable in cases of changes in law and *force majeure*.

Key subcontracts: This identifies the key subcontracts and explains any approval mechanism.

Contract changes: This clause will cover the answers to the following questions, which the concessionaire/project company (and their financiers) need to ask:

- Will the change work?
- Where has it been done before?
- Who will benefit?
- Does it increase project risks?
- Have lenders approved the change?
- How should extra costs be valued? (Note that unit prices for labour and materials may be agreed in advance.)

Spare parts: This establishes the commitment by equipment suppliers to maintain stocks of spare parts throughout the life of the assets.

Ground conditions and utilities: The EPC contractor will need to know details regarding access to the project site, the ground conditions of the site, and the availability and responsibility for delivering essential services for construction such as water and power.

Taxes: This clause allocates the responsibilities for payment of taxes between the project company and the EPC contractor.

General contractor responsibilities: This clause lists the contractor's responsibility with regard to health and safety requirements, employee regime, third-party interfaces, intellectual property and planning consents.

Defects liability: This clause specifies the period that must have elapsed before defect liability can be triggered, and the obligations of each party, including the impact of modifications, when such event arises.

Insurances: This identifies the policies required and the party responsible for arranging them.

Change in law: As described in section 2.4 above on the concession agreement.

Force majeure: As described in section 2.4 above.

Termination: As described in section 2.4 above.

Assignment: As described in section 2.4 above.

Dispute resolution: As described in section 2.4 above.

Governing law: As described in section 2.4 above.

2.6 Operations and maintenance contract

Just as for the EPC contractor, arm's-length issues can prevail in the operations and maintenance (O&M) contract. In addition, the O&M contract will be for a much longer period than the contract for construction – it may extend over the full life of the concession or assets.

Hence, while many of the O&M clauses share similarities with the EPC contract, it is impossible to fix the prices over such an extended period. As a result, unit prices are agreed at the outset for key items such as labour and materials, with overall periodic budget targets, and tariffs are adjusted for inflation using agreed indices.

One area of some uncertainty will always be maintenance costs, as the amount of maintenance to be undertaken will depend on the usage of the assets. Thus, it is normal for such costs to be regularly reviewed and the burden of extra costs to be equitably shared.

Clearly, the O&M contract does not become effective until the EPC contract has been completed. However, it is normally prudent to plan for the operator to be available on site a short time before the completion date (eg, one month), so as to become acquainted with the assets being built and, possibly, receive some training from the EPC contractor in the use of the equipment. In such a case, some 'mobilisation fees' might be justifiable.

Just as for the EPC contract, financial bonuses and penalties should be embodied in the contracts to reflect better-than-contracted and poor performance, respectively. In the event of shell companies being contractors, performance guarantees may also be required.

Lastly, given the extended period of such contracts, a benchmarking mechanism may be introduced every few years (eg, every five or seven years), when tariffs are reviewed against market prices and adjusted accordingly.

2.7 Supply contract

Some types of infrastructure and PPP concession will involve certain key supplies which will be needed throughout the concession period – for instance, fuel for a power plant.

First, any such supplies must come from a reliable source and meet the required technical specifications.

Secondly, such supplies should ideally be committed as to price and volume throughout the concession period or asset life. In practice, that may not be possible. It may be possible to fix the volume of key supplies, but the price might vary with market circumstances. On occasion, it might be possible to hedge some of any such price risk, but care should be taken in using capital market instruments such as swaps. Projects have been known to collapse due to unforeseen interruptions to revenues during the contract period, or delays in project completion, with the swap arrangements taken on by the project sponsors to mitigate such supply price risks still applying.

Thirdly, sponsors and financiers should also ensure that the necessary infrastructure for delivery and site access for essential supplies is in place, and also plan to keep on site some spare key supplies as a contingency. The project engineer will advise on how much essential supplies should be stored on site, but it should be remembered that:

- it is normal that the cost for such storage facility be included in the original capital cost estimate for the project;
- such storage is of no use unless filled with key supplies, which, in turn, also have an initial cost and financial value; and
- the value of the storage facility and the key supplies therein need to be covered under the project's insurance policies.

Normally, financiers will be prepared to accept that the funding of the first two items above be included in the overall capital costs package.

Lastly, it is prudent to identify a secondary source of supply for key materials in case the original source is unavailable. Any disruption to the supply of key materials can be a difficult issue to resolve, and that risk may have to be added to the insurance package, thus increasing project costs.

2.8 Sales contract

(a) Preface

Such terms and conditions as are included in a sales contract might, in the event, be covered by the concession agreement for a PPP. However, in both cases financiers will seek to have:

- a creditworthy buyer or payee;
- a long-term commitment from the buyer or beneficiary of services provided; and
- fixed prices and volumes for the service delivered, if possible.

Like the operations contract, the sales contract or arrangements will not become effective until project completion has been achieved. Hence, such contracts will include statements, as part of the conditions precedent to effectiveness, as to the commitment of the project company to complete construction according to a given schedule. If this is not accomplished, then the customer/buyer can usually seek an alternative supplier, and/or receive some liquidated damages via a performance bond from the contractor or concessionaire to cover the incremental costs incurred.

In summary, the sales contract will include items similar to the other contracts described above, such as:

- conditions precedent;

- period of contract;
- payment;
- *force majeure*;
- extensions to contract and implications for tariffs;
- termination;
- end of contract;
- assignment;
- immunity;
- dispute resolution (eg, international arbitration); and
- governing law.

(b) Specific clauses

There are a variety of payment structures seen in cash flow project financing transactions.

Take-or-pay contracts: This payment mechanism, which is common for oil and gas pipeline projects and in the mining sector, consists of an obligation for the buyer to pay at least enough to cover operating costs and debt service (and, possibly, some dividends) even if the product is not delivered to the buyer.

Process project contracts: This structure, which is common in the power and water sectors, includes two components:

- Capacity payment – a payment related to the capacity of the assets to produce the output or service required (eg, [x] per megawatt for a private power plant or [y] per cubic metre of treated water for a water treatment plant). Such payment will be based on:
  - the fixed O&M costs;
  - debt service payments; and
  - possibly some element of profit (eg, dividends) to the project company; and
- Delivered service payment – a payment related to the variable costs of production covering:
  - the actual costs of producing [p] megawatt/hour or treating [q] cubic metre of water; and
  - the balance of profit to the project company.

Such a payment structure is common in power generation and water project financing deals, and is underpinned by a range of performance tests relating to:

- planned capacity at contract signature;
- the actual capacity, as tested, on completion;
- ongoing capacity at payment dates; and
- procedures for testing and distribution of results.

There may also be clauses relating to the following issues:

- Who makes decisions (and following which process) as to how much the plant should produce or process at any one time;

- How and where production or processed volumes are measured;
- When the plant may be closed down for maintenance (ie, scheduled outrages); and
- Who is responsible and pays for inter-connection facilities.

Other issues to consider are:

- Once a project is physically completed under an EPC contract, there will be a period of testing when the plant produces a service (eg, power), but the plant has not been contractually handed over as ready to use. If the plant produces power during testing, that power should reasonably be sold. In such circumstances, normally the payments cover the costs of production, but not capacity.
- In the event of *force majeure*, it is normal for the buyer to continue to pay the capacity component under such payment structure, even though the delivered service payment is cancelled. This may seem unfair to the buyer, but it should be noted that under such event 'capacity' remains available.

  In addition, a *force majeure* event has a limited time span – if the event is not resolved after 180 days maximum, the contract moves to termination, so the buyer's exposure is, in fact, limited.
- There will also be additional payment clauses relating to adjustments to tariffs for inflation, currency fluctuations, and natural wear and tear of equipment, which reduces output efficiency.

Tolling contracts: This structure is a variation on the process project structure, the difference being that there is no component for profit for shareholders in the payment structure (ie, it is a not-for-profit contract).

Contracts for difference (CfD): These are increasingly often used in the energy sector. Under this structure, the seller agrees to deliver specified volumes of output to the buyer at specified future dates and the buyer will pay market prices. However, at the outset, or signature, of the CfD contract, a 'strike' price is agreed which thereafter is usually increased by annual inflation.

However, if at any one future delivery date, the actual (market) price for output is greater than the agreed strike price for that date, the seller compensates the buyer for the difference. If the market price is lower than the strike price for that date, the buyer compensates the seller for the difference.

In effect, this mechanism is a minimum price contract.

Availability payments: Under this mechanism, which is common under PPP concessions, the concessionaire makes the assets available for use. Availability is measured against defined performance measures. Technically, if no availability is made, no payment is due.

More detailed descriptions of these mechanisms are provided under the sector descriptions in the chapter titled "Transport – roads and highways" in Part 2 of this book.

Figure 7.1: CfDs

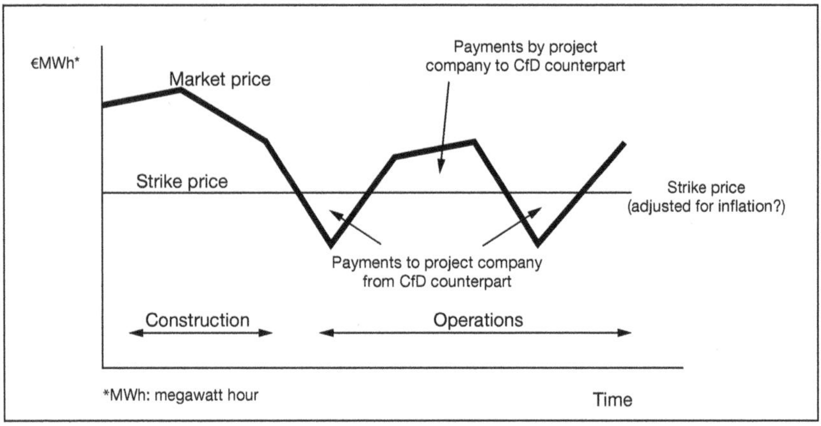

Source: author

2.9 Loan agreement

The loan agreement will reflect the terms and conditions laid down in the term sheet (for more on this, see the section on commercial bank loans in the chapter titled "Sources of finance"). Typically, the clauses will cover the following issues.

(a) Introduction

- Loan agreement context;
- Inter-creditor arrangements; and
- Definitions.

(b) Drawdown procedures

- Certification;
- Conditions precedent;
- Representations and warranties;
- Injection of sponsor equity; and
- Periodic information required by lenders.

(c) Interest payments

- Basis for calculating interest payments due;
- Margin (eg, 2% over six-month LIBOR);
- Capitalisation of interest during construction if relevant;
- Payment dates; and
- Notices.

(d) Fees

- Negotiation fees;
- Administration fees; and
- Commitment fees.

(e) ***Loan repayment***

- Repayment schedule;
- Dates for payment; and
- Prepayment/cash flow cascade issues.

(f) ***Conditions***

- Effectiveness;
- Suspension/termination/prepayment;
- Ratios and covenants to be maintained;
- Project and reserve accounts to be maintained;
- Reporting dates;
- Negative pledge;
- Events of default; and
- Cash flow models.

(g) ***Inter-creditor issues***

An inter-creditor agreement is needed whenever there is more than one lender (see section 2.10 below).

(h) ***Legal jurisdiction***

Usually loan agreements will be subject to an established international jurisdiction such as English or New York law.

2.10 Inter-creditor agreement

Multiple lending sources need coordination. The key components of an inter-creditor agreement are as follows:

- There needs to be coordination of the conditions precedent as to the terms for achieving effectiveness for all the loan agreements. It is undesirable that one loan has achieved effectiveness (ie, is available to the borrower to use) while other loans in the debt package have not.
- There needs to be coordination between all the lenders as to loan drawdowns. Some loans, such as export credits, can be used only to fund specific assets.
- There needs to be uniformity of representations, warranties and undertakings for each loan.
- Mechanisms need to be agreed between different lenders as to how to manage requests for amendments and waivers.
- In the event of default on any one loan, there needs to be coordination of rights and obligations between all lenders and agreement as to the action to take.
- There needs to be coordination between lenders if security is to be enforced.
- If the borrower wishes to prepay one of the loans, or if loan repayments are to be accelerated, there needs to be agreement between all lenders as to which loans this applies to and how.
- In respect of coordination between all lenders, agreement is required as to

how the coordination is managed, how decisions can be reached, and when rights can be subrogated or delegated.

2.11 Shareholders agreement

In summary, the shareholders agreement for the concessionaire or project company is very similar to that for any normal company. The main components are:

- parties to the agreement;
- conditions precedent;
- business of the concessionaire/company/joint venture;
- memorandum and articles of association;
- capital (initial issued and paid-up capital);
- initial shareholdings;
- capitalisation of project costs – that is, the funding structure of the company's business (equity and debt);
- equity (subscribed in cash and in kind);
- project funding (the amount to be raised, and allocation of responsibility for this);
- restrictions on sale and transfer of shares (this item is common in such deals). If a shareholder wishes to sell its shares (eg, the contractor after the project is completed), the other shareholders may have the right to buy the shares before they can be offered to a third party;
- contingency funds (arrangements for stand-by equity and finance). It is common that original cost estimates are exceeded for infrastructure projects, no matter how efficient the project management. On such occasions, if the original debt/equity ratio for the project had been 75/25, then for additional funding lenders might insist that the additional funds be provided on a 50/50 basis – that is, proportionately more equity than originally input. Both standby equity and debt need to be arranged and committed, possibly underpinned by a guarantee or ILOC;
- dividend policy (how and when dividends are paid);
- management and control of the company (long term and day-to-day);
- allocation of directors and managerial roles;
- nomination to the board;
- financial year;
- meetings;
- non-competition undertakings (this is common in project finance and PPP concessions). Participants in one such project are prohibited from supporting a similar deal in the same location for a certain number of years. Such constraint can be politically sensitive in some markets;
- duration and termination;
- arbitration (usually dispute resolution under one of the recognised arbitration regimes;
- tax; and
- jurisdiction.

3. The project engineer

Given that private infrastructure projects entail a huge amount of detail and monitoring of performance, the PPP concessionaire, or project company, and the PPP grantor (ie, the government or government agency) may appoint an independent project engineer. His role and responsibilities will be agreed between the parties, and the contractor and operator will also be co-signatories if they are separate entities to the concessionaire.

The project independent engineer will typically:

- check the design, construction, materials and quality of the works;
- check compliance with the project timetable;
- monitor the payment schedule with availability of funds;
- confirm invoices;
- ensure that the contractor has put in place quality control procedures;
- inspect works in progress;
- review the production of the operations manual;
- advise on variations, as they arise;
- assist the contractor, as may be necessary, to achieve project completion;
- ensure that the contractor complies with the completion certification procedures;
- prepare a list of outstanding works;
- supervise the contractor during any defect liability period; and
- report to signatories every month.

The engineer's fees will be paid by the concessionaire/project company.

The project process

1. Project/public-private partnership unit

For many governments, employing private sector companies and capital to develop infrastructure and deliver public services may be a new concept. The procedures and transactions are complex, combining technical, commercial, financial and legal issues.

Many governments have set up a specialised team of experts (or public-private partnership (PPP) unit) to support governments and government agencies through the process. Indeed, when it comes to implementing such deals, private companies and financiers will take some comfort from the fact that the host government may have taken this initiative, as it will help the government's understanding of the issues and limitations in subsequent negotiations.

The key parameters for setting up such a unit are outlined below.

1.1 Aim and role

The aim and role of the PPP unit is to:

- develop, confirm and establish government PPP policies;
- identify PPP policy shortfalls and to adjust PPP guidelines;
- disseminate PPP policy issues to government ministries and agencies;
- advise on 'on/off' balance sheet status of PPPs, and monitor contingent liabilities for government;
- set standards of PPP proposals, procedures, bid evaluation and documents;
- provide guidance, coordination and support to government sponsors of PPPs;
- set standards for public sector comparators and value-for-money assessments – that is, to:
  - set discount rates;
  - set the basis for 'whole life' costs;
  - assess the impact of inflation and advise on mitigation measures;
  - review taxation issues;
  - make 'optimism bias' adjustments, if applicable;
  - define the basis for risk assessment;
  - provide assistance with the assessment of subjective costs and benefits;
- prioritise projects for the host government, whether:
  - by minimum value;
  - by need and timetable; or
  - on the basis of regional, economic and political criteria;

- advise government on legal and procedural changes necessary for PPPs;
- advise government on risk mitigation and cost minimisation; and
- incubate PPPs.

1.2 **Other issues to resolve**

Location of the PPP unit: The unit needs to have access to decision makers. Accordingly, it is often close to the Ministry of Finance.

PPP unit staff: The availability of expert staff for the PPP unit can be a problem.

Public relations: The PPP unit can help the public to understand the benefits (and weaknesses) of PPPs, and help to raise the public profile of the concept.

2. Planning structure

The process of most infrastructure projects is as described in Figure 8.1 below.

Figure 8.1: The process flow

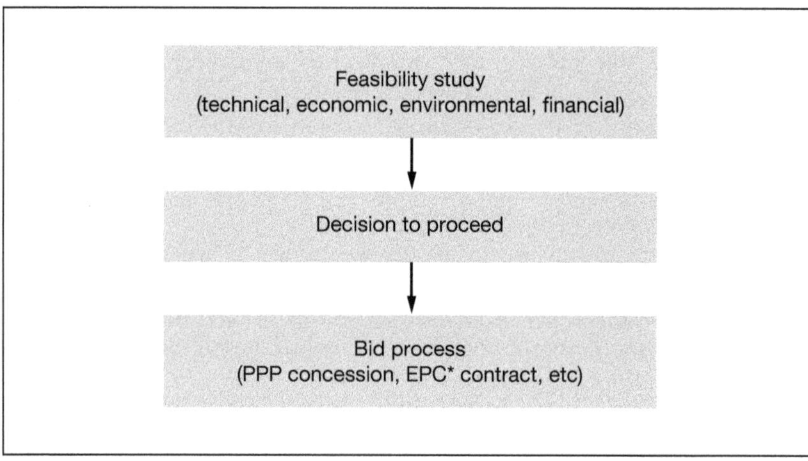

* EPC: Engineering, procurement and construction

Source: author

Typically, the feasibility study will establish value for money for the proposed development, and this study may be developed into a business plan or project information memorandum (PIM) which it turn can be used by prospective investors and lenders to evaluate the opportunity.

3. Business plan/PIM

The items to be included in such business plan/PIM could include:

- project summary;
- project participants/ownership;
- project description (technical and physical);

- project's national/macroeconomic benefits;
- host government role and support;
- legal framework, licensing regime and sector regulation;
- description of the project's market and revenue potential;
- corporate and financial structure of concessionaire/project company;
- cash flow analysis (data, base case assumptions, sensitivity analysis, risk assessment and mitigation);
- security structure for loans;
- project agreements; and
- environmental, climate change and social issues.

The items to feature in the appendices could include:

- draft project company shareholders' agreement;
- product/services market and demand study;
- country report and economic review;
- technical studies;
- draft supply contracts (ie, project inputs);
- draft sales contracts (ie, project outputs);
- draft construction contract;
- draft operations and maintenance agreement;
- government decrees;
- export credit agency (ECA) support letters;
- draft loan agreements;
- draft guarantees; and
- insurance arrangements.

Given that the above could involve a significant volume of data, project sponsors often create a data room where such information is kept. Participants to the transaction (eg, potential contractors, operators, investors and lenders) can gain access to the data room to study the details, under a confidentiality agreement.

4. Financial adviser

Additionally, given the complexity of private sector-funded infrastructure developments, such as for PPPs, many government sponsors will appoint a financial adviser:

- to provide the sponsors and/or government with an independent perspective as to risks and rewards of a proposed project;
- to review financial aspects of existing plans;
- to advise and guide on investment aims and objectives;
- to confirm financial 'bankability' of the proposed infrastructure project;
- to recommend the optimum funding structures applicable;
- to assist in the preparation of the project documents;
- to identify sources of finance available and their terms and conditions;
- to identify financial risks and mitigation methods;
- to assist the sponsors and/or government before and during the bidding process;

- to advise on the contractual negotiations with the winners;
- to help lenders and investors with the due diligence process; and
- to advise on project monitoring procedures.

5. Bid preparation and notices

For the host government that intends to grant a licence to a private sector PPP concessionaire or project company, the normal steps in a bid process are as described below.

5.1 Preparation

That phase consists of:

- setting the objectives and priorities of the project and its sponsors;
- preparing the technical, economic, commercial, financial and environmental reviews;
- conducting pre-feasibility studies and preparing the PIM, and placing them in the data room; and
- determining the bid evaluation criteria.

5.2 Pre-qualification

This phase involves:

- determining the criteria for pre-qualification (eg, experience), the resources available, the competence needed, the level of financial strength required and the staff and management wanted;
- issuing the pre-qualification notice; and
- assessing and announcing pre-qualifiers.

5.3 Tendering

This phase consists of:

- drafting bid documents and contracts;
- publishing the PIM to pre-qualifiers;
- issuing requests for bids to pre-qualifiers;
- preparing and testing procedures for bid evaluation; and
- undertaking 'competitive dialogue' for PPP concessions.

5.4 Evaluation and detailed negotiations

This phase involves:

- evaluating bids;
- negotiating with the preferred bidder and confirming funding proposals;
- undertaking due diligence (investors and lenders);
- setting up the PPP concessionaire/project company;
- obtaining and approving licences, regulatory approvals, etc;
- finalising government support; and
- signing all contracts and financial agreements – that is, reaching financial close.

The contractors, operators, lenders and investors will have to respond to the above accordingly.

6. Procurement laws and infrastructure

Most countries will have in place national laws and regulations governing the way government ministries and state agencies procure and award contracts for public services. Usually, this will include a two-step evaluation process, comprising a technical and a financial component, with no negotiation possible thereafter.

Private sector infrastructure projects and PPP concessions are inherently complex and payment may, in whole or in part, depend upon the standard and quality of the output service delivered by the private entity. Experience has shown that it is very difficult to define precisely at the outset the output specification that the private parties must meet. As a result, the outcomes can be sub-optimal.

To overcome this issue, it is now generally accepted that in such transactions, after pre-qualifiers have been determined, an additional step, called 'competitive dialogue', is introduced into the bid process.

At this point in the process, the government counterpart informs pre-qualifiers of its proposed output specification for the public services to be delivered, and pre-qualifiers are asked to comment as to adjustments, variations, acceptability, etc. Responses are 'open book' between the parties (ie, available for all to see). Following that dialogue, the government counterpart defines a final specification for the bid against which tenderers offer their proposals.

This procedure may conflict with existing national procurement laws and regulations, so adjustments may be called for if governments wish to take advantage of private capital investment in infrastructure.

7. Timetable and bid costs

In undertaking private sector infrastructure projects, governments often ignore the issue of timescale. The fact is that:

- cash flow infrastructure project financing deals take twice as long to prepare and progress to financial close than conventionally funded projects (ie, with corporate or government guarantees for lenders). The reason is that in project financing, investors and lenders need time to undertake their due diligence as to the veracity of the proposals presented; and
- cash flow infrastructure project financing deals cost twice as much to prepare and progress to financial close than conventionally funded projects. Investors and lenders will need experts to assist them in the evaluations, and governments will need extra advisers.

As a rough guide, from conception to financial close, a $100 million infrastructure project will take:

- nine to 12 months, with upfront costs of 3%–5% of the project cost, for a project structure supported by a conventional corporate or government guarantee; and
- 18 to 27 months, with upfront costs of 5%–8% of the project cost, for a cash flow, project finance structure.

Most of the upfront project costs will have to be paid on or before financial close. However, for project financing deals, it may be possible, through negotiation, to capitalise some of the costs into the overall funding package – in other words, financiers will take such costs into account in the project funding, so in effect refinancing the upfront costs paid out by the developer.

8. Innovative proposals

Many national procurement laws prevent governments or state agencies from accepting innovative, or uncalled-for, project proposals. Yet, some governments have also not been as proactive as they should have been in developing national infrastructure to match economic development, and the private sector has come up with proposals to clear the backlog.

One way to overcome the issue of governments not being allowed to accept innovative proposals is to use what is known as the 'Swiss challenge' procurement mechanism. In brief, the 'challenge' works as follows:

- An innovator presents a proposal for an infrastructure project, and the host government accepts the concept.
- The government conducts an international competitive bidding process for the project, based on the innovator's general specification.
- The government choses a winner from the competition.
- If the winner's price is lower than the innovator's offer, then the innovator is given a set period – say, one month – to 'better' the winner's price. If achieved, then the winner is compensated for its bid costs, and the innovator is awarded the contract. If the innovator fails to better the winner's price, then it may/may not receive any compensation.
- If the winner's price is higher than what the innovator first offered, the innovator is awarded the contract, and the winner of the competition receives payment for its bid costs.

This mechanism has been used in cases involving development banks (also known as 'international financial institutions' or IFIs), which normally demand strict compliance with procurement regulations. That was for instance the case for the Quito Airport PPP with support from the Inter-American Development Bank, and the Manila Water PPP with support from the Asian Development Bank.

9. Raising the funds

Funds are raised in the four steps outlined below.

Step 1: The project company/concessionaire will inform selected banks about the project, issuing to them an outline business plan.

Step 2: Interested banks may respond, providing an outline term sheet.

Step 3: The project company/concessionaire selects a lead bank and negotiates a mandate letter.

Step 4: The project company/concessionaire may also contact IFIs, ECAs, and other financial sources regarding their proposed project.

10. Mandate letter

The mandate letter will include clauses covering:

- the parties to the mandate;
- the background to the mandate;
- the mandated activity;
- the timetable for the mandate;
- the fees for the mandate, if applicable;
- payment for out-of-pocket expenses;
- termination of the mandate; and
- responsibilities and indemnities of the parties to the mandate.

11. Due diligence

Due diligence is the checking process that the investors and lenders will undertake before finally committing funds to the project. Further, if there are any additional costs incurred (eg, for lawyers or auditors), then the project company/borrower will usually have to pay the fees.

Due diligence consists of three main components: technical due diligence, financial due diligence and legal due diligence.

Technical due diligence: Investors and lenders may seek independent, third-party professional advice as to the design and technical specification of the proposed project, and seek advice as to the commercial prospects and experience with such technologies.

Financial due diligence: This is to enable lenders and investors to check the integrity of the cash flow model, the veracity of the projections and the underlying assumptions. Investors and lenders may often have access to the developer's computer model, under a confidentiality and 'no liability' arrangement, so that they can undertake their own sensitivity analysis. For complex projects, participants may also have the project model audited by a third party, not least because such model may be used at a later date for budgeting and tariff adjustment negotiations.

Legal due diligence: The legal advisers to the investors and lenders will review items such as:

- issues relating to title to property;
- enforceability of contracts;
- licensing and permits required;
- outstanding litigation, if any, of participants;
- environmental issues and liabilities;
- local laws on insolvency, expropriation and compensation;
- relevant statutory instruments required for the project;
- warranties and indemnities proposed for participants;
- corporate and executive liability issues; and
- mechanisms for repatriation of profits to investors.

12. Project monitoring

Project monitoring is a key component of the project process, yet it is invariably given lower priority than project preparation. Keeping control of costs and monitoring performance is essential to ensure that private investors and lenders receive their just rewards.

There are a number of project management systems used by major corporations and governments. One common model worthy of note is the Earner Value Management System (EVMS), often adopted in North America.

In essence, the objectives of project monitoring are:

- to relate time-phased budgets to specific contract tasks or statements of work;
- to provide a basis to capture work progress assessments to be compared against the baseline plan;
- to collate and compare technical, schedule and cost performance data;
- to provide valid, timely and auditable data/information for proactive management; and
- to provide managers with practical summaries for effective decision-making.

The system involves a range of criteria and measures, covering:

- organisation;
- planning, scheduling and budgeting;
- accounting considerations;
- analysis and management reports; and
- contractor and customer benefits.

Increasingly, in many countries the use of EVMS-type regimes is becoming mandatory for the project management of large, complex infrastructure-type developments.

13. Standards of probity and conflicts of interest

Infrastructure and PPP developments comprise investment in assets to deliver public services. There is therefore an expectation and, indeed, a demand that standards of probity and governance be maintained by all participants, both during the construction period and throughout operations.

Developers and operators of infrastructure projects might thus collectively be described as 'utilities' delivering public services; they invariably require, under national legislation, a licence to provide such services. The standards imposed may be embedded in the licence, or feature in a separate document.

Some governments accordingly impose regular 'fit and proper person' tests on their infrastructure licensees. The tests provide, at least in theory, the opportunity to monitor the performance of the utilities, impose corrective measures if performance is below expectations or accepted standards, and revoke the licence in the event of complete failure.

As investors worldwide increasingly use offshore tax havens to channel investment in such ventures, host governments to private infrastructure projects will wish to ensure that licensees do not abuse their position, in particular on issues such as national taxation and corporate transparency. Regular monitoring of a licensee's corporate affairs is advisable.

A second issue which needs to be addressed is conflicts of interest.

Conflicts of interest in the procurement and implementation of infrastructure projects can be defined, as below by the EU Parliament, as:

A set of circumstances that creates a risk that professional judgement or actions regarding a primary interest will be unduly influenced by a secondary interest.

Unlike fraud, misrepresentation, etc., the concept of conflict of interest does not necessarily imply any wrongdoing on the part of the individual or organisation, but may be an indicator, precursor or result of corruption.

The term 'concept' covers both perceived and actual conflicts of interest. Further, such conflicts can affect the procurement process and/or the delivery of a contract.

The procurement and implementation of infrastructure projects often involve inherent conflicts of interest among participants. These conflicts need to be identified, managed and disclosed to all the transaction's stakeholders as soon as, and even ideally before, they arise.

A dual measure which can be used to minimise and avoid undue conflicts is:

- to demand that all participants declare, at the outset of procurement, any potential or actual conflicts; and
- to exclude from the project process, without possible appeal, any participant that fails to disclose a conflict or possible conflict as and when it might arise.

A PPP unit could take on the role of administrator and adjudicator in such matters. As with any conflict, however, the adjudicator's perception may not coincide with what the (possibly) conflicted party believes to be the facts of the case.

Part 2: Practice and experience

Part 2 will review the experience of using private capital across a range of infrastructure sectors and the key issues faced. The underlying terms and conditions of finance, as described in previous chapters, will be similar across the sectors, although adjustment may be needed to fit each specific case.

Indeed, a comparison of a loan's terms sheet for a solar panel farm with that for a public-private partnership (PPP) highway shows that, apart from differences in the use of funds and some commercial components such as payment mechanisms, the underlying funding terms and conditions are very similar.

Financial risks are the obvious common element to all infrastructure projects, but a number of other factors can enhance success or bring about failure. Indeed, it is arguable that, due to the time, care and attention which financiers put into preparing and implementing cash flow-type infrastructure projects, very few of these projects have gone into liquidation for purely financial reasons or flawed financial structuring over recent times (including during the 2007–2009 financial crisis). That is not to say that some projects have not failed (eg, PPP cash toll roads in Spain), but these failures were due to injudicious project preparations such as over-optimistic traffic forecasts rather than financial shortcomings.

Where relevant, references are provided as to further reading.

Transport – roads and highways

1. Key features

1.1 Highways

The main characteristics of highway projects are as follows:

- Completion risks can be significant, but manageable;
- Environmental issues need to be reviewed early in the project cycle;
- Government support is needed for land acquisition;
- Traffic forecasts are an art, rather than a science;
- Cash toll projects are possible, but take longer to transact;
- Financiers prefer public-private partnerships (PPPs) paid against 'availability' payments;
- In emerging markets, foreign exchange risks can be a major risk; and
- There are many international examples of PPP-type highway projects.

1.2 Urban roads and road maintenance

In urban road and road maintenance projects, it is difficult to ring-fence the risks. Very few PPP-type urban road and road maintenance concessions have been implemented successfully.

1.3 Motorway service areas

Motorway service areas are structured as property/retail outlet transactions.

1.4 Car parks

Car parks are often overlooked as a sector for private investment, even though many municipalities have spare, unused land and such projects are cash-based business with limited/minimal investment required.

1.5 Street lighting

Street lighting is a growing sector for PPP application. They are low risk ventures, and easy to implement and manage. The prime risk lies in the creditworthiness of the concession grantor (eg, a municipality).

2. Key risks for highways

2.1 Completion

Financiers will require the project to be completed to time, cost and specification.

It is common for the construction period of road projects to last two to three years. Negotiating fixed price contracts for such a period can be difficult. In addition, when contractors start work on site, unforeseen costs or alternative ways of overcoming a particular topographical feature can arise, so cost increases and/or overruns are not uncommon. The construction contract needs to anticipate comprehensively such issues.

2.2 Traffic

Irrespective of the payment method to the private sector developer or concessionaire – whether cash tolls or availability payments – data regarding the possible traffic for a proposed highway is essential.

For instance, traffic forecasts will determine the revenues from cash tolls, and so the ability of the developer or concessionaire to service project debts. However, whichever payment mechanism is used, potential private sector owners of such highways will wish to know the forecast traffic in order to assess what level of maintenance costs they need to include in the prices to be included in any bidding process.

The remainder of this chapter will show that building highways with private sector capital on the basis of cash tolls has had a very chequered history. Not only have traffic forecasts been too optimistic on occasion, but people's willingness to pay, particularly in emerging markets or where the highway in question is the first cash-toll highway in the country, has also been overestimated. This has resulted in a number of disasters.

These experiences show that government promoters wishing to develop highways as private projects are better off using availability payments. This mechanism has the advantage of removing the traffic risk from the developer. Accordingly, the developer, supported by investors and lenders, can focus on:

- completing the project successfully;
- ensuring that the highway is made available for use under the performance terms of the concession, which is rarely a major risk area; and
- assessing the creditworthiness of the payer of the availability payments.

Another advantage of this mechanism is that the time taken for the lenders and investors to undertake their due diligence before committing to fund the project is invariably shorter: traffic forecasts do not have to be verified in such depth under such a scheme.

Lastly, availability payments should not stop the host government from introducing tolling too (although the level of such tolls and the revenues that they generate may be insufficient to cover all operational and finance costs). Tolling introduces to the travelling public the principle of having to pay to use the highways.

2.3 Environment

Major highway projects can face significant environmental risks as they can stretch over many miles of country. Hence, it is essential that such projects comply with standards such as the Equator Principles (discussed in the chapter on risk, not least to widen the availability of funding by the major project financing banks.

2.4 Land acquisition

Highway projects require significant areas of land. Such land might have little value unless a road is built on it, while some land might not be readily available without governmental intervention and support. Generally speaking, private developers of highway projects will not be prepared to carry the risk of land acquisition. That risk is usually left with the host government or relevant ministry.

2.5 Currency

Infrastructure projects require long-term funding (debt and equity) to cover capital costs. In emerging markets, that often means that the currency of funding may be different from the local currency, which is used to pay capital and operating costs, and generate revenues. As a result, there is an inherent mismatch between the local and funding currencies, with the former usually the weaker of the two. Hence, over a 15–20-year time horizon, there is the possibility that the local currency will devalue against the currency of funding, which may lead to debt service difficulties and, ultimately, default.

This risk arises both for cash toll highway projects and for those where payment to the developer is by availability payments. However, in the latter case it may be possible for the developer to avoid this risk by the host government payer covering any foreign exchange risks arising.

2.6 Case histories

(a) Southeast Asia

In the late 1980s/early 1990s Malaysia, Thailand and Indonesia were all actively promoting private sector, cash toll road projects, which were successfully built and operated for a time.

However, in 1997–98 an economic recession hit the region, and the Indonesian rupiah and Thai baht devalued significantly against the US dollar, which was the currency of much of the projects' debt. The result was that the project companies had difficulty servicing their debts and restructuring took place. The Thai projects, including the Bangkok Expressway, also were subject to political interference from the government, which added to the difficulties.

In Malaysia, the ringgit did not suffer so badly due to the natural resource exports (natural gas) which supported the currency. As a result, the $1.6 billion North–South Highway and other private highway (expressway) projects weathered the storm.

(b) ***Mexico***

In the same era, Mexico implemented an ambitious programme for 5,500 kilometres of toll-road projects with an estimated cost of $13 billion. Seven PPP-type deals were actually completed at a cost of $5 billion with mainly Mexican developers, dominated by construction companies. Typical funding consisted of equity (29%), US dollar loans from Mexican banks (52%) and government funds (19%).

The outcome was disastrous:

- The projects suffered from massive cost overruns (the developers were primarily contractors which were also building the projects);
- Traffic forecasts were too optimistic; and
- The local capital market could provide loans only of up to five years' maturity, so the long-term project debt necessary to establish project viability was denominated in US dollars.

In 1994, the Mexican peso, which was the currency of revenues and costs, was devalued. The result was that not only did the project companies collapse, but the contractors, Mexican banks and the economy as a whole were also affected. International (essentially, US) support was required to restructure the projects and the economy.

These experiences show that, where possible, infrastructure project funding should come from long-term local capital markets. If this is impossible, then steps need to be taken to mitigate, or avoid, the inherent foreign exchange risks.

(c) ***United Kingdom***

By the mid-1990s, project financing banks, which might be expected to fund up to 80% of the costs of a private infrastructure project, were beginning to be wary of cash toll projects, particularly in emerging markets.

In 1995–1996, the UK government set up the PFI (Project Finance Initiative) Executive to promote PPP-type deals, following on from the privatisations of telecommunications, ports, airports, power and water utilities, among others, in 1986–1991, and the implementation of transport projects such as the Channel Tunnel (Eurotunnel) and the Dartford Bridge.

The first four deals, which consisted of upgrading existing and building some new highways, were known as design, build, finance and operate (known as DBFO) deals, which were implemented in 1996–1998. They were based on 30-year concessions, and the payment mechanism was termed 'shadow tolls', whereby the project company/concessionaire received revenues based upon an agreed tariff up to a certain volume of traffic, paid by the Highways Agency (ie, the UK government), with additional revenues paid at set tariffs for incremental traffic – in other words, traffic risk was partly transferred to the concessionaire. The projects were:

- the M1–A1 Yorkshire link – a 29km section of road built at a cost of £180 million by Yorkshire Link (made up of Trafalgar House (Kvaerner) and Balfour Beatty);
- the A1(M) road – a 21km road built for £125 million by RMG (Amec, Brown & Root (Halliburton), Dragados and A McAlpine);

- the A419/A417 road – a 51km road built for £50 million by RMG; and
- the A69 road link – an 83km road built for £14 million by Road Link (H Boot, Christiani & Nielsen, Cogefar-Impresit, Morrison Project Investments Ltd, Pell Frischmann and ASTM-SINA).

The projects were successfully completed and operational.

An analysis after the event (National Audit Office, HC 476, 1997–1998) provided details of the transactions, as executed. One significant feature of the review was a breakdown of the bidding costs for the private bidders and the costs for the government counterpart. The total costs amounted to approximately £15 million each for the first two projects, £13 million for the third and £10 million for the fourth.

From this data, it is clear that for small, low value projects, PPP-type funding solutions are not cost effective. Indeed, the A69 road link did not achieve a positive benefit/cost ratio as a PPP as well. The A419/A417 road was marginal as a PPP in the circumstances, but as its funding was combined with that for the A1(M) road, there were some synergies, which reduced costs.

Hence, project value is a key issue when considering when to use the PPP-type funding mechanism for infrastructure developments (see in Part 1 the chapter on the options for governments for more on this issue).

M6 Toll: The United Kingdom has only one toll road, known as 'M6 Toll', which provides an alternative route around Birmingham to avoid congestion at the junction of the M5 and M6 motorways. The road was first proposed in 1992 and called the Birmingham North Relief Road or BNRR. Following a bidding process, a PPP-type concession was awarded to a joint venture named Midland Expressway between Trafalgar House, a major UK contractor, and Autostrade, an experienced Italian toll-road operator and part of the IRI Group.

There then followed an extended period of public consultation as to the route, planning, etc, and it was not until 1998 that the project was finally approved by an act of parliament.

By then the shareholding of the consortium had changed. Trafalgar House, which held 75% of the shares in Midland Expressway, was no more, and its shareholding had been acquired by the Macquarie Infrastructure Group (MIG), a Luxembourg-based private equity fund, with Autostrade holding the balance. (MIG later bought out Autostrade.)

Financial close was reached in May 2000 for a project funding of £830 million, of which £685 million was senior bank debt with a 16-year maturity, £145.5 million was subordinated debt at 12% interest rate, and £1.5 million was shareholder equity.

Unusually, the PPP concession extended over 53 years, and the tariff level for tolls is set by Midland Expressway itself, without government interference. The argument used to justify such freedom for tariff-setting was that if the tariffs were too high, drivers would use the alternative routes (which were more congested).

The road was completed in December 2003, and opened for use. It soon became clear that usage was lower than forecast as the tariffs were too high, so Midland

Expressway reduced them, at the same time as drivers started to realise the time saved by using the link.

However, Midland Expressway has paid minimal, or no, UK corporation tax to date. This is due to the presence of the high-interest subordinate debt in the funding structure, and the allocation of the interest costs against taxable profits, thereby minimising corporation tax liability. Indeed, the subordinate debt is set up such that it is repayable whenever the shareholders wish, which provides some corporate flexibility in this matter. The forecast annual debt service cover ratio was around 1.5.

By 2006, the project had been operational for nearly three years and was meeting all its costs. A syndicate of international City-based banks proposed a restructuring of the project debt – in effect, a securitisation – and offered Midland Expressway a £1 billion debt package with a legal maturity of August 2015. This loan was then used to repay the outstanding senior debt, which at that time had been reduced to £620 million, and the balance of £392 million returned to the MIG Fund as a special dividend.

Following this, MIG made a commitment to the UK government to invest a further £112 million in new infrastructure in the area of M6 Toll to improve access.

Lessons: The above project structure and subsequent events are somewhat unusual. The private project company has ended up so highly indebted that questions are raised as to its sustainability. It is also an example where investors – in this case, private equity funds – may put profitability before the sustainability of a public service. It remains to be seen whether this project will survive over the full extent of its concession without additional financial support.

For a long time, M6 Toll was effectively owned by its creditors, but media reports in early 2017 indicated that M6 Toll had been sold to IFM, a major Australian pension fund, for an undisclosed sum.

(d) Central Europe

With the collapse of the Berlin Wall in 1989, the possibility of developing infrastructure projects as private sector ventures opened up in Central Europe. One of the prime attractions was that, if suitably structured, the financial obligations for servicing debt for such projects could be kept off national balance sheets, which for governments with limited budgetary availability was a boon.

Cash toll highway projects were proposed in the Czech Republic (eg, D5 and D47) and Poland (eg, A1: North–South and A2: East–West), but due to unpredictable traffic forecasts or uncertainty over users' willingness to pay, and lack of economic viability and/or governmental support, such projects foundered before reaching financial close. (Note that the two Polish projects were finally funded as cash toll projects years later, but not without EU and governmental support.)

M1/M15 and M5, Hungary: In 1993–1994, a proposal was put forward to upgrade and expand the M1/M15 Budapest–Vienna motorway, with a branch up to Bratislava (M15). This was a key project for central and eastern European traffic. A concession was awarded to a Franco-Austrian-Hungarian consortium and the funding structured as a cash toll, build, operate, transfer (known as BOT)/PPP type, and supported by the European Bank for Reconstruction and Development – the development bank formed in 1991 to finance economic developments in Central Europe and the former Soviet Union.

The motorway opened in 1996 to much international acclaim, but it soon became clear that revenues were only 70% of those forecast, primarily due to optimistic traffic forecasts and a lack of willingness to pay by users. By 1998, the concessionaire company was in financial difficulties and the finance had to be restructured with Hungarian government support.

This debacle left commercial lenders with a jaundiced view of such projects and highlighted the difficulties of financing cash toll projects.

By then, though, the Hungarian government had attempted to implement the M5 Budapest–Serbia PPP motorway on a similar basis to the M1/M15 motorway. However, following the experience of the M1/M15 project, the government changed the structure to an availability payment mechanism. The M6 Budapest–Croatia motorway was similarly funded against availability payments in 2005.

Lessons: After the experiences in the above projects, commercial lenders were becoming averse to supporting cash toll projects without any additional security for debt service payments. A number of alternatives have been attempted internationally, some successful, some not. The straightforward availability payment mechanism has become more established, though, with a number of successful precedents set.

(e) Venezuela

In the mid-1990s, Venezuela, like many emerging markets, passed a PPP concession law to permit private investment in public service infrastructure.

The first project to be attempted under this law was a PPP concession for the upgrade and operation of the existing 17km Caracas–La Guaira *autopista*, linking Caracas, the capital, to La Guaira on the coast, where the main international airport and regional port are located. The highway passes through some spectacular scenery, rising from the coast to an elevation of 350m, with three 300m to 500m viaducts (one of which needed to be replaced), and two 300m tunnels. The region is also periodically subject to earthquakes. The highway was already tolled, but the concession also included the operation and upkeep of the old road over the mountains, which was free to use, but much slower and twisty.

After a bidding process, a Mexican consortium called Aucoven was awarded the concession on a cash toll basis. Work started on the upgrades, which turned out to be more expensive than expected, so Aucoven requested toll increases, an event which had been foreseen under the original concession agreement. By then, the government had changed and the economy had become weaker. The government nevertheless allowed the toll increases, but the travelling public protested against these increases by organising demonstrations on the highway. The government backed down, and tolls were reduced. This made it impossible for Aucoven to cover its costs.

In due course arbitration proceedings were initiated before the World Bank's

International Centre for Settlement of Investment Disputes. After a while, Aucoven was awarded compensation.

Lessons: It is crucial to include viable dispute resolution clauses in the concession agreement. Public service concessions always have a political dimension.

2.7 Availability payment mechanism

The underlying principle for an availability payment mechanism, which is widely used in PPP projects in many sectors, is that if the PPP concessionaire fails to deliver the contracted service, no payment is made. Accordingly, it is vital to define very closely at the outset what the PPP service comprises.

The availability payments, sometimes called 'unitary payments', should cover:

- the concessionaire's operations and maintenance costs;
- debt service payments (interest, fees and repayments); and
- a return, or profit, for the shareholders.

Such payments are paid periodically (eg, monthly), so it will be for the concessionaire to manage cash flow to match debt service payments, which might arise every six months.

Further, the availability payments will be payable, once the underlying service is delivered (ie, on project completion) over the lifetime of the PPP concession, which could extend to 30 years.

Such payments, therefore, include adjustments to account for inflation, particularly for operations and maintenance costs. It is usual to separate out key components of the latter (eg, labour and materials), and agree in the concession agreement the indices to be used relating to these activities.

As such indices, which must relate to the currency of payment, may not be published until some time after the date to which they apply, further adjustments to payments might be necessary. It must also be added that in some emerging markets these indices may not be reliable or not relate closely to the underlying activity, so estimates have to be made against an agreed formula.

The question arises as to whether finance costs (ie, debt and equity) should be similarly inflated. The scheduled debt service costs should become identifiable once project completion is achieved, and these will remain unaffected by future inflation. Therefore, any inflation formula should arguably not apply to debt service. For equity, which typically represents between 20% and 30% of project capital costs, there are arguments to support both cases (ie, no or some adjustment), so this is a matter for negotiation before the concession agreement is signed. Preferably, the host government should state its demands in this respect in the PPP bid documents.

Different governments adopt differing procedures for tendering such PPP projects. Some request bidders to offer just one, all-in periodic availability payment, while others break down such availability payments into its components, as above.

Whichever is the adopted mechanism, it should always be remembered that PPP concessions are long-term deals – like a marriage! Whereas the two parties (host government and PPP concessionaire) may negotiate hard at the outset, ideally they should maintain a cooperative relationship throughout the life of the deal (ie, up to 30 years). If one of the parties is unhappy with the relationship, then the PPP service to be delivered will suffer. If there is a total breakdown in the relationship, everyone loses out, and the service to the public collapses.

The next question is how to measure availability, or performance. The normal approach is to adopt a points system, whereby any failure to meet the performance standards set for the PPP service to be delivered attracts a certain number of penalty points.

For a PPP motorway project, the points regime will typically comprise:

- a level of penalty points allowable within each payment period for which the concessionaire is not financially penalised. This represents the principle that no concessionaire is perfect;
- a level of penalty points within each payment period above which each point is given a value and the aggregate within that period is deducted from the periodic availability payment due; and
- a further level of penalty points within each payment period above which a multiplier is applied to each point incurred (eg, 2×) and the aggregate within that period is deducted from the periodic availability payment due.

Variations to the above scheme may be applied, under which the aggregate penalty points per period are compared with the totals for the previous or subsequent periods, and any increase or decrease (which reflect an improving or deteriorating performance respectively) are recognised either as bonuses or additional penalties.

In addition, incentives may be introduced for the concessionaire to carry out maintenance at times when the motorway is less used (eg, multiples are applied to penalties incurred for maintenance activities during the rush hour, whereas maintenance during offpeak or weekends may avoid such multiples).

Similarly, penalty points may be incurred per 100m per hour of closure (ie, non-availability) of the inside, as opposed to the outside, lane or for failing to keep drains clear, signs lit, snow cleared, etc. A typical penalty regime might comprise 20 to 30 performance targets for the concessionaire.

Lastly, such a system, of which there are now a number of international precedents, carry the following additional features:

- The monetary value of each penalty point is based on best estimates. Clearly, the value has to incentivise the concessionaire to deliver the PPP service as defined in the concession agreement. However, it should not unduly penalise the concessionaire. Lenders, which provide 70% to 80% of project funding, will examine carefully the penalty regime to satisfy themselves that a concessionaire will receive an adequate amount under the periodic availability payments to meet operations and maintenance costs, plus debt service, under normal, reasonable conditions. If such debt service payments come under threat, lenders may exercise their step-in rights. After all, they will take security over the project assets so long as their debt is outstanding.

Hence, the penalty points regime needs to focus on the inherent impact on the equity component of the availability payment.

- Who measures and collates the penalty points? For a motorway, it is impractical for the government counterpart to monitor performance over a, say, 100km stretch of PPP motorway 24/7, 365 days per year. In many instances, therefore, the concessionaire measures its own performance.

In emerging markets such a suggestion may seem extreme and open to abuse, but it is pragmatic. However, under such regime the government counterpart – that is, the PPP concession grantor and the obligor for the availability payments – will reserve the right to demand to see the PPP concessionaire's penalty book without notice, and, in the event of cheating, the concessionaire will incur heavy penalties, with possible termination for repeated offences. In reality, at this stage of a PPP project lenders' interests in ensuring optimal performance by the concessionaire coincide with those of the government, as that is the best way for the lenders to receive full repayment of their loans.

- The aggregate value of penalty points incurred in any one period will be deducted from the periodic availability payment before any indexation to reflect inflation is applied to the availability payment.
- Adjustments may need to be applied to the availability payments to reflect changes in maintenance costs. If the actual traffic using the motorway is higher than originally forecast, this will not impact the amount payable for availability, but will increase maintenance costs. Usually, unit prices for additional maintenance will be included under the original concession agreement.
- A regime of 'scheduled outages' – that is, periods when the highway will be closed for regular maintenance – will be agreed between the concessionaire and government for each year.

Case histories: The guidelines as to whether PPP highway projects, paid for by availability payments, are on or off balance sheet for the host government are open to interpretation. Indubitably, such payments represent contingent liabilities for the concession grantor (ie, host government), but whether such obligations are interpreted as direct financial liabilities remains unclear. Hence, some governments have adopted different approaches to mitigating traffic and willingness-to-use risks in such projects.

Not long after the M1/M15 debacle in Hungary, Croatia successfully developed the Bina Istra highway as a cash toll PPP. This project enjoyed a number of advantages, however:

- There were precedents for toll roads in Croatia;
- The government provided a support mechanism for the concessionaire by guaranteeing that the debt service reserve account was maintained at the required level (ie, indirectly guaranteeing debt service); and
- The government paid for some of the tunnelling costs, which removed this risk from the concessionaire.

With such a scenario, the first phase of the project was successfully funded in

1999 with export credit agency and bank debt, and later refinanced in 2004, along with the funding of the second phase, by accessing the international bond markets. A similar structure was used for the Macelj–Zagreb motorway in 2004.

Israel undertook the $1.2 billion Cross-Israel cash toll highway with the government providing a revenue support mechanism if traffic is less than expected, and a profit-sharing mechanism, described as 'very complex', for any traffic upside. As a result, very long-term (28-year) debt was raised as part of the funding.

Chile has successfully adopted a similar mechanism for a number of PPP cash toll projects. In these projects, the concessionaire carries revenue risk within a band (say, more or less 10% of a projected target) agreed at the outset, but any amounts above these limits are returned to the government, and, likewise, any deficits below this limit are made up by the government. As a significant portion of the finance may be raised in US dollars but revenues are in Chilean pesos, there is a similar banding support mechanism for the US dollar/Chilean peso exchange rate. It is understood that Colombia and Mexico are now following a similar system for their PPP highways.

One other notable characteristic of the Chilean system, which has bolstered the expansion of PPPs in Chile across all sectors, has been the development of a long-term local capital market. Following the deposing of President Allende and arrival of General Pinochet in 1973, the economy was on its knees. The government demanded that those in employment pay a certain proportion of their salary into a pension fund, some publicly managed, some private. Such pension funds seek both short-term investments to meet immediate pensioners' needs, and long-term investments to satisfy those who will not retire for some years.

Over time, this created a long-term capital market, and as privately owned and controlled infrastructure and public service projects require long-term funding, a ready source of capital in local currency to support PPPs.

Economists have argued about the expedience of such policies, but the impact in Chile, and more recently in Peru where a similar policy has been adopted, has underpinned the argument that private infrastructure in emerging markets is best funded with long-term local capital.

In this context, it is noteworthy that South Africa, which for many years restricted the remittance of foreign exchange, has also developed with some success privately owned and controlled private sector, cash toll highways using long-term local capital (eg, N1/N4 and N3).

Nigeria, more recently, tried to repeat this model for the Lekki–Epe Expressway in Lagos, but although traffic demand was significant, users' unwillingness to pay resulted in the project receiving bad local publicity and a demand from sponsors that the project be structured on availability payments.

2.8 Availability v cash tolls

The above discussion leads to the conclusion that:

- the availability mechanism allows highway PPP projects to proceed more expeditiously. The timetable to reaching financial close will be shorter than for a cash toll project. However, whereas there are now a number of successful

precedents for the availability performance regime, the focus is on the creditworthiness of the availability payer, which carries the traffic risk. Further, such a structure is more overtly a direct obligation on the host government; and
- the cash toll mechanism takes much longer (often twice as long) to reach financial close and there are just as many project successes as failures.

Nevertheless, there is growing recognition internationally that users of public services should pay some fee towards the investment and operations of the underlying assets. Even if a PPP highway project is funded against availability payments, host governments should consider imposing tolls (cash, vignettes, or licences) whose revenues may, or may not, cover all the payments to be made under the availability mechanism. At least, such tolling accustoms the users to paying fees for the services delivered.

Case histories – the impact of the financial crisis: Before the 2007–2009 financial crisis, finance costs were low and the European Union was keen to develop infrastructure in its newer member states. Consequently, private sector infrastructure projects, including highways, and PPPs were widely promoted. At the same time, some of the more hard-pressed governments, such as Greece, Spain, Portugal, Ireland and Italy, perceived the potential off balance sheet advantages of pursuing such deals.

A number of PPP-type highways were implemented, some as cash tolls, some with availability payments, often strongly supported by EU/European Investment Bank funding against a perceived economic cost/benefit justification.

As the financial crisis unfolded, many such projects came to grief. Either traffic and, hence, revenues dropped significantly for cash tolls, or governments had difficulties meeting availability payments due to budgetary constraints. Many such projects have had to be restructured and one or two were declared bankrupt (Spain).

The above was a clear message that such funding structures are not a free lunch. Governments and project sponsors need to be clear about the inherent risks and potential contingent liabilities created by their support.

It is interesting to note the greater conservatism of northern European governments in this respect, where there have been fewer PPP highway projects promoted over the years than in southern Europe. Germany, Austria and the Netherlands have undertaken only a few.

However, one significant recent development was the implementation of the €250 million N33, Assen–Zuidbroek highway PPP as a 23-year concession to upgrade 38km of single to double carriageway. The project costs were funded with a conventional debt/equity (90/10) package, with payments to the concessionaire to be on an availability basis. However, at the outset (ie, at financial close), a major state-owned pension fund, APG, agreed to refinance 70% of the bank debt on project completion at a fixed interest rate. Hence, there is a committed bridge between bank funding and the bond market at completion for a large part of the debt.

It is to be expected that such a mechanism will be adopted for similar projects in future given that under Basel III regulations, as imposed by the Basel Committee for Banking Supervision, bank lenders are constrained from lending long term, yet bank finance has greater flexibility than the bond markets to meet costs during the construction period.

3. Risks for other road-related sectors

3.1 Motorway service areas

Whilst such facilities are an essential component of long-distance highways, generally speaking they are funded in a manner similar to retail/restaurant outlets, on a medium/long-term lease from the landowner. As such, they represent property, rather than infrastructure, financing.

3.2 Urban roads and maintenance

As mentioned in section 1.2 above, the key issue with such projects is that it is difficult to ring-fence (ie, control) the risks. Hence, private sector operators will not show great interest. Furthermore, such schemes are often labour rather than capital intensive.

That said, there have been two such road maintenance PPPs – Portsmouth and Birmingham – in this sector, but the outcomes are unknown.

3.3 Car parks

Many municipalities have spare urban land, while at the same time experiencing parking shortages.

Car parks are simple projects to implement and are cash generators.

Whilst hardly classified as 'infrastructure', such projects represent potentially attractive opportunities to entrepreneurial property developers.

There is one drawback, though. For large-scale car parks, where more sophisticated parking management and payment collection mechanisms may be employed, there are only a limited number of major operators in the field, so open competition is constrained.

3.4 Street lighting

Over the past five to 10 years, a number of street lighting projects have been implemented successfully as PPPs in the United Kingdom. Typically, a PPP concessionaire will take over and operate between 10,000 and 20,000 street lights and signs in a city. The investment usually entails replacement of the existing lights with new light standards and energy-efficient and long-life bulbs, thereby reducing energy and labour costs, over a period of years. The concession may also include maintenance of street signage and furniture.

The unexpected outcome of such projects has been that better lighting in urban areas has often reduced street crime, and in turn this has led to greater community activities at night given the added security in the areas.

Transport – bridges and tunnels

1. Key features

The key features of bridge and tunnel projects are as follows:

- The completion risk is usually manageable;
- Traffic risk remains a major issue, but it is usually more predictable than for roads and highways;
- Currency risks can be an issue over the long term; and
- There is a possible contribution from enhanced property values (for more details on this subject, see the chapter titled "Transport – rail").

2. Key risks

2.1 Completion

As for highways, building bridges or tunnels to time, cost and specification is a key risk area. Fixed price contracts for tunnels through mountains are generally not available (unless the geology is well understood), and if they are, there will be an upper limit to the fixed price.

2.2 Traffic

As for highways, traffic represents a key risk. However, this risk is usually more manageable, particularly if the bridge or tunnel links two urban areas. A number of privately funded bridges and tunnels, but not all, have exceeded traffic forecasts once built.

2.3 Environment

Given that tunnels and bridges are limited in area, the environmental risks may be more easily identified and controlled. That said, in the case of estuarial crossing, natural habitat issues might be a major constraint.

2.4 Land acquisition

The land required for bridges and tunnels may be much smaller than for highways, but acquiring the project site may, as for highways, be difficult environmentally, socially and politically. Hence, this risk is usually carried by the host government.

There is also the issue of the land under the sea, estuary or river over, or under, which the project goes. Such land may be owned by a different government agency to that which promotes bridges and tunnels, and special permits may be required, which can take time.

2.5 International borders

Major bridge and tunnel projects may span from one country to another. The same might apply for oil and gas pipeline projects and power transmission lines, although it is understood that no binational private highway projects have been built and funded as one project to date.

To overcome this risk, an international treaty, specific to the project, is required to satisfy lenders and investors. Such treaty will define the parties' roles, responsibilities and obligations, as well as the regulations to which both governments will adhere in respect of the project, protecting investor and lender rights.

One caveat can be that such treaty might take months, if not years, to negotiate in some cases.

2.6 Currency

As for highways, availability of foreign exchange to cover financing costs represents a key risk over the long term for bridges and tunnels that are cash-tolled and funded in a different currency to that used for revenues and costs. Similar measures as for highways need to be taken.

3. Case histories

3.1 Dartford Tunnel

Historically, the United Kingdom has been at the vanguard of implementing infrastructure projects as privately funded ventures.

The earliest public-private partnership (PPP)-type project was the Dartford Bridge, which provides the crossing over the Thames on the eastern portion of the M25 motorway circling London. The project cost £226 million, including the purchase by the project company of the existing operational twin-bore tunnel under the Thames, reaching financial close in 1987 and project completion in 1991.

Unusually, the project company's capital was pinpoint (only £1,000), provided by the contractor, Trafalgar House. No dividends were payable. The balance was made up of bank loans and loan stock/bonds, which had an overall maturity of 12 years, plus the net revenues from the existing tunnel operations. Given the uncertainty over traffic forecasts and with this funding structure, debt was due to be repaid whenever the project company/borrower was able to. Once all the debt was repaid, then the project would revert to state ownership.

In fact, traffic demand was greater than forecast, so the debt was repaid early, and the project returned to the state. Interestingly, under the Dartford-Thurrock Crossing Act 1998, which governs this project, once the bridge and tunnel return to state ownership, then tolls should be charged by the state to cover ongoing costs only. Such tolls, however, continue to be levied at 'commercial' levels!

Lessons: This project is one of the few PPP projects globally which has successfully reached the end of its concession period and ownership returned to the state.

3.2 Channel Tunnel/Eurotunnel

In the annals of infrastructure project financing, Eurotunnel holds a special place. While Eurotunnel has been a technical and economic success, financially the project has been a disappointment to investors and lenders. The original investors enjoyed discounted travel fares but received no dividends, and lenders received interest, but no principal, repayments.

The project, which was built between 1986 and 1990, cost approximately £8 billion, of which the original debt represented 81% of capital. The concession was initially for 55 years, later extended following refinancings.

A project-specific treaty between the United Kingdom and France (Treaty of Canterbury) governs the execution of this binational project and the rights and responsibilities of the host governments. The treaty states that the concessionaires were not to receive any financial guarantees (ie, the tunnel had to be funded as a stand-alone cash flow financing), and neither the French nor British government was allowed under the treaty to intervene except on issues of security or if a commercial dispute was not resolved within six months. This was to be of some significance some years later, when Eurotunnel got into financial difficulties, as by that time the majority shareholder was a French state entity.

Further, a target was set by both governments that rail travel time between Paris and London was to be under three hours once the tunnel was open: a target met on the French side by the TGV (*train à grande vitesse*, or high-speed rail), but not until 2003 on the UK side with the opening of the Channel Tunnel Rail Link (now known as 'HS1').

Construction was undertaken by a consortium of UK and French contractors, Trans-Manche Link JV. The construction contracts were overpriced – unsurprisingly, as the consortium companies were, to a large extent, negotiating the construction contracts with themselves (as contractors). Added to this, there were some changes to the underlying specifications of the rolling stock, which similarly increased final costs.

On project completion, the operator was Eurostar, a joint venture made up of SNCF (French state railways: 55%), London & Continental Railways (a private UK consortium, which won the Channel Tunnel Rail Link concession: 40%) and SNCB (Belgian state railways: 5%).

There were significant uncertainties as to how much traffic would be attracted away from the cross-Channel ferries, which were using more than one port on both sides of the Channel, so could offer greater flexibility than the fixed-link tunnel. In the event, initial traffic forecasts for the tunnel were over-optimistic. The result was that Eurotunnel did not achieve the initial forecast traffic levels until many years after opening. Consequently, revenues, after meeting operational costs, could cover only interest payments and not debt repayment.

Raising the equity was also a challenge and unusually undertaken by an initial public offering. That equity offering proved insufficient and a second offering was required, which raised the proportion of equity in the funding structure to 22%.

Similarly, raising the debt presented major difficulties, as the project's economics required debt with 18-year maturity, which was somewhat longer than had been the norm for financing such projects. Notwithstanding the support of the European Investment Bank, many banks declined the opportunity to take part. Ultimately, though, the international profile of the project helped to raise the debt, albeit from a syndicate of 200 banks.

By 2006, Eurotunnel still had not repaid its debts, so a restructuring of the debt was seen as essential for the long-term sustainability of the business.

The size of the syndicate of lenders meant that, when it came to refinancing the Eurotunnel debt (first in 1996 and later in 2006), the administrative difficulties of undertaking that exercise were significant – even though many lenders by 2006 had sold their Eurotunnel debt in the secondary market at a discount. After the restructuring, the Eurotunnel debt was reduced from £6.8 billion to £2.8 billion, with an extension of the concession to 2086 (ie, 100 years overall).

By 2010–12, the Eurostar trains, built by Alsthom (France), had been operational for 20 years and replacements were planned. Under EU Procurement Regulations, an international public tender was required, and while Alsthom offered an updated version of its rolling stock, Siemens offered a cheaper, higher passenger capacity and more energy-efficient alternative, the E320 Velaro. Eurostar awarded the contract to Siemens.

In due course, this led to an international dispute between the French and German governments, and the matter was ended with Eurostar's decision being upheld in the UK courts, with Alsthom being offered a smaller contract to refurbish some of the existing coaches.

Lessons: Eurotunnel represents a key component of Europe's transport infrastructure of significant economic value. Technically, it was well executed for the day, but some of the commercial and financial features were less than optimal and somewhat over-ambitious and optimistic.

3.3 Severn Bridge and Skye Bridge

In the same era, two other major cash toll bridges were built in the United Kingdom across estuaries: the Severn Bridge (1992, £522 million), carrying the M4 motorway to South Wales, avoiding a significant detour, and the Skye Bridge (1991, £27 million) in Scotland. Both bridges link up a relatively prosperous region of the United Kingdom with a less prosperous region, both provide significant time gains, so are a quasi-monopoly, and both projects were structured financially similarly to the Dartford Crossing described above.

However, these bridges did not avoid controversy, primarily over the issue of toll levels, in that their users' willingness and ability to pay differ significantly from that forecast. The net result has been that the concession for the Skye Bridge was terminated early and the Welsh government has had to support indirectly the Severn Crossing.

Lessons: Notwithstanding their economic benefits, cash toll bridges (or tunnels), just like roads, are usually financially successful only when traffic forecasts are robust and the willingness of users to pay is established by precedent.

3.4 Second Tyne Tunnel

This project (2007–10, £397 million) under the River Tyne in Newcastle, United Kingdom, was undertaken as a cash toll venture, but had the benefit of receiving cash tolls from the existing, operational first tunnel during construction. Furthermore, the traffic forecasts were well established. Hence, a debt/equity ratio of 85/15 was achieved and the project successfully executed.

3.5 Mersey Gateway

This 1km, cable-stayed bridge (2014, £717 million) in the northwest of England is targeted at relieving congestion at other cross-River Mersey bridges in the region. It will be cash-tolled, with discounts for local residents. However, the PPP concessionaire will be paid against availability payments as there are alternative cross-Mersey routes available to users, giving rise to traffic uncertainty.

In March 2014, financial close was achieved for a 26.5-year PPP concession awarded to FCC (Spain), Kier (United Kingdom) and Samsung (South Korea).

The funding structure includes a UK government support mechanism to the local municipality, Halton, which is responsible for paying the availability payment, in the event that a shortfall in toll revenues arises and Halton is not able to cover all costs. Furthermore, the UK government has provided a guarantee for the £257 million project bonds, quoted on the Dublin Exchange.

Lessons: With traffic uncertainties, governmental support is often required to sustain financial bankability and to capture the economic benefits.

3.6 Other bridges and tunnels

(a) Europe

The experience of cash flow-financed bridges and tunnels throughout Europe has been similar to that of the United Kingdom in that traffic volume uncertainties have undermined the consistency of traffic forecasts, resulting in the need for third-party support.

Thus, the Rio-Antirion Bridge (Greece), Vasco Da Gama Bridge, Lisbon (Portugal), Limerick Bridge (Ireland) and Oresund Bridge (Sweden–Denmark) have needed governmental support in one form or another. The Lord Foster-designed Milau Bridge (France) and the Warnow Tunnel (Germany) have also suffered traffic uncertainties, although some 500,000 tourists each year go to view the stunning architecture of the former.

As for roads, the fallback position is to fund against availability payments, so the traffic/revenue risk is carried by the concession grantor.

The alternative is for the host government to guarantee minimum net revenues to ensure debt service cover, as has been provided by the Turkish government for the $1.45 billion, single bore, 2x2 lane, 5.4km tunnel under the Bosphorus, plus 3.8km of access roads, awarded as a PPP to a Turkish–South Korean consortium in 2012.

(b) *Australia*

Australia developed PPP-type deals for investment in public service assets in the early 1990s. However, in respect of tunnels, the Melbourne City Link was plagued with controversy over toll collecting systems, and in Sydney the Cross City Tunnel and Lane Cove Tunnel (2006 and 2007) failed to achieve the forecast traffic volumes, so fell into unrepaid debt.

Lessons: While experience shows that completion risk for a bridge or tunnel can be effectively managed, traffic risk, as for highways and roads, remains a key constraint on stand-alone, cash flow financings.

Transport – rail

1. Key features

1.1 Inter-city/high-speed rail

The main characteristics of inter-city/high-speed rail (HSR) projects are as follows:

- The investment costs in track, bridges, tunnels and stations are high;
- As for roads, environmental/social issues can be significant;
- High traffic volumes are needed to establish financial viability;
- Government subsidies are often required; and
- The optimal project and corporate structure for successful railway projects using private capital, in whole or in part, remains elusive.

1.2 Rolling stock and vehicles

Rolling stock and vehicles often represent an attractive leasing business. Maintenance can be outsourced to the private sector.

2. Key risks for inter-city/HSR

2.1 Costs and completion

New inter-city railway lines, particularly if they are HSRs, are costly projects. Overall, the investment in infrastructure (cement, concrete, track and electrification) often represent over 90% of project costs.

Experience on European HSR systems shows that the cost per kilometre for construction can range from $10 million to $50 million, depending on the topography and whether the line passes through urban areas, where tunnelling may be necessary. Costs can be even higher, such as the UK Channel Tunnel Rail Link ($8 billion equivalent for a 108km line – or $80 million per kilometre). The high costs on this occasion were due in great part to the tunnelling through the outer suburbs of London.

For conventional two-track line, the costs – including electrification – could be much lower (eg, $7 million to $9 million per kilometre). Single bore rail tunnels add to costs (eg, $50 million to $100 million per kilometre), and modern passenger train-car sets might cost $5 million to $6 million per railcar.

Thus, the bulk of the costs comes from track and infrastructure. These high costs mean, however, that fixed price turnkey contracts are often unattainable.

That said, once built, rail tracks and the associated physical infrastructure last for many years and maintenance costs are relatively low compared to capital cost (although there have been indications that some HSR lines have required more maintenance than expected). Nevertheless, cost recovery for track infrastructure extends over a very long period, often much longer than the maturity of funding available.

2.2 Traffic and financial viability

In many countries there is significant demand, both from passengers and freight, for rail networks – not least because governments are keen to move traffic away from the roads to help support climate change policies and relieve congestion. However, given the heavy costs of building railways – and upgrading existing railways to take modern rail traffic – the revenues from passenger fares and freight are invariably insufficient to cover costs. Hence, public subsidies in some form are required to sustain financial viability, if economic viability is established in the first place.

The result is that few, if any, international rail passenger systems are financially viable on their own. There are, however, some long-distance freight railways which are financially sustainable, usually based on the transportation of a key commodity (eg, a mineral) or container traffic (eg, across North America).

Accordingly, railway systems tend to fall into the two corporate structures described below.

Figure 11.1: Vertically integrated model

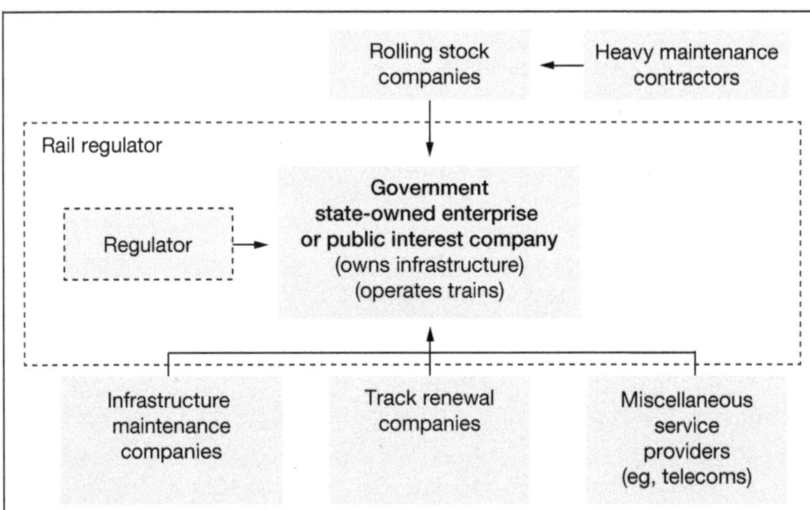

Source: author

Vertically integrated: A single entity owns the infrastructure and provides the transportation services. It is usually state-owned, but there are also a few private companies – for instance, for freight.

This structure has been well tested. Other characteristics include the following:

- The demand and use of the railway facilities for passenger versus freight traffic needs to be carefully managed so as not to provide unbalanced usage;
- Third-party access is possible, but needs some regulatory framework;
- Cost-efficiencies are possibly achievable; and
- Monopoly service can prevent competition.

Figure 11.2: Vertically separated model

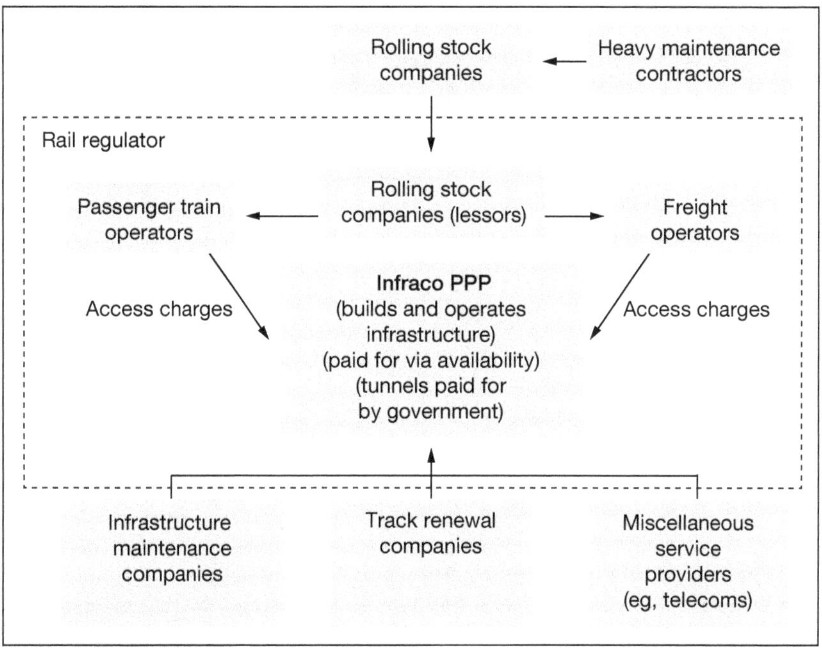

Source: author

Vertically separated: One entity (often state-owned) owns the infrastructure. Separate entities provide the transportation services; they can be state-owned or private.

Characteristics of this structure include the following:

- There are fewer precedents and less experience of this structure to date;
- The passenger/freight interface needs to be managed for usage so as to provide fair opportunity and competition;
- Third-party access is mandated; and
- Cost efficiencies are possible via competition.

The United Kingdom followed the vertically separated structure with the privatisation of its operators and later the infrastructure provider, Railtrack, quoted on the London Stock Exchange in 1994. Railtrack owned the track and stations, and charged private passenger and freight operators for using that infrastructure.

However, in due course Railtrack was found to be financially unviable, and in

2002 Railtrack became Network Rail, a state-controlled, not-for-profit company. Some 80% of Network Rail's revenues still come from direct government grant, with only 20% coming from operators (ie, passengers and freight).

In Europe and elsewhere, the vertically integrated structure is more commonly found, with state-owned entities (corporately separate) owning and operating the track and trains respectively. Nevertheless, the trend is towards having more than one operator in any one system, introducing an element of competition.

2.3 Environment

As for private PPP-type highways, rail projects may entail significant environmental and social risks. Early review is, therefore, called for.

2.4 International borders

Conceivably, inter-city rail projects may be cross-border (eg, Eurotunnel (United Kingdom-France), or the Perpignan-Figueres TGV (*train à grande vitesse*, or high-speed rail) PPP (France-Spain). An international treaty, specific to the project, is required to allocate inter-governmental roles and responsibilities, and to satisfy lenders and investors.

2.5 Land acquisition and planning

As for highways, the land required for rail projects may be significant. This risk is usually carried by the government.

The potential contribution from enhanced property values should be mentioned here.

Enhanced property values: Whenever a road, railway, bridge or tunnel is built, experience has shown that the value of land contiguous with the entrances or exits (ie, transport nodes) of the infrastructure increases comparatively more than normal values increase. For example, analysis showed that, for the extension of the London Underground Jubilee Line from Waterloo to Canary Wharf in 2001, if one had been able to capture the enhanced values of properties close to the Underground stations (ie, the incremental value created as a result of building the extension), the enhanced value could have paid for the extension itself (Don Riley, "Taken for a Ride", Centre for Land Policy Studies, 2001).

This phenomenon is not new. In 1975–77, when the Hong Kong Mass Transit was being built, HKMTRC, the mass transit company, also developed the areas above the stations for commercial use, and, more significantly, the area above the extensive maintenance yards in Kowloon for residential apartments. Within a few years, the HKMTRC property company was a larger entity than the metro itself.

This issue has been approached in a number of different ways by a number of governments, and not just for private infrastructure projects. In France, companies with more than 20 employees are charged a specific municipal tax which is directed towards developing local transport projects. When the extension to the Dublin metro was built, commercial developers within a certain distance of stations had to pay a *praecipium* to gain planning consent. Similarly, in London businesses are being charged an additional municipal tax to help pay for Crossrail 1.

To date, the optimum mechanism for capturing enhanced property values has not been established. The prime problems concern:

- the method for measuring the enhancement or incremental value;
- the capture of the incremental value (eg, via a tax); and
- the timing mismatch – the enhancement comes after the infrastructure has been built, so the enhancement is not available to support funding of, and pay for, the infrastructure at the outset of construction.

So far, the railway sector has been less advanced in harnessing this phenomenon than the urban transit sector. With the huge areas of space above stations and maintenance yards in many railway systems, the potential asset value is vast. It is not just property value that can be enhanced, too – power production may be another option to explore. Thus, the new extension to Blackfriars station over the Thames in London is covered in 4,400 photovoltaic solar panels, which provide 50% of the station's power demand.

3. Case histories

3.1 United Kingdom

Mention has already been made of the Channel Tunnel Rail Link (CTRL) between London and the Channel Tunnel, built as a private, PPP concession by London & Continental Railways, at least initially, for around £5 billion. At the outset, the project was to be funded under a conventional, cash flow-type debt/equity structure, with the equity being drawn first, followed by a bond issue.

However, the bond issue was not underwritten at the outset, and by the time the bond was to be issued the market had become unconvinced by the underlying business model of CTRL. In the end, construction could proceed only with government financial support.

Ironically, the only other bidder for CTRL was a group of contractors, largely from the Channel Tunnel project, which assembled a more conventional bank loan debt package. With commitment fees presumably being paid, CTRL would have had the debt funding available when required.

3.2 Kenya/Uganda

A similar story arose with the rehabilitation of the Mombasa–Nairobi–Kampala railway line (the Rift Valley railway) undertaken as a PPP concession in 2005–7. The concession was awarded to a South African consortium after a public competition, but when the time came to inject equity funds, the shareholders were unable to provide the funding.

As with CTRL, the deal collapsed, emphasising the fundamental project financing principle to have all funds committed at the outset of project construction.

3.3 France and the Netherlands

Apart from the corporate viability issues facing railway projects, traffic uncertainties, as for roads, also prevail.

Not surprisingly, the trend, therefore, is towards structuring the payment for such projects against availability criteria.

The HSL-Zuid project between Amsterdam, Netherlands, and the Belgian border, as well as a number of recent French TGV links (eg, Perpignan–Figueres, the Brittany–Pays de la Loire TGV, and the Tours–Bordeaux lines) have all been so funded.

One novelty in the French PPP scene is the '*cession Dailly acceptée*' mechanism, whereby post-completion there is an assignment of receivables from the French state, up to a level of 80% of the bank debt outstanding, which mitigates debt service risks for lenders. (Traditionally, lenders have not been able to take security over state assets in France, which is one of the normal security measures taken by project finance lenders.)

Lastly, it is worth noting that all of the $40 to $50 billion-worth of railway projects currently being built in the Gulf countries are effectively government-funded.

4. Key risks for rolling stock and vehicles

Review of rail, bus and mass transit systems around the world shows that, even for state-owned transport companies, the rolling stock, engines and vehicles are often leased on a long-term basis.

The industry is well established, and the advent of PPP-type funding mechanism for infrastructure projects has little impact on this business.

Transport – metros, mass transit, light rail and trams

1. Key features

1.1 Metros and mass transit

The key features for these types of transport project are as follows:

- The investment costs in track, tunnels and stations are high;
- The projects are complex to construct;
- Government subsidies may well be needed to ensure financial viability; and
- Enhanced property values may play a role.

1.2 Light rail and trams

The key features for these types of transport project are as follows:

- The costs in infrastructure are lower than for heavy metro systems;
- Traffic forecasts are usually uncertain;
- The metro service needs to be integrated with other transport modes operating in the same area such as buses; and
- Bus-ways can be cheaper and quicker to implement.

2. Key risks and case histories for metros and mass transit

2.1 Key risks

(a) ***Costs and completion***

The cost and completion risks are similar to those for roads and railways, but tend to be greater. Constructing metros in cities, whether above or below ground, entails interfaces with many public utilities (eg, water, electricity, gas, telecoms). It also creates significant public inconvenience. These interfaces increase the inherent risks; this in turn explains why such projects are deemed complex.

(b) ***Traffic***

Traffic projections can be uncertain, unless the various transport modes are integrated. Taxis and buses could divert traffic away from the new metro as they are much more flexible in terms of the routes that they can use compared to metros.

(c) ***Financial viability***

Given traffic uncertainties, financial viability can be fragile. To the author's knowledge, the only metro in the world which is able to pay for its investment and cover its costs through fares is the Hong Kong Mass Transit (HKMTRC).

Initially, that project was funded with debt raised against UK government guarantees as it was too early for public-private partnership (PPP)-type structuring. However, HKMTRC was floated successfully on the Hong Kong Stock Exchange in 2000, and is a successful transport company with investment grade debt. In recent years, HKMTRC has been selling its expertise globally; it will be the operator for London's new Crossrail 1 link.

2.2 Case histories for metros and mass transit

(a) London Underground PPP

A number of attempts have been made to undertake metro projects as private ventures or PPPs, the most (in)famous being the London Underground PPP, awarded in February 2002.

The overall PPP concession structure comprised three complementary, 30-year PPP concessions, representing groups of existing, operational Tube lines. After an international bidding process, two concessions went to one consortium, Metronet (made up of Bombardier, WS Atkins, Balfour Beatty, Thames Water and SEEBoard), the third to TubeLines (made up of Bechtel, Halcrow, Ferrovial, Amey and Jarvis).

The estimated capital investment envisaged amounted to £20 billion, spread over a 20-year period. Given that this investment, in effect, was to rehabilitate the existing system plus undertake some upgrades, there was much uncertainty as to the actual costs to be incurred. Accordingly, the concessions were structured so that there would be a cost review every seven and a half years, which would duly affect the tariffs and revenues due to the concessionaires.

Lessons: Towards the end of the first seven and a half-year period, the PPPs collapsed for a variety of reasons, some of which should have been foreseen:

- No country had attempted such a large and complex mass transit PPP before (ie, there were no precedents);
- The PPP involved taking over existing assets, many built 100 years or more ago, and there was no definitive asset register. Consequently, defining investment costs was an impossible challenge open to variations;
- The availability payments structure was overly complex; and
- The resulting PPP concession agreements were over 3,000 pages long.

More importantly, at the end of the first seven and a half-year period, the PPP Arbiter – an innovative, somewhat experimental, role – had to negotiate, on behalf of concession grantor Transport for London (TfL) (ie, the UK government), the investment programme for the next seven and a half years with each concessionaire.

Unsurprisingly, there was disagreement over the cost estimates for this next investment programme. In particular, there were significant differences between the views and estimates of the arbiter on the one hand, and the Metronet consortium on the other, which was primarily made up of contractors and equipment suppliers (see also the reasons for cost overruns for Eurotunnel).

The PPPs were abandoned. The two Metronet concessions were taken back under the control and operations of TfL. Subsequently, TfL terminated the TubeLines concession as well, albeit for different reasons. TubeLines had reportedly kept tighter controls over project costs.

As the original PPPs had been structured as conventional project financings, the lenders to the concessionaires had, technically, security over the project assets (ie, London Underground), so long as their debts (between £3 and £4 billion) were outstanding.

On termination of the PPP concessions, however, a deal was struck between TfL and the lenders to restructure the underlying debts, most probably because the lenders did not relish the idea of exercising their security rights in the event. As for TfL, it needed money/bank loans to buy out the original lenders.

(b) Caracas Metro, Venezuela

After Hong Kong, Caracas was the next major city to build a new metro in the late 1970s. It was a natural candidate, with a population of 2.5 million living in a long narrow valley, a track record of major traffic jams and a creditworthy government. However, Venezuela had no other passenger railway, apart from a defunct link to the coast built by British engineers in the 19th century, so the new metro would be a novelty.

As with other metros since, stand-alone financial viability was impossible, so the government created a state-owned metro company, CA Metro de Caracas, with strong management, and required it to pay the investment costs for the rolling stock and equipment through the fare box. The infrastructure (tunnels, stations, etc) was funded directly by the government.

Notwithstanding the metro company's responsibilities, the debt covering the equipment contracts was also guaranteed by the government: it was too early for using a PPP mechanism, and Venezuela was a somewhat unknown risk to many banks. This structure ensured that the project not only had the funding required, but had it in a timely manner.

A key component of this project was the strong management. The president, the vice president and the finance director of CA Metro all retained their positions from project conception, through the five years of construction and then the first 20 years of operations. Construction costs were also tightly controlled (there was no overall turnkey contract).

In addition, CA Metro demanded to take responsibility for keeping the streets clean within 100 metres of every station, and provided its own fleet of buses to bring passengers from outlying districts. The result was that the public took pride in their metro. Graffiti in the stations and on coaches was minimal.

Lessons: Financiers should review closely the experience and abilities of the project company's management team for such complex projects.

(c) ***Dubai Metro***

In 2004, Dubai planned a new $4 billion metro on a stand-alone PPP basis. A PPP-type concession was awarded to a Japanese–Turkish consortium for a part underground, part above ground system. It soon became clear, however, that the long-term debt funding could not be raised. In the end, to ensure project completion, the Dubai government provided the support necessary to raise the funding.

Today, the line provides an excellent service – it is an economic success and has been extended with additional lines.

(d) ***South Africa and Nigeria***

In 2006, Johannesburg initiated the construction of the $4 billion (ZAR24 billion), 80km Gautrain urban system. A PPP-type concession was awarded to a South African–Canadian consortium, supported by RATP from France (which runs the Paris Metro) for operations.

In line with the constraints described above for earlier metro projects, 85% ($3.4 billion) of the project costs were funded by the South African government. Of the balance, 15% was consortium equity and 85% debt in rand (South Africa has a long-term local capital market, so foreign exchange risks could be minimised). It is understood that Gautrain is now carrying more passengers than forecast.

Lagos, Nigeria is also planning and has part-completed two new metro lines. The funding details are unclear, but it is understood that, following experience elsewhere, the infrastructure will be funded directly by the government, while the equipment will be funded through fares.

Overall, this model is probably optimal for many projects of this type.

3. Key risks and case histories for light rail and trams

3.1 Key risks

As for heavy metro, the key risks for light rail and tram systems are project completion and traffic. Overall, there are many similarities, although the infrastructure component of project costs might not be so dominant.

3.2 Case histories

(a) ***Croydon Tramlink, United Kingdom***

In 1996, the first UK PPP-type, stand-alone light rail system was built in Croydon, a suburb 12 miles south of London. The system was 28km long and had access to 18km along existing railtrack, 3.5km on streets and 6.5km on new alignment. The investment cost was £200 million, and a 99-year PPP concession was awarded to a contractor/equipment supplier consortium.

The project was completed, but when it started to operate it could not cover its costs, and so got into financial difficulties.

When the concession was awarded, the local bus company operator had agreed that buses would feed passengers to the light rail system and not compete. However, once the light rail started to operate, the buses continued to compete. The result was an arbitration case and the original consortium was bought out by the government.

Lessons: It is important to integrate all modes of urban transport to achieve optimal results and obtain private sector involvement.

Since the Croydon Tramlink project, there have been a number of similar and successful light rail projects both in the United Kingdom and elsewhere. However, these other projects involve payments to the PPP concessionaire on an availability basis (eg, Nottingham (United Kingdom), DLR Extension (United Kingdom), Line 5 of the Milan Metro (Italy) and Tenerife Light Rail (Spain)).

(b) Bogota Bus Way, Colombia

One option for overcoming the high costs and extended construction period for metros and light rail, and provided that land is available, is to build a bus way.

For many years, the municipality of Bogota, Colombia, had been toying with the idea of building a heavy metro, but never reached starting point. Then in 2000, a PPP-type bus way was proposed and implemented. The project comprises 13km of dedicated 2x2-lane bus way along main highways in the city, with extensions to the suburbs. By 2007, the system had been extended to 84km, covering a total network of 387km. The specially designed buses have a capacity of 160 passengers, and can operate along both the bus way and normal roads.

The initial cost was $210 million, with the government building the bus way and acquiring the buses, which were leased to private operators. The operators collect the fares, with tariffs set by the government, and the operators receive a certain proportion to cover their costs and profit (the target investor return is 15% per annum).

Lessons: Overall, the Bogota Bus Way has reportedly been a success, and it is easy to see how practical and flexible such an infrastructure development could be.

If land is available, it can provide a much cheaper and quicker alternative to fixed track metros or light rail.

Transport – ports

1. Key features

The key features for these types of infrastructure project are as follows:

- Ports incur high investment costs in jetties, wharves and breakwaters; such costs can represent up to 75% of the total, the balance being cranes and equipment.
- The life cycle for jetties, wharves, etc is very long (30 to 50 years).
- Cranes, gantries and warehouses have a 10- to 15-year life cycle.
- Environmental issues can be significant in port developments.
- Traffic/throughput forecasts are somewhat speculative.
- Major shippers rarely commit to use a port for more than three to five years.
- Ports can often be regional monopolies.
- Landside access infrastructure (road and rail links) is important.
- Adequate seaward access to port is also important.
- Very few, new stand-alone private ports have been built in recent years.
- The 'landlord model' is favoured in most countries for the corporate structure (see section 2.1 below).
- Some ports have a military/naval interface.

2. Key risks

2.1 Costs and completion

Given the distribution of costs between infrastructure and equipment for most ports, fixed price, turnkey contracts for building new ports are rare. Taken as a whole, many ports are economically viable – that is, they bring significant benefits to the host economy – but not financially viable.

Hence, the landlord model is often preferred, whereby the host government, or its agency, develops, funds and builds the new infrastructure, and leases land to private investors to develop terminals as public-private partnership (PPP)-type concessions. Assuming that the infrastructure is in place when such concession is awarded, then the private concessionaire should ensure timely project completion to cost, so as to start operations as soon as possible.

Under the landlord model, the concessionaire will charge shipping lines fees for onloading/offloading and storage, and will make lease payments, often linked to profitability or container throughput (on the basis of key performance indicators), to the landlord. Port dues, payable by shippers for navigation, dredging, etc, may be payable directly to the port authority/landlord, or via the concessionaire.

2.2 Traffic, revenues and currency risks

In many instances a port may represent a monopoly entrance/exit point for the host country. Even if there are alternative ports available, such ports can still operate monopolistically within a region. Hence, the host government will always wish to ensure that public interest requirements are met.

Further, the shipping market, particularly international container shipping, is highly competitive. Shippers will move to those terminals where the operations are the most efficient, turnaround times are short and tariffs lowest. As mentioned above, shippers will rarely commit to using a particular terminal for more than three to five years. This means that long-term sales or throughput contracts, of the type which support PPP concessions in other sectors, are just not available for ports. The inherent project risks to investors and lenders are, therefore, higher.

For this reason, more conservative debt/equity ratios are prevalent in port projects – for instance, 70/30, or 60/40, rather than 80/20 or 90/10 for some PPPs. The landlord model is also preferred, where the infrastructure (jetties and wharves) costs are the responsibility of the landlord (ie, the host government).

One advantage across the port sector is that many, if not all, the fees charged (eg, from shipping lines) and revenues paid are in hard currency (eg, US dollars). Accordingly, if, as usual, long-term debt is provided in hard currency, currency risks are minimised.

A word of caution must be expressed with respect to potential investors in port operations. Over recent years, existing port operations have become seemingly attractive investments for life insurance and pension funds, often led by private equity, investment bank managers. In order to estimate the value of a target port, the value of current earnings before interest, tax and debt amortisation (better known as EBITDA) is identified from corporate accounts, and a multiple applied based on comparisons with similar port operations. Unfortunately, on a number of occasions the multiple applied has been too optimistic, and the investors have come away most disappointed.

2.3 Environment

As for other PPP-type transport projects, ports entail significant environmental risks. Early review is, therefore, called for of such issues.

2.4 Access infrastructure

Developers often overlook access infrastructure:

- Landside – an efficient port operation needs good landside connections (eg, road and rail) to the hinterland. For a new port development, it is quite possible that for every dollar spent on developing the port 'inside the fence', another dollar has to be spent 'outside the fence' on improving port accessibility.

  With the landlord model, such investment would be for the landlord (ie, the state or government) to meet.

  If the landlord also owns the freehold of the land in the port, usually this results in more holistic planning of the overall access infrastructure than if the port land is owned by the PPP concessionaire. This issue has been highlighted by the inconsistency of access infrastructure planning for UK ports, which were privatized (including freehold of the port land) almost 25 years ago.

- Seaward side – many ports are sited in estuaries or bays, where the entrance might be quite narrow. There have been too many precedents where plans for new ore handling or container terminals have been developed with adequate quayside depths for the proposed shipping, but review of the seaward access has shown limitations as to water depth at the entrance or access channel, turning circles for ships, etc.

  One remedy is to dredge the access channel. However, dredging is an expensive activity, and a dredged channel one day is filled up again by the tide the next.

3. Case histories

3.1 Container ports

(a) DCT Gdansk, Poland

There have been many examples of private container port projects implemented throughout the world. Most have followed the landlord model, and quite often the container port concession itself has been funded on a corporate, rather than cash flow, project financing basis – the concessionaire often being the subsidiary of a major shipping line.

One example of a completely new private container port in recent years has been the 36ha DCT Gdansk Container Terminal on the Baltic coast in Poland. The terminal was developed in 2007–9 with a capacity of 500,000 twenty-foot equivalent units (TEU) containers, plus 150,000 TEU roll-on/roll-off (or Ro-Ro) (ie, vessels designed to carry wheeled cargo, such as vehicles driven on and off the ship on their own wheels or using a platform vehicle, such as a self-propelled modular transporter), with 15m quayside depth (ie, capable of taking the larger container ships operating today). The 650m berth had three post-Panamax cranes and five rubber tyre gantries (ie, mobile) cranes.

Experienced European contractors constructed the port. The key risk, however, was traffic and potential revenues.

An assessment of the market showed that there was a similar container terminal at Gdynia, 18km distant, but located up an estuary, limiting expansion to take larger ships. Further, in comparison with other Baltic container ports, Gdansk would be ice-free. Lastly, it was noted that Gdansk had good existing road and rail connections to the hinterland.

However, despite these advantages and even though the Polish market lacked adequate container port facilities, financiers were unsure about the ultimate success of Gdansk. The project was funded with a conservative debt/equity ratio of 50/50. By 2012, the success of Gdansk was assured, and with the commercial support of a deal with Maersk, the port was expanded to 1 million TEU capacity.

(b) ***US ports – political risks***

In 2006, Dubai Ports World (DPWorld) took over the UK shipping line P&O, which also operated a number of container port concessions throughout the world, including six in the United States.

Even though the US government approved the deal, Congress opined that DPWorld was, in effect, a sovereign fund, and that P&O's US ports were strategic assets. In due course, DPWorld had to sell these assets to the investment arm of AIG, a US insurance company.

Lessons: This was a salutary tale as to how governments may consider ports to be strategic assets, and that political risks associated with such investments need to be addressed by private investors as part of their due diligence.

(c) ***Rotterdam World Gateway***

One of the few cash flow port project financings in recent times has been the Rotterdam World Gateway (2012), a €720-million development for a 2.35 million TEU container terminal on a 110ha site. The facility has 14 quay cranes, 59 auto-guided vehicles, 32 auto-stackers and 16 auto-cranes, reflecting the high-tech nature of a modern container terminal. The shareholders in the 25-year concession are five of the top container shipping lines and port operators: DPWorld (30%), APL (20%), MOL (20%), Hyundai (20%) and CMA CGM (10%).

Although funded after the financial crisis, the project attracted 20-year loans, with cash sweeps reducing final maturity to a notional 16 years.

3.2 General purpose ports

General purpose ports offer multiple revenue streams, commercial interfaces and heterogeneous activities, such as general cargo, fishing, agricultural products, etc. Consequently, the opportunities for developing long-term PPP-type concessions are minimal. Funding is usually undertaken on a corporate or governmental security basis.

3.3 Oil/gas/mineral terminals

The beneficiaries of such projects are invariably major international energy or mining companies. Such terminals, in value terms, also represent a small portion of the overall investments that such multinationals make in developing their projects. Such companies also often have strong balance sheets.

Hence, for such companies it is often more expedient and timely to fund the terminals that they need on a corporate, rather than a cash flow project financing, basis.

3.4 Cruise ship terminals

As for ore terminals, such projects are usually funded on a government or corporate basis.

However, given that the indirect beneficiary of a cruise ship terminal could be a municipality where passengers visit, such a project could be undertaken as a PPP, with the concessionaire paid on an availability basis. This could work well for a tourist destination served by a number of cruise ship lines, where no one line is prepared to risk the investment for just a few visits, or visitor traffic is high risk.

However, to date there are few precedents.

3.5 Naval and military

Many ports have a military interface. That interface needs to be carefully and sensitively managed. However, some of the naval activities might be quite suitable for use of the PPP funding mechanism.

The United Kingdom offers a number of successful examples:

- the provision and management of portside stores for the Royal Navy (a PPP concession was awarded to a supermarket chain); and
- the provision of six Ro-Ro ships for Royal Navy use, when required (a PPP concession was awarded to a commercial shipping line with ships built to military specifications).

3.6 Port services – dredging, navigation and dry docks

Such projects or activities are usually funded on a governmental or corporate basis.

Transport – airports

1. Key features

The key features for these types of project are as follows:

- Airports incur high investment costs in runways and aprons.
- The life cycle for runways/aprons is very long – 30 to 50 years.
- Passenger and freight terminals have 10 to 20 year life cycles.
- Access infrastructure, as for ports, is an essential component of costs.
- To mitigate traffic forecast uncertainties, scheduled flights are preferable to charter traffic.
- Most airport developers want their project to become a hub, but there are downsides to being a hub.
- Airports can often be regional monopolies.
- Significant terminal revenues can come from retail activities.
- Some airports have a military interface.
- As with ports, the 'landlord model' is favoured in most countries.

2. Key risks

2.1 Costs and completion

Given the different life cycle of runway/apron assets on the one hand and terminals on the other hand, the landlord model, as for ports, is often preferred. Today, very few greenfield airports are built, and those that are usually require financial support from the host government.

Under the landlord model, the government funds the runways and aprons, but the passenger/freight terminals are built and operated by public-private partnership (PPP)-type concessions.

2.2 Traffic, revenues and currency risks

The economic and financial viability of most airports depends largely on passenger traffic rather than freight. Key to the volume of passenger traffic will also be the proportion of scheduled flights to charter flights. Clearly, the former provide a more robust traffic flow, but over the medium term such flows can change significantly for economic and political reasons. Traffic forecasting in the airline/airport sector can thus be somewhat speculative.

One advantage across the airport sector is that many, if not all, the fees charged (eg, from airlines) and the revenues generated are in hard currency, (eg, US dollars).

If, as is usually the case, long-term debt is provided in hard currency, then currency risks are minimised.

As hinted at above, the main use of private capital in airport developments has been in the investment and management of passenger and freight terminals.

However, as with other PPP-type project financings, traffic throughput has to reach a certain watershed below which the PPP structure is not cost-effective to implement. What that watershed might be varies widely, but a throughput of 0.5–1 million passengers per year is a starting point, the decision as to the actual number often dependent on whether that traffic is generated by scheduled or charter flights.

A more recent trend, particularly in Europe, has been that every major airport operator aspires to be a hub attracting a wide range of international flights, and providing easy national to international transit possibilities. Whilst there are International Civil Aviation Organisation (ICAO) regulations and limits as to how much airports can charge airlines (and therefore passengers) for landing, taking off and processing passengers through the terminals and the associated support services, such hubs can represent major concentrations of flight activity, in turn creating local congestion and access infrastructure problems. Not all passengers will transit.

Another feature of modern airport terminals is the potential for developing retail activities (eg, shops, bars, restaurants, offices, hotels, etc). Many airports, especially in emerging markets, have yet to exploit these opportunities fully. The accounts for London Heathrow Airport operator BAA (now Heathrow Airport Holdings Ltd after divesting Gatwick, Stansted, Edinburgh, Glasgow and Southampton Airports), owned by an investor group led by Ferrovial (Spain), show that more than 50% of Heathrow's revenues are generated from commercial retail activities.

2.3 Environment

Similarly to other PPP-type transport projects, airports entail significant environmental and social risks, such as noise. Early review is, therefore, called for in the project process.

2.4 Access infrastructure

Airport developers often overlook this risk. An example of this issue is provided by the plans for London Heathrow's third runway, which, if built, is expected to attract an additional 30 million passengers per annum. Of these, maybe 50% will transit, so 15 million will leave from/arrive at the airport from other UK locations.

Heathrow is a fully privatised airport, owning its freehold, but scant attention in the plans was given to the infrastructure required to provide access for these 15 million passengers. A landlord model approach, where both the airport site and surrounding area come under the planning control of one authority, might have taken that issue into account.

Without adequate access infrastructure, the full business potential of an airport will not be realised. Furthermore, for every dollar spent on facilities inside the airport fence, up to another dollar might be required for investment in access infrastructure.

3. Case histories

3.1 European airports

In the United Kingdom, Manchester, Cardiff and Newcastle Airports are majority-owned by the municipality, while the other key airports (Heathrow, Gatwick, Stansted, Luton, Bristol, East Midlands, Liverpool, Teesside, Belfast International), are all privatised operations. Accordingly, any new investments in the latter category's terminal facilities are private deals, not exposed to public scrutiny.

In mainland Europe the landlord model prevails, with the freeholds, or land ownership, at Schipol (Netherlands), Paris Charles de Gaulle and Orly (France), Frankfurt, Berlin Brandenburg and Munich (Germany) and Madrid (Spain) all owned by the state or regional governments.

An attempt was made to develop the new Brandenburg Airport in Berlin as a PPP-type deal, but that collapsed before implementation.

Notwithstanding this ownership structure, many of these airport facilities/ passenger terminals are in fact operated by private concessions. Again, however, many of the details of such concessions remain confidential.

Spata Airport, Athens, Greece: One complete, new airport which was structured as a PPP was Spata Airport, Athens for the 2004 Athens Olympics. The cost was just over €2 billion, but a review of the detail shows that the Greek government maintained 55% of the shareholding in the PPP concession company, with 45% held by Hochtief (Germany), and the debt was largely supported by the European Union, the European Investment Bank and the Greek government. Thus, in effect the funding was structured as a conventional government-secured project.

Overall, this airport, taken together with the significant investment in access infrastructure, was very expensive and its economic, never mind financial, viability questionable.

3.2 Quito Airport, Ecuador

Another stand-alone and noteworthy airport investment project was the new airport in Quito, Ecuador, implemented in 2006 at a cost of $600 million.

Quito had needed extra airport capacity for many years, but government planners had deemed the very high mountains surrounding Quito and the capital's high altitude major constraints to the expansion of the existing airport, not least on safety grounds. The government had allocated land, further away from Quito and on flatter land, where a new airport could be built. However, the frequent changes of government meant that no project was brought forward to execute.

Eventually, a consortium of US/Canadian companies presented the Ecuador government with an innovative proposal for a PPP-type concession for a new airport at the new site with a 3.6km runway and terminal facilities for 3.3 million passengers per annum.

This was just what the government required, but the proposal did not comply with Ecuadorian procurement laws for public service investment.

The government then proceeded with a 'Swiss Challenge' procurement process.

Under the challenge, as described in the chapter on project process, the basic specifications from the proposal received are taken and used as the basis for an international tender for a PPP concession. A winner is chosen from that competition, and the price compared with the initial offer. If the initial price is the lowest, the winner of the competition is compensated for some of its bidding costs and the PPP concession is offered to the developer behind the initial proposal. If the initial price is higher than the winner's price, then the developer behind the initial proposal is usually given a few weeks to adjust its price. Again, after that, the lowest price wins the PPP concession, and the loser receives some compensation for bidding costs.

The process is not without controversy and variation. However, in the case of Quito, it was acceptable to, and funded by, a development bank, the Inter-American Development Bank (IADB), and the United States' Overseas Private Investment Corporation (OPIC).

The initial proposal was structured as a classic private infrastructure, 35-year PPP concession, with 15% equity and 85% debt from IADB, OPIC and export credit agencies.

The new airport is now operational.

3.3 Medina Airport, Saudi Arabia

Another noteworthy example of a PPP-type airport concession was provided by the $1.2 billion Medina Airport expansion, implemented in 2012. A private Saudi–Turkish consortium won a 25-year PPP concession to expand airport capacity at Medina from 6 to 8 million passengers per annum, with the prime traffic arising from pilgrims on the Hadj. There are, however, no traffic guarantees and the financing, on a debt/equity ratio of 65/35, had to be *Sharia*-compliant.

This was the first PPP in Saudi Arabia outside the power and water sectors.

4. Air traffic control

One area of air transport infrastructure often overlooked is air traffic control (ATC). Below a certain altitude, civil airliners come under the control of local airports, whereas above that altitude the aircraft move along predetermined motorways in the sky, usually operated under separate international air traffic control.

When a civil airliner overflies any country, the country below is entitled to charge a fee for using its airspace. Such fees are controlled by the ICAO, depending upon the aircraft type and other criteria, and are paid in hard currency, usually US dollars.

Airlines pay for their use of the airspace over Europe via an international company, Eurocontrol, which is headquartered in Brussels and has all EU member states as its shareholders. Eurocontrol interfaces with the UK National Air Traffic Service (NATS), a PPP concession managing the UK airspace, whose shareholding is made up of the UK government (49%), the Airline Gp (including BA, Virgin, EasyJet) (42%), NATS staff (5%) and Heathrow (4%).

Apart from air traffic control, ATC companies also impose safety regulations, and navigational training, among other activities.

Interestingly, in the United States the ATC systems are all state government-owned and controlled, whereas Canada has adopted a novel PPP structure called NavCanada for ATC systems.

In 1995, Canada's individual, provincially owned ATC systems needed upgrading and re-equipping, and some provinces lacked the funding necessary to cover the overall C$1.5 billion investment required. The Canadian ATC systems together managed approximately 7 million flights per annum (at that time, NATS was managing less than half that number). In 2014, NavCanada managed 12 million flights per annum, making it the second largest ATC system in the world by traffic volume.

The Canadian federal government created NavCanada as a non-share, not-for-profit company (ie, a crown corporation), in which the government vested the existing ATC assets throughout Canada for C$1. NavCanada pays no dividends, has to make a return on capital through the revenues generated from over-flight fees, and is an agency within the Ministry of Finance.

In addition, NavCanada has 15 directors: five from the aviation industry, two from the unions, three from the government and five more, including the chief executive, chosen by the directors. Directors cannot be elected officials or associated with equipment suppliers, and NavCanada can set over-flight tariffs at whatever level it likes, within ICAO regulations, providing that NavCanada achieves a target return on capital.

On funding, NavCanada did not enjoy a government guarantee for its debt, but was able to securitise future revenues to raise the necessary C$1.5 billion to acquire new equipment, etc.

The above corporate formula has been a success, and provided the flexibility for NavCanada to change tariffs to meet unforeseen circumstances – for instance, the downturn in traffic post-9/11 – without having to resort to periodic regulatory negotiations such as those that take place in the United Kingdom every five years.

The model has many merits and could easily be applied across other sectors and in other regions with potential success. It effectively marries public interest requirements (eg, air safety) with private sector profit motivation.

The author would like to recommend *Managing the Skies: Public Policy, Organization and Financing of Air Traffic Management* by Clinton V Oster and John S Strong for further reading on this topic.

Power generation – thermal (coal, oil, gas)

1. Key features

In thermal power generation, typical project capital values range from $70 million to $1 billion and project life usually spans 20 to 25 years. Other considerations and characteristics include the following:

- There are many international precedents for private independent power producers or plants (IPPs);
- Developers need to ensure that grid connections are available; and
- IPPs are often combined with desalination plants in hot climates such as Gulf countries.

1.1 Market structures

Stand-alone, private sector power generation projects historically have been funded against the security of long-term sales contracts (ie, 'bulk purchase' contracts). This provided lenders with the secured revenues that they sought.

Figure 15.1: Deregulated power system

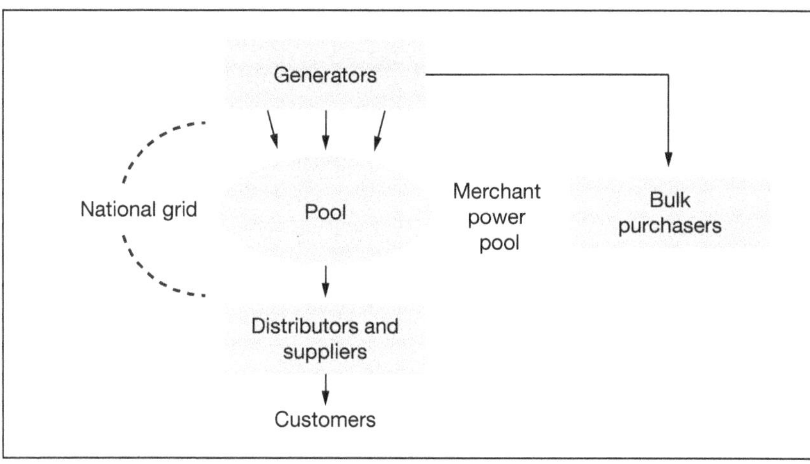

Source: author

In more recent times, many markets have moved to a 'pool' system, in which a regulator requests generators to quote prices for amounts of power to be supplied to the grid for a future period, and the regulator selects the lowest offers. As there should be excess (or reserve) generation capacity in the system, generators are not guaranteed that any power that they produce will be sold. In other words, the regulator has introduced a degree of competition into the supply of power by generators. Such a structure is known as a 'merchant power pool'.

In reality, the power structure in many countries today is a mix of merchant power and bulk purchase. Many power technologies are not very flexible and cannot be turned on and off at will, even though such units may produce the cheapest power on average (eg, nuclear).

Furthermore, the introduction of competition between generators increases the uncertainty over the generators' revenues, and thereby the inherent revenue risks. So, for IPPs supplying merchant power, more equity might be needed than for IPPs supplying bulk purchase markets – for instance, a debt/equity ratio of 75/25 might apply, rather than 80/20.

1.2 Power generation types

When discussing power systems and characteristics, it is important to recognise the differences between power sources and in particular their:

- inherent cost – Figure 15.2 gives data for:
  - cost per installed megawatt (MW);
  - typical plant size;
  - typical operating life; and
  - 'levelised cost' – that is, an estimate of average power costs;
- availability – some power types have unpredictable availability (eg, wind); and
- response time – some power types take time to reach full production capacity from start-up.

Note that the data above may be open to dispute, but the intention is to emphasise the differences rather than the precise values quoted. The values for solar power are omitted due to the significant changes seen in that market over the past five years.

2. Key risks

2.1 Costs and completion

Given the possibility for the construction contractor to ring-fence risks, fixed price, turnkey contracts are often available in this sector.

2.2 Revenues, currency and financial viability

Power projects naturally sell their power to local markets, with revenues denominated in local currency. However, particularly in emerging markets, the long-term capital for funding could be in a different, harder currency than the currency of revenues and some operating costs. This translates into an inherent foreign exchange risk.

Figure 15.2: Power station unit costs (estimated)

Power type	Cost per installed MW ($/kW)	Typical unit size	Typical operating life (years)	Levelised cost* ($/MWh)
CCGT	1100	350MW	25	130 (±40%)
CCGT uprated	1300	350MW	30	140 (±35%)
Coal with FGD	1500	650MW	30–40+	150 (40%)
Nuclear	5000 estimated	1000–1,500MW	50+	90 (±40%)
Hydro	3000+	5–500MW	15–20	N/A
Wind (onshore)	1350	3MW/turbine		140 (±30%)
Wind (offshore)	2500	3–5MW turbine	15–20	195 (±40%)
Solar	N/A	N/A 25	N/A	N/A

* Levelised cost is total cost of building, financing and operating plant type over its life, expressed in today's values
kW: kilowatt
MWh: megawatt hour
CCGT: combined cycle gas turbine
FGD: flue gas desulfurisation

Source: author

To overcome this risk for IPP-type funding, either:

- tariffs in the sales contract (power purchase agreement or PPA) are denominated in the currency of funding – that is, the exchange risk is passed on to the power purchaser; or
- there is a clause in the PPA stating that, in the event of a devaluation or revaluation of the local currency against the currency of funding within the period of the PPA, then sales tariffs are adjusted to compensate the power generator/seller (ie, IPP).

The situations described above (devaluation/revaluation) have indeed arisen in a number of emerging markets in recent years and, when host government purchasers or utilities have failed to adjust tariffs – particularly in the event of a devaluation – resolution has been sought via international arbitration under the New York Convention. In most cases, investors/lenders have won their case. This demonstrates the value of including such international arbitration clauses in the PPA.

2.3 Technology

Developers often overlook this risk. The equipment supplier's excellent reputation for technological expertise and quality is no reason for the project company to accept the latest machine, just out of the research and development laboratory. Investors and lenders to IPPs prefer to fund proven technologies. As part of their due diligence, they will seek confirmation from their consultants that the technology and equipment proposed for a new venture have a proven track record of successful, medium-term performance.

2.4 **Environment**

Environmental issues can be prominent in power projects – for instance, coal, where flue gas desulfurisation is necessary to gain acceptance.

2.5 **Grid connection**

Many power developers tend to overlook access infrastructure, just as port and airport developers tend to overlook it. This is however a key risk for renewable energy in particular, such as wind energy where the generators may be in remote sites.

3. Case histories

3.1 Typical emerging market IPP

Here are the details of a typical emerging market IPP:

- Capacity = 2x600MW coal-fired, mine-mouth power station;
- Cost = €1.2 billion;
- Construction period = 36 months;
- Turnkey engineering, procurement and construction (EPC) contract with international contractor and suppliers;
- Funding:
  - Equity = 30% (€360 million): investor input supported by an irrevocable letter of credit. Investor is an international power utility/operator;
  - Debt = 70% (15 years repayment, on an annuity basis);
  - Export credit agencies (ECAs) = €350 million;
  - International financial institution (IFI) A loan = €170 million (see section 3.2 of the chapter on the sources of financing in Part 1 of this book for a description of IFI A/B loans);
  - IFI B loan (from commercial banks) = €250 million;
  - Local banks = €70 million;
  - Debt service reserve account = €60 million;
  - Insurance and maintenance reserve accounts are required; and
  - Standby debt facility (5%) = €60 million.

Below are the typical terms and conditions for such a project.

EPC contract:

- Fixed price, turnkey contract;
- EPC contract limit to liquidated damages = 20%;
- Early completion bonus and profit shared 50/50;
- Performance guarantees for output, fuel quality and heat rate;
- Three-year warranty for turbines; and
- International arbitration for dispute resolution.

Operations period:

- 15-year, fixed price fuel supply contract;
- Fuel supply guarantees as to energy content, etc;
- 15-year operations and maintenance contract;

- 15-year supply contract for limestone for flue gas desulfurisation;
- 15-year contract for ash and gypsum removal;
- Two months' supply of fuel and limestone to be kept on site;
- Pass-through for price of alternative fuel supplier, if different; and
- Target load factor = 85%.

Revenues:

- 15-year sales contract with creditworthy, state-owned utility;
- Payment structure:
  - Capacity (per MW tested) – fixed costs, debt service and profit = paid in euros
  - Variable (per megawatt hour produced) – production costs = paid in local currency; and
  - Minimum sales = 65% of forecast demand.

Finance:

- Interest rates and fees are undisclosed;
- Average debt service cover ratio (DSCR) = 1.25;
- Minimum DSCR = 1.15 (ie, trigger for lenders' step-in rights);
- Default DSCR = 1.05;
- Dividend lock-up if DSCR = <1.20;
- Operator to retain shares in IPP for minimum of five years;
- 50% cash sweep at Year 10 and 100% cash sweep at Year 12;
- Negative pledge except for €25 million;
- Lenders take security over project assets; and
- Equity drawn pro rata with debt after 5% contractor down-payment.

3.2 General IPPs

The above terms and conditions apply across many IPPs undertaken in both developed and emerging markets. It should be added that, with many investors being conscious of climate change and environmental issues, new coal-fired developments are few and far between; they are being replaced largely by gas for base load capacity.

Notwithstanding this technological trend, the underlying financial characteristics and features remain as quoted above.

Some of the more unusual structures and experiences seen, however, are described below.

3.3 IPPs in the Gulf

Over the past 15 to 20 years a number of IPPs have been developed in Gulf countries, not just as power plants, but also with water desalination plants alongside them – water being an essential commodity in such climates. These plants are termed 'independent water and power projects' (IWPPs). However, plants using reverse osmosis desalination – the commonly employed technology for desalination – consume significant amounts of electricity in the production of clean water.

Gulf countries experience their period of highest demand for power in the summer months (for air-conditioning/cooling), which is also the period for maximum demand for water. Further, the inherent economics for power and desalinated water production respectively are such that it is more profitable to produce power than water.

So, to balance demand in these markets, the IWPP PPA or the regulator requires that, for every megawatt hour of power produced and sold, a commensurate volume (in cubic metres) of water be produced and sold too.

3.4 Jorf Lasfar IPP, Morocco

In 1997–98, a $1.5 billion, 3×350MW coal-fired IPP was successfully developed in Morocco by ABB (Sweden) and CMS (United States) – the first IPP in North Africa. Power is sold to ONEE, the state-owned power utility.

One of the issues to be overcome was that, under Moroccan law, power plants are public property – that is, lenders could not take security over the IPP's assets. Accordingly, a special agreement (*'droit de jouissance'* or right of occupation) was signed, which satisfied lenders.

In 2012, Jorf Lasfar 5 and 6 (2×350MW) were added as an IPP, with the investor group, TAQA from Abu Dhabi, funding 25% of project costs with equity, and the balance raised as loans from South Korean and Japanese ECAs, plus international and Moroccan commercial banks. Given the success and precedent of the first Jorf Lasfar IPP, the arrangement of the funding was straightforward with minimal difficulties.

3.5 ContourGlobal, Togo

Many emerging markets suffer from lack of power generation capacity. Such was the situation in Togo in 2009, when the government had planned to build a combined cycle gas turbines (CCGT) plant in 2006. However, the project was badly affected by the delayed completion of the West African Gas Pipeline, bringing gas from Nigeria.

However, entrepreneurial US investor/operator ContourGlobal, staffed by experienced power utility operators and supported by a US hedge fund, was offered to build and fund a $192 million, 100MW (comprising six dual fuel engines from Wartsila, Finland) power plant, with 50% of production destined for the Togo market and 50% for Benin. Wartsila provided a fixed price turnkey contract, and the project was supported by a 25-year PPA with the state-owned power utility, CEET. Payments for power were structured as capacity payments in US dollars and variable costs in the Togo currency (the CFA franc), which is linked to the euro.

The funding was provided as 25% ($47million) equity and 75% ($145 million) debt through a 20-year loan from the United States' Overseas Private Investment Corporation.

The project was completed in 18 months and is operational. It offers a timely, if expensive, alternative to a CCGT, and offers more flexible operational characteristics – for instance, with six units, fuel sources can be changed and one unit out of action does not significantly impact overall performance.

3.6 Green Frog, United Kingdom

The UK power generation market is characterised by ageing coal and nuclear power plants, and the replacement projects have not necessarily kept pace with demand. Sector reserve capacity is considered by many to be too low.

National Grid plc, quoted on the London Stock Exchange and responsible, with regulator OFGEM, for ensuring that capacity meets demand, had become aware of this problem in 2011. As a result, it implemented a number of short-term operating reserve mini-IPP projects to bridge the gap.

After a bidding process, a portfolio of these mini-IPP projects was awarded to Green Frog, an investor-led consortium. Overall, the extra capacity planned was 20MW, made up from 52x380kW back-up diesel units at different locations throughout the United Kingdom. The cost was £75 million, of which £60 million was provided as debt, supported by a 15-year PPA with National Grid if power production was called for.

The payment structure, therefore, was as for a conventional PPP – that is, against availability. The availability payments made by National Grid covered fixed cost, debt service and shareholder profits. If the units were called upon to deliver power to the grid, then the extra costs of production were paid by National Grid as a pass-through.

As for Togo, this project was simple to implement and low risk. However, the cost of the power produced is high compared to other sources, and the IPPs use heavy fuels, which are less environmentally acceptable.

3.7 Pamir, Tajikistan

Land-locked Tajikistan has a small, poor economy. In 2002, it was decided to upgrade the Pamir 1 power station from 14MW to 28MW at a cost of $26 million, and a 25-year concession was awarded to an international consortium, Pamir Energy Corp, made up of the World Bank's International Finance Corporation (IFC) (30%) and the Aga Khan Foundation for Economic Development (70%) to build the plant and operate the existing power system.

The debt/equity ratio was 60/40, with the IFC providing part of the debt and the balance coming from the World Bank via the government of Tajikistan.

The main problem was that the existing tariff for customers at that time was only 0.4 US cents per kilowatt hour, well below what was required to make the system and project financially viable.

The Swiss aid agency, SECO, agreed to provide Tajikistan with a grant over a number of years to make up the difference between the revenues collected and the revenues required to make the project and system economically and financially viable. Over the interim period, the government agreed to increase consumer tariffs such that after five years the grant support would no longer be required.

It is not known how successful this use of grant money has been, but it represents one way of overcoming financial viability issues in very poor markets.

Power generation – hydropower

1. Key features

Capital costs for hydropower projects are three to four times higher per installed megawatt (MW) than for thermal power. Other key features include the following:

- Fixed price contracts are not readily available, so construction/completion risks can be significant.
- Hydro projects have minimal operating costs.
- Environmental issues can be significant, both on site and downstream.
- Very few large hydro independent power plants (IPPs) have been implemented to date.
- Mini-hydro (run-of-river) projects are still expensive per MW, but are easier to implement and so offer an attractive alternative. In addition, they can be developed as IPPs.
- In some cases the civil engineering (dam) can be split from the powerhouse (turbines, etc), with the former funded by the government and the latter structured as an IPP.
- Hydro projects can generate carbon credits (although this is controversial).

2. Key risks

2.1 Costs and completion

Given the high costs of building large dams, fixed price contracts are not available. In addition, for a hydro project involving a large dam, the cost of the powerhouse could represent less than 10% of the total cost.

For mini-hydros it may, however, be possible to pass cost and completion risk to the construction contractor.

2.2 Revenues, currency and financial viability

Hydro projects are no different from thermal power stations with regard to market, revenues and currency risks. As a result, the same risk mitigation measures apply.

Hydro projects have a rapid response time, which means that they are often used as standby facilities. Consequently, the commercial and financial viability of a project will depend on how and by whom power will be requested from the plant. Investors and lenders will look closely at the contractual arrangements in this respect.

2.3 Technology

The two prime areas of risk are the dam and the power generation equipment. For the dam, the main risks arise from possible leakage around the abutments when the lake behind the dam is close to full. This problem can be mitigated by the injection of an impermeable membrane into the adjoining bank, or hill. Many unknown issues can arise from such measures, though, which can lead to significant cost overruns.

For the power equipment, the turbines are often mounted vertically, rather than horizontally as for conventional power, and the rotation speed is much slower. Indeed, a hydropower turbine can reach full production within minutes of start-up. As such turbines have slower moving parts and operate at lower temperatures than, say, a combined cycle gas turbine, hydro turbines can last for many years, commonly 20 to 40 years, and even up to 100 years.

Another issue for dams is the water supply. Droughts have occurred in many countries where dams have been built, and private investors and lenders are loath to assume such risks. Usually, it will be for the host government to underpin water volumes.

However, water supply, river management etc is the responsibility of a different institution from the one responsible for power. Indeed, in many countries water is a public commodity, only for 'use' by public entities. It follows that the acquisition of the relevant permits and licences is a condition precedent to project implementation.

Apart from the hydrological risk, many dams are in seismic zones, which creates an extra hazard that private investors and lenders may prefer to avoid.

2.4 Environment

Environmental issues for hydro projects can be significant, and possibly insurmountable. For many years in the late 1990s the World Bank declined to fund hydro projects because of the environmental, social and political risks potentially involved.

However, with the arrival of the Equator Principles (a risk management framework adopted by financial institutions for determining, assessing and managing environmental and social risk in projects) and the UN Principles for Responsible Investment guidelines for investors, hydro projects are back on the agenda, not least because of the potential climate change benefits.

Nevertheless, environmental studies and reviews are often critical path items in project preparation for hydro schemes. Not only have the dam and its environs got to be reviewed on such aspects, but so too must the environmental and economic impact on communities who live upstream and downstream of the dam. Hydro projects have foundered because of a lack of such considerations.

2.5 Grid connection

Just as port and airport developers tend to overlook access infrastructure, so do hydropower developers with grid connection – a potentially expensive oversight as hydro schemes may be in remote locations, a long distance from the grid. Further complexity may arise from the fact that grid investment, construction and management may fall within the remit of a different utility from the beneficiary utility.

In such circumstances, it is common for a hydro developer to take responsibility for building the grid connection, even if the associated costs are funded by the beneficiary utility.

2.6 Conclusion

Given the difficulties of developing large hydro schemes, mini-hydros offer, on many occasions, more attractive outcomes, lower risks and greater bankability.

3. Case histories

3.1 Bujagali, Uganda

In the annals of attempts to develop privately financed large hydro projects in emerging markets, Bujagali holds a special place.

In the early 1990s, when many conventional IPP-type projects were being implemented in developed countries, AES (which had become the largest IPP utility in the United States) was awarded a $510 million contract to build a 250MW run-of-river hydro IPP, plus 100km of transmission line, at Bujagali, on the Victoria Nile in East Uganda.

The proposal was highly controversial with non-governmental organisations. After spending $75 million on the preparations and environmental studies with little progress to show, AES pulled out in 2003. By that time the World Bank, which had initially been supportive, was likewise withdrawing its backing from any large hydro projects.

Before long, the proposal was resurrected. Although costs had risen to $880 million, a consortium made up of Sithe Global (a major US power utility), the Aga Khan Foundation for Economic Development and the government of Uganda (as a non-voting shareholder) was awarded to contract to complete the dam.

The funding package comprised:

- $198 million (23%) equity, with $115 million of this covered by political risk insurance from the Multilateral Investment Guarantee Agency (World Bank); and
- $682 million (77%) debt, provided by:
  - the International Finance Corporation (World Bank) A/B loans ($130 million and $115 million respectively);
  - the European Investment Bank ($175 million);
  - the African Development Bank ($110 million); and
  - balancing loans from Proparco (France), FMO (Netherlands) and KfW (Germany).

The government carried the water supply risk and the sales contract (power purchase agreement or PPA) was, in effect, a take-or-pay contract with the government. Financial close was achieved in 2007, with project completion in 2011/2012, almost 20 years after the project was originally proposed.

A similar structure was employed on the 1,070MW Nam Theun II run-of-river hydro project in Laos near the border with Thailand, with EdF (France) as prime sponsor, in 2005. On that occasion, 90% of the power under the take-or-pay PPA goes to EGAT, the state-owned Thai utility. Nevertheless, that project also struggled to reach financial close.

3.2 Boyabat, Turkey

A more recent, and unusual, major hydro IPP has been the $1.2 billion 510MW Boyabat scheme on the Kizilirmak River in Northern Turkey, funded in 2010.

At the time, Turkey's economy was growing rapidly, and domestic capacity struggled to meet demand. Further, the power market was being restructured, with a number of utilities privatised, although the final structure of the proposed grid system was perceived as unclear. In any event, Turkey was moving from a bulk purchase-type market to a 'pool'/ 'merchant' power scenario. Given such uncertainty, therefore, investors and lenders were not prepared to support new conventional power plant projects until market clarity was established, so years of national power shortages were forecast.

A private consortium of Turkish investors supported by Turkish banks then obtained the necessary licences and permits, and was awarded a 49-year public-private partnership (PPP)-type concession to build Boyabat.

The debt/equity ratio for the funding was 65/35, and there was, surprisingly, no PPA. However, given the rapid response time of hydro, the business plan for Boyabat was based on taking advantage of the premium tariffs available from the pool at peak demand.

The base case for lenders gave an average debt service cover ratio (DSCR) of 1.2 at a tariff of €0.08 per kilowatt hour (kWh), somewhat higher than the renewable energy feed-in tariffs available in Turkey.

The risks for this project are unusual. Unsurprisingly, only Turkish investors and lenders funded the project, which is located in a seismic area – a significant risk to international participants.

3.3 Vez Svoghe, Bulgaria

As mentioned earlier, mini-hydros can offer lower risk and more bankable private sector project opportunities.

One such example is Vez Svoghe on a tributary of the Danube in Bulgaria, where there are 9×3MW mini-hydros built in sequence in three phases for a cost of €75 million. The debt/equity ratio was 65/35, with Petrovilla (Italy) and the local municipality providing the equity, and a development bank (European Bank for Reconstruction and Development) and commercial banks providing the debt under an A/B structure.

The usual water licences, security over project assets, DSCR covenants, reserve accounts, dividend and share lock-ups were imposed. Another constraint was that the second phase of the project could not be initiated until the first phase was completed to budget.

One additional feature was that this project was accepted as eligible for carbon credits under the Kyoto Protocol (which extends the UN Framework Convention on Climate Change). Under the scheme, for every megawatt hour (MWh) of power produced, a carbon credit is granted, providing additional cash flow to investors and lenders. Such carbon credits are later converted into cash (ie, monetised) via a special fund set up by development agencies to support such projects in emerging markets.

In recent years, however, experts have claimed that such projects should not benefit from such carbon credits given the projects' overall carbon footprint.

3.4 Marine power

There is increasing discussion as to the use of tidal power, but to date there have been no IPPs. Like for hydro, the inherent costs in building such projects dictates that very long-term capital is required, and project financiers have not yet been attracted to these ventures.

Power generation – nuclear

---

1. Historical features

Although commercial nuclear power plants (NPPs) have been operational in many countries for over 50 years, not one has been funded as a stand-alone, cash flow, project financing anywhere in the world. That said, there have been two notable exceptions:

- Dunkerque/Gravelines, France, where the NPP was built as a dedicated unit in the 1980s to provide power for an aluminium smelter. However, both the NPP sponsor, EdF, and Pechiney, the smelter owner, were state-controlled at the time; and
- Olkiluoto 3, Finland, a 1,600 megawatt (MW) EPR (ie, third generation pressurised water reactor – see more on this in section 2 below) currently under construction, but suffering significant delays and cost over-runs. In many ways it, too, is a dedicated power unit, with sales to industrial customers and municipal utilities.

In the United States, which has 100 operational NPPs – more than any other country (France has 58 NPPs) – nuclear power represents 20% of electricity supplied to customers. These NPPs have been developed as private and state-owned utilities, funded corporately.

2. Key features

The commercial NPPs in existence today are very large, typically 1,000–1,600MW each unit. They are consequently also very expensive – for instance, $6–$8 billion per unit. Theses costs make it challenging to attract private financiers to fund the projects.

In addition, the construction periods are very long (four to five years minimum). The combination of lengthy construction period and overall costs means that fixed price, turnkey contracts are just not available.

The choice of reactor type is also limited. There are four main types available today:

- EPR (from Areva, France);
- AP1000 (from Westinghouse/Toshiba, Japan);
- VVER 1000/1200 (from two Russian organisations); and
- APWR (from Mitsubishi/KEPCO, Japan).

The interchangeability of design, equipment and fuel rods is even more limited.

NPPs are not rapid response generating plants. It takes four to six weeks for a reactor to reach full production or close down. Yet, once into full production they produce cheap power (see Figure 15.2 in the chapter on thermal power generation). As such, NPPs represent base load capacity in any system.

The slow response time of NPP operations, though, makes them un-attuned to the flexibility required to respond to the demands of a pool or merchant power market (see in this respect the downfall of British Energy for precisely this reason, when changes in market structure were introduced by the UK government between 1998 and 2001).

Safety and planning issues clearly prevail for any NPP proposal. However, national policies towards nuclear power can vary from government to government, and the political cycle of any government may be shorter than the normal operating licence for an NPP.

NPPs historically have been licensed for 30 years' operations. Many are now close to the maturity of their licences. The question arises, therefore, as to whether they are to be closed down or the licences extended.

Close examination of the integrity and condition of many of the reactors built post-1980 shows the reactors to be in good condition, with the possibility of another 10 or 20 years (or even longer) of useful and safe life. Accordingly, the commercial dilemma arises as to whether it is optimal to:

- close down the plant and build a new NPP or a conventional power unit; or
- re-equip the peripheral equipment of an existing NPP, so as to prolong the life of the reactor.

Many countries are now adopting the latter option as the most economical approach.

The fuel sources for uranium are regionally and globally different from coal, oil or gas, and arguably from more politically stable countries. However, there are, for obvious safety reasons, only a very limited number of internationally available enrichment facilities, which in turn raises the risks of transporting enriched fuel or waste product around the world.

The methodology for dealing with spent nuclear fuel has yet to be satisfactorily resolved, and the decommissioning of NPPs is a very long and costly process.

On the plus side, NPPs do not emit carbon dioxide or noxious gases (although they absorb more carbon dioxide in their construction than other power types). Yet, to date, under the Kyoto Protocol and national/local climate change regulations such benefit is not recognised (although at the time of writing some US states have introduced support mechanisms for nuclear power based on this benefit so as to keep older plants operational for longer than might otherwise have been the case, judged against normal climate change criteria).

As to funding sources, some international financial institutions (IFIs or development banks) ban, in their charter, any funding for NPPs (eg, the World Bank/International Finance Corporation), while others could fund them, but choose not to as a matter of policy (eg, the European Bank for Reconstruction and

Development (EBRD) and the Asian Development Bank). That said, the EBRD manages the Nuclear Safety Account, which provides grants and loans for safety upgrades on existing operational NPPs.

Export credit agencies, by contrast, provide special terms for NPPs with up to 18-year loan maturities.

Considering all of the disadvantages outlined above, the question might rightly be asked whether nuclear power has a place in any power system, particularly post-Fukushima?

The disasters at Chernobyl, Three Mile Island and even Fukushima can arguably be put down to human error. The most recent, Fukushima (March 2011), was caused not so much by the earthquake (there are a number of other NPPs around the world close to fault lines), but by the subsequent tsunami. The NPP had been automatically cut off from the grid when the earthquake occurred, but the back-up generators were needed to keep coolant circulating through the reactor and spent fuel rod tank. Unfortunately, the tsunami took out the back-up generators, sited close to the sea wall, leading to the subsequent disaster. It is conjecture as to what would have been the outcome if Fukushima had been so designed as to protect the back-up units.

A few weeks after Fukushima, a tornado passed right over an NPP in the southern United States. As at Fukushima, the NPP was cut off from the grid, but the back-up units did their job and kept the plant cool. Within 36 hours, the NPP was back on the grid.

The nuclear world after these events is very safety-conscious. Irrespective of national politics, there is extensive international exchange of information, operational experience and technical know-how. It is right for a prudent public, however, to question procedures and monitor developments continuously. In the end, the promotion of nuclear power will be a subjective and personal judgement.

3. Future prospects

Notwithstanding Fukushima and the other NPP accidents, a number of countries are currently planning or building new commercial-size NPPs, using government or utility financing sources. For example, China has 21 NPPs under construction.

What of the future? Given the magnitude and costs of the currently available commercial NPPs, financiers will continue to struggle to find a formula which allows such projects to proceed as cash flow, project financings. They are just too big.

The obvious answer, which strangely has eluded the industry to date, is to design and build smaller NPPs. Interestingly, China, Russia and the United States are all developing their own programme of smaller units (eg, 50MW to 150MW, which will be much more bankable and possibly commercially available and licensed within five to 10 years. Watch this space!

As few NPPs have been built and completed over the last 20 to 30 years, there is a dearth of knowledgeable and experienced engineers to design, build and operate such units. Nations needs to address this if nuclear is to progress.

Similarly, the number of contractors with the ability to shoulder the commercial risks of construction of such NPPs is limited today. This problem needs addressing.

Support via Kyoto-type subventions seems appropriate given the arguable climate change benefits of NPPs.

The solution for long-term waste storage and decommissioning is not yet available. However, taking a 30-year perspective (a short time in the nuclear sector), it seems likely that an acceptable physical or chemical methodology will be found.

Meanwhile, many utilities with operational NPPs are putting off the closure dates and seeking licence extensions. Consequently, NPPs will remain a core component of many national power systems for some years to come.

Power generation – renewables (wind, solar, geothermal, biomass)

1. Kyoto Protocol

The Kyoto Protocol (www.unfccc.int) was adopted by the UN Framework Convention on Climate Change (UNFCCC) in 1997 and entered into force in 2005. There are 192 parties to the convention, including the European Union and all UN members, except Afghanistan, Sudan and the United States. Some of the key features of the protocol are outlined below:

- Under the protocol many countries agreed to legally binding targets, limiting by 2012 their country's emissions of greenhouse gases (GHG) to 5% below 1990 levels. The initial commitment period was 2008–2012, and the second, 2013–2020.
- The 2015 Paris Agreement, which entered into force in October 2016, complemented the UNFCCC with the specific aim, as from 2020, of holding the rise in the global average temperature this century to below 2°C above pre-industrial levels and, ideally, to adopt efforts to limit the temperature increase to below 1.5°C. Each country/signatory is to set its National Determined Contribution to achieve this target with the first review in 2018.
- Under the Kyoto Protocol, each signatory commits to an emission reductions target under its National Allocation Plan, the emissions being defined in terms of tonnes of carbon dioxide (CO_2).
- Developing countries, including India and China, are exempt from committing to binding targets under the protocol, but are still encouraged to reduce GHG emissions – for instance, by supporting renewable energy projects, improving energy efficiency and reducing deforestation.
- The trading of emissions quotas is allowed between developed countries, which can also receive credit for financing emission reduction projects in developing countries.
- The main GHG gases identified by the protocol are methane (CH_4), nitrous oxide (N_2O), hydro-fluorocarbons (HFCs) and sulphur hexafluoride (SF_6). The GHG impact of these gases varies significantly and, in determining the differential values, reference needs to be made to the UNFCCC data on global warming potential (GWP; usually the 100 year data). However, as an example, some HFCs have an impact at least a thousand times greater than one tonne of CO_2.
- The protocol defines three mechanisms for use by developed countries (also known as 'Annex 1 countries') – two are project-related, the third is trade-related.

1.1 Clean Development Mechanism (CDM)

The CDM mechanism has two aims:

- to assist developers of emission reduction projects in emerging markets (ie, non-Annex 1 countries); and
- to assist parties from Annex 1 countries to meet their targets, by investing in emerging market emission reduction projects.

The (somewhat bureaucratic) institutional framework and participants in the CDM are as follows:

- the project developer, or implementer, is known as the 'project proponent';
- the government of the host country (emerging market) sets up a designated operational authority, which approves and regulates proposed projects. The authority also oversees the CDM Executive Board (see below);
- the CDM Executive Board registers and supervises a CDM project;
- independent consultants, which are designated operational entities (DOEs) accredited by the CDM Executive Board, validate proposed projects in terms of their carbon emission reduction benefits, additionality (ie, benefit related to additional or incremental cost), etc.

The CDM accreditation process works as follows:

- The project proponent prepares a feasibility study for the proposed project;
- In addition, a project design document is prepared which includes information as to how the project is to be implemented and monitored; and
- The proposal and project design document are validated by the DOE, approved by the designated national authority, and registered with the CDM Executive Board.

The approved CDM project then generates certified emission reduction credits (CERs – that is, credits for each tonne of CO_2 saved), which accrue to the investors in the developer company – that is, to the project proponent. The CDM project also counts against that country's national target for GHG reductions.

For a CDM project in an emerging market, the CERs may be monetised either directly in the market or via special funds set up by development agencies to assist such developers in emerging markets to convert CERs into cash.

For the same CDM project in the emerging market, in the event that one, or the only, investor is from an Annex 1 (developed) country and wishes to obtain CERs which can be applied against emission reduction targets in its own country, the investor must first obtain confirmation from the emerging market authorities that:

- the proposed CDM project contributes to sustainable development; and
- the project would not be implemented without such investment – that is, it is additional.

Further, a forecast (baseline) has to be given as to the emissions which would arise in the absence of the CDM project. The case is then approved by the DOE, and the CDM Executive Board registers the CDM project and issues CERs, when generated, against the baseline projection. The developing country investor can then place these CERs against targets in its domestic market.

In the early years of the CDM, this procedure allowed some investors to manipulate the emission reductions market by allowing them to make small investments in non-Annex 1 countries in projects which produced high GHG emission factor multiples (eg, HFCs) rather than making the intended investments in reduction projects in their host countries. For every dollar invested in such emission reduction projects (eg, a refrigerator manufacturing plant, where HFCs are employed as coolants), the number of CERs so generated was much higher than for every dollar invested in, say, a flue gas desulphurisation facility at a lignite power station in the developed country.

This loophole has now been closed, although some aspects of the procedure are still open to interpretation.

1.2 Joint implementation

Under joint implementation (JI) projects, a developed country (Annex 1) entity invests in an emission reduction project in another Annex 1 country, and is able to place the CERs accrued in its domestic market.

The accreditation process for such projects is somewhat complex, and there are limits as to how many CERs the host country may allocate.

1.3 International emissions trading

Various international trading platforms have been set up for the trading of CERs, allowing governments and accredited entities to cover shortfalls in meeting targets, as well as selling surplus CERs. The main platforms are the European Union, London and the United States.

However, in recent years some countries have had excess allowances (CERs), so the markets have been over-supplied, depressing the value of CERs and in turn depressing the attractiveness to investors of investing in emission reduction projects. Furthermore, computer hackers have on some occasions interfered in the transaction process, which has not engendered confidence in the trading procedures.

2. Renewable energy projects

2.1 Key risks

The key risks are very much the same as for conventional power, but with some added features.

(a) Costs and completion risks

Given the possibility for the construction contractor to ring-fence risks, fixed price, turnkey contracts are often available in this sector.

With regard to the overall cost of renewable energy projects, however, it is worth noting that many such projects are operational only intermittently – when the wind blows, when the sun shines or when the tide comes in or out. Consequently, when comparing the system cost of renewable energy against other sources, the cost of back-up, reserve capacity or power storage should be taken into account. Unfortunately, only a few commercial-size, power storage technologies have become available or schemes undertaken (eg, for pumped storage or batteries).

(b) ***Revenues, financial viability and political risks***

Renewable energy power sources are inherently more expensive than conventional power and nuclear. Renewable projects need subventions if they are to achieve financial viability and be attractive to private investors and lenders.

Under the Kyoto Protocol, the signatory countries have set up various mechanisms (outlined below) to support renewable projects, some more successful than others.

Quota schemes or carbon credits:

- The host government (or European Union) imposes emission targets on electricity distributors and suppliers as to the levels of renewable energy that they must supply customers annually, as evidenced by carbon credits or certified emission reduction credits (CERs), compensated periodically (eg, annually). Similarly, targets for the amount of renewable energy that they consume in any one period (again evidenced by CERs) may be imposed on major consumers of power.
- Under such scheme, the renewable energy generators receive CERs for units of renewable energy generated.
- To manage such a scheme, the certification is represented in units expressed as tonnes of CO_2 per megawatt hour (MWh). For example, the certification in the United Kingdom is represented by Renewables Obligation Certificates (ROCs), where 1ROC = 1MWh of renewable energy. To convert this into CERs, one needs to have an emission factor, which can vary according to the alternative, or replaced, power source.
- Typically, emission factors are as follows:
  - Renewable energy sources = 0.00
  - Coal = 0.30
  - Heavy fuel oil = 0.26
  - Natural gas = 0.19
  - Electricity taken from the grid* = 0.43

  *(*this figure reflects grid make-up and transmission losses and will vary country to country)*
- From these emission factors, it is possible to calculate the periodic CO_2 emitted from any one source per unit of power generated.
- For any power plant or manufacturing consumer:

  CO_2 emitted (in tonnes) = power consumption × emission factor for the power source.
- The countries which have adopted such a system include the United Kingdom, Australia, Belgium, Poland, Sweden and the US states of California, Maine and Texas. Thus, in these areas the traded instruments are ROCs, not CERs.

- The rationale for these systems, often termed 'cap and trade', was that they were seen as fairer as they provide participants greater freedom of action. However, they are perhaps more complex and less transparent than might have been hoped, and many such systems are being allowed to run their course, then closed.
- When reviewing the revenue stream for renewables projects in these countries, the cash flow contribution from ROCs needs to be identified; sometimes it is included in the sales price to the customer/distributor, sometimes it is a separate stream.

Revenue support mechanisms: There are two types of revenue support mechanism – feed-in tariff (FiT) and FiT Premium. Each type is reviewed in turn.

FiT:

- Under such a payment mechanism, which is increasingly commonplace in the renewable energy sector, all the renewable energy generated by a plant is contracted and sold at an elevated tariff, or is given priority sale in a 'pool' system. The elevated tariff will be sufficient for the renewable energy developer to cover all operating costs, maintenance and finance. The FiT may also be indexed for inflation over time.
- In effect, the higher FiT makes up for the lack of ROC-type compensation, as under the quota scheme. However, it also means that if the plant is available and can produce power, then the power will be sold, debt service payments covered and investor returns guaranteed.
- In some countries, the FiT support is 'grandfathered' – that is, it is fixed for the period of the project no matter what the host government does. Alternatively, the support may drop away with time, meaning that the FiT declines (as for some wind farms in China).
- The countries which have adopted this type of support scheme include Austria, Brazil, Canada (Ontario), China, France, Germany, Greece, India, Portugal, Japan and Turkey.
- On occasion, particularly in the early years of wind and solar developments, the FiTs awarded were excessively high. This highlighted the fact that two questions must be answered:
    - Can the customer – usually, a state-owned or major utility – pay? In other words, is it creditworthy?
    - Will the FiT be sustained at the elevated level over time?
- These issues have arisen in particular in Spain, Portugal and Greece in recent years with the downturn in their economies. The ultimate customer for power, the public consumer, may no longer be able to pay the elevated prices. In turn, the utilities drop into financial difficulties and the host government, which often regulates the prices, reduces the FiT, leading to disputes.
- In such event and in many emerging markets, investors and lenders to such privately funded renewable energy projects and sales arrangements may be protected by international arbitration provisions in the underlying contracts.

There are precedents of investors and lenders gaining redress and compensation in such circumstances.

- In the European Union, such contractual arrangements may not pertain, and the fall-back position for investors and lenders is to claim unfair treatment under the EU Energy Charter – an untested case.
- Hence, apart from inherent revenue risks, political risks need to be assessed too.

FiT Premium:

- A variation on FiT is where renewable generators receive a fixed premium per MWh of renewable energy generated, but they sell into a pool or wholesale market, as is the case in Spain and Denmark. However, the same political risks apply as above.
- A more complex arrangement is found in Ireland and the Netherlands, where generators sell into a wholesale market and payments are made to counterparties based on a target and average market price.

Alternative subvention methods: To support renewable energy, some countries have adopted additional subsidy mechanisms such as tax benefits or credits, investment incentives, favourable capital allowances, loan guarantees, loans at concessionary interest rates and grants for research and development.

It is difficult to assess how successful such schemes have been. However, it has to be said that some offer much less complex and more transparent ways of promoting and evaluating the true costs for supporting renewable energy projects, and some place the true risks for project success with the developers, which is appropriate. In recent times, the FiT mechanism has become the favoured mechanism, mainly due to its simplicity and transparency.

(c) Technical risks

Technical risks with renewable energy projects are often overlooked. However, if financiers are to fund such projects with long-term (10- to 15-year) equity and debt, will the technology perform to the standards expected throughout that period?

Specific technical risks will be described under each renewable energy category below, but one has to recognise that the technologies used in this sector are often innovative and there is only limited long-term operational experience for many.

2.2 Renewable energy types

(a) Wind power

Summary:

- A typical commercial wind farm consists of 3MW or 5MW turbines. These can have towers that are 80–120m tall and weigh 150–280 tonnes. The nacelle itself could weigh 40–70 tonnes and have a rotor diameter of 90–100m. Consequently, installation presents some challenges.
- The costs for offshore wind vary significantly from those onshore. In general

terms, the installed cost of offshore is twice the cost of onshore. The difference is partly due to the extra costs and difficulties in installing foundations, and partly the need for large, heavy-lift barge cranes to lift the turbines into place.

- Typically, the breakdown of capital costs might be as shown below:

		Onshore	*Offshore*
Turbine and tower:	Turbines	30%	18%
	Rotor blades	25%	15%
	Tower	25%	12%
Turbine installation		–	5%
Foundations		6%	17%
Foundation installation		–	8%
Electrical installation		9%	15%
Administration and finance		5%	10%
		100%	**100%**

- For wind, the revenue risks may be significant. How often does the wind blow and at what force? With low wind, no power may be produced. Similarly, at high wind force, it may be too dangerous to operate the wind turbine.

  In developed markets, wind measurements may have been taken for many years. But how reliable is the data and were the measurements made at the same location as a proposed project?

  In emerging markets, such wind data may not be readily available, which is an added risk for developers.

  The United Kingdom is considered as probably the most windy country in Western Europe. Early privately financed wind farms were built on the premise (ie, base case assumptions for financiers) that the wind would blow enough (but not too much) to generate power for around 28% of the time. In fact, later studies showed that that figure was closer to 22–23%, so the projects underperformed.

  For offshore wind, which is a newer sector, the opposite seems to be the case, although it might be early days to make such assessment. Wind measurements have shown that power has been produced for around 35% of the time.

  Nevertheless, wind forecasting, like traffic for roads, remains an art form rather than a science in most regions. Nature can be unpredictable!

  - With respect to wind-specific technical risks, notwithstanding the normal warranties and performance guarantees available for major manufacturers of equipment, over the long term (ie, 10–15 years) questions are being raised as to the following aspects:
  - Equipment life – some studies have shown that, after 10–12 years, the gearing and rotor bearings in the turbine/blade rotation mechanisms become worn and inefficient;
  - Fire – in very high winds, although the blade direction and pitch can be adjusted to achieve optimal power generation, it might be necessary to

stop power production for safety reasons. On occasion, the forces on the turbine installation under such a scenario have been so great as to cause fires in the machinery;

- Noise – wind farms built close to residential areas have been accused of noise pollution. The studies are inconclusive, but the issue cannot be dismissed as trivial; and
- Power capacity – equipment manufacturers are, as always, developing and producing larger and larger wind mills. Not only are 5MW units now readily available, but also 7MW and even 10MW units are being proposed. These units are, of course, that much bigger and heavier, and there is less operational experience for prudent project financiers to rely on if they are to provide long-term capital.
- A final risk area is the grid connection. Wind farms are often located far from the existing grid. The costs for such connections, particularly if offshore, may be significant.

In many countries, the grid is operated and managed by state-owned entities, so the grid connection, in theory, may be their responsibility. In practice, to ensure timely availability of such connection, it is often the developer which implements the construction of the grid connection, even if the utility pays its costs.

Typical wind farm – emerging market:

Project	50 × 3MW windmills, onshore
Capital cost	€275 million
Debt/ equity ratio	75/25
Debt	15-year repayment International Finance Institution (IFI) A/B loan with commercial banks
Equity	From equipment supplier and investors, supported by an irrevocable letter of credit (ILOC)
Construction	Fixed price, engineering, procurement and construction (EPC) contract with supplier
Revenues	• FiT specified under the national renewable energy law • Power purchase agreement (PPA) for 12 years with state-owned utility • FiT increases annually with inflation • If power produced, priority sale to state-owned utility • After [x] MWh of power sold, FiT drops to normal pool tariff* **this condition may not apply in all countries*
Finance	• Base case = P90 (>90% confidence of forecast exceeded) • Base case (P90): average debt service cover ratio (DSCR) = 1.30; minimum DSCR = 1.21 • Base case (P75): average DSCR = 1.40; minimum DSCR = 1.32 • Cash sweep after Year 12 (ie, when PPA matures

- No dividend paid if DSCR <1.14
- Default DSCR = 1.06
- Shareholder retention of minimum 51% while loans outstanding
- Normal reserve accounts required (eg, debt service reserve account (DSRA) and maintenance reserve account (MSRA))

(b) Solar power

There are two main types of solar power: photovoltaic (PV) and concentrated solar power (CSP) (or concentrated solar thermal in the United States).

PV systems:

- PV projects comprise an array of PV panel modules, connected as a 'string' to an invertor which converts the direct current generated by the panels to alternating current for supply to a grid. Typical capacity is 0.5MW per module.

  The invertor usually represents about 10% of the overall cost and has a useful life of approximately 10 years.
- Overall, a PV plant may have a useful life of 20–25 years, although there is some concern that after 10–12 years some types of panel deteriorate and are less effective.

  Manufacturers may provide some guarantees against degradation, but there are also issues of soiling and, in some countries, dust storms to fight against.
- Traditionally, PV solar panel modules have been made up from crystalline silicon materials in wafer form. While well-established, such material is also expensive. In recent years, other, newer materials have become available, but there remain some doubts as to their long-term efficiency and reliability. Nevertheless, over the past five years international prices for PV panels have dropped by more than 50%, to the customer's gain, but a few manufacturers have also gone bankrupt along the way.
- An added issue is that solar power is a relatively new industry internationally. Today, most of the polysilicon and solar panel manufacturers are based in China and the Far East. Many are not 'high street' names in the international markets, compared with suppliers in the conventional power sector. Concerns, therefore, exist as to the long-term reliability and performance of some materials and their suppliers, an issue which is important for long-term providers of project capital.

CSP:

- CSP uses mirrors or heliostats to concentrate direct normal irradiation (DNI) onto a centralised point, and the heat focused thereby is used to power a power generator. The heated material, known as heat transfer fluid (HTF), can be salt or water/steam, depending on the plant set-up. The former may be used for horizontal parabolic troughs, whereas the latter might be used for central receivers or towers. However, the HTF temperatures are high (eg, 400–500°C; salt solidifies at 220°C).
- CSP plants, being more dependent on direct sunlight, have moving parts and

sophisticated control systems. They are, therefore, more expensive per installed MW than PV plants. Like PV plants, they have to contend with soiling and dust storms.

- Whereas a PV plant may cost €3,000 per installed kilowatt (kw), CSP may cost €4,000–5,000 per installed kw.
- The same issues as for PV arise with respect to reliability and the performance of suppliers and operators, given that it is relatively a new industry.

Solar power revenues:

- Obviously, solar power plants will depend on direct sunlight, or just light, for power production. Such measurement should present no major issues, in principle. However, there is a tendency for promoters to be too optimistic.
- The main criterion used is the performance ratio (PR) of any particular system. This ratio, expressed as a percentage, represents the actual production generated from a solar plant (in MWh) versus the maximum expected production (also in MWh), given the direct current capacity of the plant.

  Typically, with a PR of 75–85%, financiers will take the P90 (ie, over 90% confidence that the forecast will be exceeded) as their base case. An indicative average DSCR in such case could be 1.40.
- However, the risk is somewhat higher than for conventional power with regard to:
  - how efficient any particular plant might be;
  - how much light or sunlight will actually fall on such plant and be converted into power; and
  - how such plant will perform over the long term.

Typical European PV solar power project:

Project	50MW PV power project
Capital cost	€225 million (€4,500 per installed kw)
Debt/ equity ratio	70/30
Debt	15-year repayment, bank loan, re-financed on completion with bond issue
Equity	From equipment supplier and investors, supported by ILOC
Construction	Fixed price, EPC contract with supplier
Revenues	• FiT @ €0.25 per kwh, defined by the national renewable energy law • PPA for 20 years with state-owned utility • FiT increases annually with inflation • If power is produced, priority sale to state-owned utility
Finance	• Base case = P90 (>90% confidence of forecast exceeded) • Base case (P90): average DSCR = 1.25; minimum DSCR = 1.18 • Base case (P75); average DSCR = 1.32; minimum DSCR = 1.25 • Cash sweep if loan life cover ratio <1.2

- No dividend paid if DSCR <1.15
- Default DSCR = 1.09
- Normal reserve accounts required (DSRA and MSRA)
- MSRA build up over three years before major maintenance

(c) ***Geothermal power***

Whereas geothermal power has been exploited for a number of years, it is only recently, with the increased interest in renewable resources, that it has come more into the spotlight.

The main zones for geothermal power to date have been:

United States	3,500MW
Philippines	1,900MW
Indonesia	1,350MW
Mexico, Italy and New Zealand	900MW each
Iceland	700MW
Kenya, Costa Rica and El Salvador	New development

Most of the above have been government or corporately financed. Only recently have project finance, independent power producer (IPP) techniques been applied to new projects.

Apart from the usual IPP risks of completion, revenues and political risks on elevated tariffs, the key risks for geothermal power concern the volume of steam available, the length of time the steam will be available for and the temperature of that steam. Fortunately, modern geological analytical techniques have increased the confidence in steam production forecasts.

One issue to note is whether the steam emitted is 'wet' or 'dry'. 'Wet steam' is relatively low temperature, whereas 'dry steam' is superheated and is readily applicable for power generation.

3. Case histories

3.1 Olkaria Geothermal, Kenya

Olkaria was probably the first geothermal IPP in Africa. Olkaria I was initially developed as a 3 × 15MW plant, financed as an equity-funded project (like oil well developments), with equity provided by Ormat Industries, a US company quoted on the NASDAQ Exchange. Ormat is one of the most experienced geothermal power plant generators worldwide, with over 1,700MW of geothermal plant in operation under its management.

The second phase, Olkaria II (2 × 35MW), was likewise funded as an equity project by Ormat.

Olkaria III (48MW) was funded in 2009 with the support of Ormat equity and some development bank funding (Proparco (France), DEG (Germany) and the East Africa Investment Fund).

In 2011, Olkaria III was expanded to 100MW with the support of the Overseas Private Investment Corporation (United States). However, the opportunity was taken to refinance phases I–III. Of the $310 million package raised, $85 million was used to refinance existing debt, $165 million to cover the expansion costs and $60 million as a standby credit.

The whole of Olkaria's power production and sales was underpinned by a PPA with state-owned Kenya Power, with Multilateral Investment Guarantee Agency (World Bank) political risk insurance and tariffs payable in US dollars.

Since these projects have been implemented, the Kenyan government has embarked on a programme of an additional 5,000MW of geothermal power over the next five to 10 years.

3.2 Rwanda IPP

Lake Kivu (30 × 55 miles) in Rwanda is the world's largest source of CH_4 (methane) and CO_2 gas concentrated in water, at a depth of 300–400m.

In 2011 ContourGlobal (which also developed Togo IPP), which employed experienced ex-AES executives and investment bankers, assembled a $142 million IPP package for exploiting this resource.

Given the technical uncertainties (ie, capturing the gas under the lake, stripping out the CO_2, and generating power with the residual CH_4), the debt/equity ratio was an adventurous 65/35.

The project was underpinned by a sales contract on a take-or-pay basis with the state-owned power utility, payable in Rwandan francs, backed up with a government guarantee.

No contractor completion guarantee was available, so ContourGlobal covered the risk.

3.3 Centrale Thermique de Belle Vue, Mauritius

This was the first IPP undertaken in Mauritius (1999). The project comprised a dual-fired 70MW power plant using coal and, when available, bagasse (the waste from sugar plantations).

The investors in the project were local sugar refiners and the power equipment suppliers (Air Liquide and Charbonnages de France, France), which provided a completion guarantee, with the debt provided by export credit agencies and local and international commercial banks on a project financing basis. The debt/equity ratio was 78/22.

The power is sold under a PPA into the local grid, with a pass-through on the price of coal; there were some concerns over the creditworthiness of the customer, the state-owned power utility.

When the bagasse is available (there are two crops of sugar cane per year), it is exchanged with the IPP for power and steam for the refineries.

3.4 Birmingham BioPower, United Kingdom

This 10.3MW waste wood, power project was funded as an IPP in early 2014.

The project cost £47 million, with a debt/equity ratio of 50/50. The equity came from the contractor (Balfour Beatty) and private equity funds, with debt (or sub-debt) coming from the Green Investment Bank and GGP Infrastructure Fund.

The fuel is waste wood (67,000 tonnes per annum consumption), which otherwise would have been left at landfill sites. The EPC contract is with MWH (United States), which has built similar plants, and Nexterra (United States/Canada), which has experience with this type of technology.

This is an innovative project, which explains the increased equity needed in the funding structure. Another potential issue is the uncertainty over fuel supplies over the long term.

3.5 Other types of renewable energy – woodchip IPP

A number of IPPs based on woodchip have been proposed and some implemented in recent years. However, the main area of risk is fuel supply. There is also the issue of transportation of fuel to the power plant.

The result is that such projects have primarily been implemented close to the fuel supply source. Projects where the fuel has to be transported over long distances often fail.

There are also a number of other, usually small, power plants using a variety of fuels (eg, stearin, tallow oil, pig manure, rubber crumb, etc), but these have yet to make a significant impact on the power market.

Oil, gas and power transmission and distribution

1. Key features

1.1 Power transmission

Power transmission projects are quick to build, but planning issues can inhibit implementation. In addition, cross-border projects need international treaty support. Such projects could be implemented as public-private partnership (PPP) concessions, but to date there are no precedents.

1.2 Power and gas distribution

In such projects it is difficult to ring-fence the risks. The projects are therefore usually undertaken as utility (ie, corporate) financings.

1.3 Oil and gas pipelines

As mentioned above, pipelines are often cross-border projects, so need to be supported by a bilateral or international treaty. Completion risks can be high as the risks cannot be ring-fenced.

These projects can be funded through cash flow, project financing, but revenue risks are often significant. PPP-type concessions with payment made against availability criteria provide an alternative structure with private capital.

Environmental risks can also be significant for such projects.

2. Power transmission – applications and experiences

In concept, long-distance transmission lines are electrical highways, so should be capable of being funded similarly to PPP highways. The construction and environmental risks should be manageable, and the revenue stream could be supported by an availability payment mechanism. However, as such projects can stretch over many kilometres, physical security of the assets can be a significant risk.

To date, few – if any – international and/or long-distance transmission lines have been funded as PPP concessions in their own right, though. Most have been financed either by governments or utilities as corporate financings.

3. Power and gas distribution – applications and experiences

With respect to local power and gas distribution, as for water, it is difficult to ring-fence and, therefore, manage the physical risks. Such project developments are therefore usually funded by governments, municipalities or utilities as corporate financings. However, where these utilities are private, they have become attractive investments for private equity, pension funds and the like in recent times.

4. Oil and gas pipelines – case histories

4.1 Baku–Tbilisi–Ceyhan oil pipeline, Azerbaijan–Georgia–Turkey

This 1,768km, 1 million barrels per day, oil pipeline from BP-operated fields in Azerbaijan via Georgia to the Mediterranean coast in southern Turkey was first proposed in 1994, when the original project company, AIOC, was set up. However, it took almost 10 years to negotiate and agree the trinational agreement to allow the project to proceed. Key issues to that agreement included the acceptance of:

- English law as the basis for the contracts; and
- international arbitration for dispute resolution.

Eventually, the project was implemented at a total cost of $3.7 billion with a debt/equity ratio of 70/30. The lead majority shareholders were BP and SOCAR, the state-owned Azeri oil company, with a number of other well-known oil companies covering the balance. The shareholder sponsors committed to throughput contracts to support revenues.

The debt comprised a mix of loans from an international finance institution (IFI) (the European Bank for Reconstruction and Development), an export credit agency (ECA) and commercial banks. Overall, at least 24 funding institutions were involved. With the international legal challenges faced by the participants, plus issues over land acquisition and political risks associated with such a multinational deal, it was rightly acclaimed as "Deal of the Year" by *Infrastructure Journal* in 2004.

It was one of the first infrastructure projects to apply the Equator Principles (a framework adopted by financial institutions for determining, assessing and managing environmental and social risk in project finance). Given the pipeline's length, the completion risk was carried by the sponsors.

4.2 Chad–Cameroon oil pipeline

Land-locked Chad was found to have more than 1 billion barrels of recoverable reserves of low sulphur crude oil in the late 1990s, but had no funds available to develop the fields and transport the oil to the Cameroon coast.

With the support of the International Finance Corporation (IFC), the private sector arm of the World Bank, a $3.7 billion package was assembled with Exxon/Mobil (United States, 40%), Petronas (Malaysia, 35%) and Chevron (United States, 25%) as sponsors, of which $1.5 billion was to develop the oilfields in Chad, and $2.2 billion for a 30", 170km pipeline to the Chad–Cameroon border and a further 1,050km pipeline to the Cameroon coast at Kribi, where a floating buoy mooring was to be built 12km offshore. Sponsors funded the oil development (ie, through corporate finance), but the pipeline's funding was more akin to infrastructure finance.

The pipeline funding had a debt/equity ratio of 64/36, with 90% of the equity from sponsors and the balance from the two governments, funded by World Bank and European Investment Bank loans. The project debt, which amounted to $1 billion, was a classic IFC A/B loan structure, with some ECA funding for the pipeline, and a capital markets bond issue secured by sales contracts with the sponsors.

The sponsors, as for the Baku–Tbilisi–Ceyhan oil pipeline, provided a completion guarantee which dropped away on completion, when the sponsors were exposed to oil market and price risks.

One of the controversial aspects of this deal was that the IFIs, in particular, wished to ensure that any revenues or royalties accruing to the Chad government were used for appropriate purposes, not for military equipment. Escrow account arrangements were set up with this intention, but that mechanism was reportedly not fully effective.

4.3 Blue Stream gas pipeline, Russia–Turkey

In the annals of pipelines this project stands out as it faced some unique difficulties and provided an innovative security structure for lenders.

The project comprised 370km of gas pipeline in Russia, 380km offshore (Blue Stream) under the Black Sea to the north coast of Turkey and 500km within Turkey. Gazprom (Russia) and Botas (Turkey) funded the onshore portions in their respective countries. Blue Stream was to be cash flow, project financed.

The cost of Blue Stream was estimated at $3 billion, with an expected throughput annual capacity of 12 billion cubic metres (bcm); SNAM/Saipem (Italy) was the contractor. At that time, Turkey's economy was growing rapidly, and there was a shortage of energy resources.

The project had to tackle some unusual technical problems, however. The offshore pipe was to consist of 2 x 24" lines at a depth of up to 2,150m. Until that time the deepest such a pipeline had been laid was 600m for the Tunisia–Italy Trans-Mediterranean Pipeline. Blue Stream was therefore venturing into the unknown. In the event, a special pipe-laying vessel was built, with a 130m high tower framework and 14,000-tonne heavy-lift gantry crane atop a 118,000-tonne crude carrier – the largest heavy-lift ship in the world at the time – to lay the pipe vertically, to avoid the danger of the pipe breaking between the stern and the sea-bed if laid horizontally.

A second technical issue was the fact that the Black Sea is in a seismic zone where hydrogen sulphide can be emitted. The project engineers forecast the possibility that, at a depth of 2,150m where the pipe was to be laid, such gas could convert into sulphuric acid and corrode the pipeline. Unsurprisingly, this made the lenders rather nervous about the technical performance of the project. In addition, the creditworthiness of the customer (Botas) and the gas throughput over the project's life had to be considered.

To avoid stalemate, a novel security package to support $2.4 billion of project debt was put in place.

For 15–20 years Italy had been importing gas from Gazprom and had in return been exporting capital goods and equipment to Russia, supported by finance from SACE, Italy's ECA. As part of that financing, an offshore escrow account arrangement had been set up in which the revenues due to Gazprom for the gas sales were deposited as security for the ECA debt.

Following negotiations with the Russian government, this escrow account was also made available as security for the Blue Stream lenders. The Blue Stream funding was put in place, and the project implemented.

World Bank negative pledge: One aspect of this transaction – the World Bank negative pledge – has wider international applications.

When the World Bank, or for that matter any other IFI, provides a sovereign loan to the government of another country, then, as part of the security for that loan, the World Bank/IFI has a lien over the borrower's assets – that is, over the borrowing government's national assets, including natural resources such as oil, gas and minerals.

Thus, where a project consists of developing the resources of a country in which the funding entails the lenders taking a lien over the project's assets (as is a fundamental condition of most cash flow, project financed deals), then an obvious conflict arises as those assets are already secured against the IFI loan.

In such circumstances, therefore, lenders to the project have to seek a World Bank negative pledge waiver, which enables the project financing to proceed. The World Bank – on behalf of the IFIs – will usually grant the waiver as long as:

- the project has an acceptable economic and financial feasibility;
- the lenders are private;
- the loans' maturity is five years or longer; and
- there is no alternative security available.

For natural resources projects in emerging markets, this is just one extra hurdle one might need to negotiate. This issue arose with Blue Stream, but a waiver was given without problem.

4.4 Nord Stream, Russia–Germany gas pipeline via the Baltic Sea

The rationale for this project was to bring Russian gas to Germany and Western Europe. The project comprised:

- 917km of 56" gas pipeline in Russia, funded by Gazprom;
- 1,222km, 2 × 48" pipeline under the Baltic Sea to Germany;
- 5 bcm underground gas storage in Germany; and
- connections in Germany to the MIDAL, STEGAL and Yamal pipelines.

The offshore portion was to be cash flow, project financed. The project cost was estimated at €5.7 billion, of which:

- €1.8 billion (32%) was to be provided by equity from Gazprom (51%), BASF and EON (15.5% each), Gasunie and Suez (9% each); and
- €3.9 billion (68%) was to come from ECA and commercial bank debt.

Whilst the project claimed economic feasibility, there was some doubt as to its long-term commercial viability, notwithstanding 25-year signed gas sales contracts with BASF, DONG, EON and Suez. This is because Gazprom, the majority shareholder in Nord Stream, had alternative routes for supplying gas to Western Europe via the existing Yamal and Brotherhood pipelines.

Another concern for lenders was that the sponsor/project company was domiciled in Zug, Switzerland, a tax haven within a tax haven.

To overcome the revenue risk, lenders proposed a typical PPP-type payment structure (ie, payments made against availability criteria, as for a highway).

The negotiations were completed and financial close reached in 2010 with a syndicate of 27 commercial banks.

One final consideration in such a project is to estimate the value of the gas in the pipeline (in Nord Stream, €700 million), and include this cost as part of the funded capital costs, amortised with project assets: without the gas in the pipeline, no sales are possible.

5. Conclusion

The financing of pipeline projects tends to follow similar characteristics. The key elements are:

- completion risk, usually covered by the sponsors;
- strong throughput commitments, and, if not available, availability payments; and
- complex environmental and political issues to overcome.

Water and waste management

1. Key features

1.1 Water

The key characteristics of water projects are as follows:

- The risks attached to water treatment plants can be ring-fenced and so potentially controlled; accordingly, the projects can be funded with private capital.
- Water distribution systems are more diffuse, so less attractive to investors. If private capital is sought, the route is normally via a privatisation of the water system, creating a utility.
- Many water system projects consist of upgrading existing assets and in many instances there is no up-to-date asset register which identifies and certifies the condition of the existing structures and equipment available.
- In many countries and cultures, clean water provision is seen as a 'God-given' right, so imposing fees on the public for water supply is politically sensitive.
- The customers for water services projects are often municipalities, so issues of creditworthiness arise.
- Many water sector projects do not achieve the threshold capital value such that the use of private funding is cost-effective.

1.2 Waste management

The key characteristics of waste management projects are as follows:

- The risks attached to waste management plants can be ring-fenced, as for water treatment, so the projects can potentially be funded with private capital.
- Many waste sector projects exceed the threshold capital value, which makes the use of private funding cost-effective.
- To date, most privately funded, waste management projects have been implemented in advanced economies where governments have to comply with strict legislation with regard to the disposal of rubbish and waste.
- Charging the public for rubbish disposal can be politically sensitive. Hence, most private waste ventures have municipalities as their customer.
- If the customers for waste management projects are municipalities, issues of creditworthiness have to be addressed.
- Some waste management projects take responsibility for collecting waste

from houses, etc, whereas for others, the municipality has responsibility to deliver waste to the plant door.

2. Water projects

2.1 Case histories

In principle, water treatment plants should represent an attractive project type to fund with private capital, provided that the project components which lie outside the fence (ie, the supply of water to be treated and the customer for clean water) are reliable and creditworthy.

One such example was the Almond Valley, Seafield & Esk Water Project, Scotland, on the banks of the Firth of Forth and undertaken by Stirling Water Seafield Holdings.

The project, which consisted of the upgrade of an existing plant, cost £100 million, funded with a 'standard' debt/equity ratio of 80/20. Contractor and water utility company investors provided the equity, part as a subordinated (or shareholder) loan, part as long-term debt via a 27.5-year, £79 million bond issue insured by Ambac, a US company specialising in financial guarantees. The viability of raising a bond issue at the outset was possible as the project enjoyed the cash flow from the existing plant's operation to service bondholders during construction.

The construction and completion risks were deemed low, and the provider of untreated water was state-owned Scottish Water, which was also the customer for the clean water under a 30-year contract. So, in many ways the project was an outsourcing of Scottish Water's activities.

The project proceeded without undue issue. Then, one day in early 2007 a pump in the plant broke down, resulting in the plant being unable to process dirty water. The excess, untreated water had to be ejected into the sea, and the public was warned to keep out of the sea and away from the local beaches.

Fortunately, the problem with the pump was resolved within 36 hours and all was well thereafter. Further, no public health issues arose, and a report undertaken shortly after by the Scottish government and the regulator showed that the project company had taken all correct measures following the accident.

However, this event raised some important issues. Firstly, was the insurance adequate to cover any liability arising with third parties if the event had had more serious consequences?

Secondly, why did the breakdown occur at all? Was ongoing maintenance at the plant inadequate, or was it unforeseeable through faulty materials in the equipment? Or was the pump due for replacement, but management had not provided the funding necessary to buy a new one – in other words, was someone accountable?

The water utility investor in the project company, which it is assumed provided the project with operational management, was Thames Water, one of the major privately owned water utilities of England and Wales – owned by private equity funds based in a tax haven. Could they, or their directors, be held accountable? In the event, the question never arose as the equipment breakdown was deemed *force majeure* and the water treatment service restored within a few days without harm to third parties.

2.2 Miscellaneous water treatment projects

(a) *General comments*

There have been a number of similar types of project, where governmentally or municipally controlled water utilities have effectively outsourced, or awarded concessions to undertake, their water treatment responsibilities to the private sector, including:

- EMASESA (Spain, 2003) – €96 million for system upgrades in Seville and environs;
- Muharraq (Bahrain, 2009–11) – $300 million for water treatment and a 16km sewer tunnel;
- Bucharest (Romania, 2002) – €110 million PPP concession for water treatment plant and system improvements; and
- St Petersburg (Russia, 2002) – €190 million water treatment plant upgrade, structured as a PPP but a municipal project.

The reported success of such projects has been mixed, highlighting the difficulties experienced in attracting private capital to this sector.

(b) *Long-distance water pipeline, Jordan*

The construction in 2009 of the 365km, $975 million Disi–Mudawarra water pipeline as a 25-year PPP concession carrying water from aquifers in southern Jordan to Amman was the first of its type in Jordan. Indeed, this project is one of the few of its type globally. It is forecast that the aquifers can supply Amman with 100 cubic metres per annum for the next 50 years, at least.

The debt/equity ratio was 80/20, with the equity provided by Gama Enerj, a 50/50 joint venture between Gama Holdings (Turkey) and GE Financial Services (United States), with the long-term (20-year) debt coming from a consortium of development banks – the European Investment Bank (EIB), the Overseas Private Investment Corporation (OPIC, United States) and Proparco (France), plus a $300 million grant from the Jordan government, funded via EIB and AFP (France).

The engineering, procurement and construction (EPC) contractor was Gama Holdings (Turkey) and the operator Suez Environment (France) under a 25-year operation and maintenance contract. The customer is the Jordan government under a take-or-pay contract.

(c) *Privatisation of water utilities*

The United Kingdom has one of the few fully privatised water systems in the world. Privatisation came about in 1989, when 10 England and Wales water utilities were floated on the London Stock Exchange, with the utilities in Scotland and Northern Ireland remaining in state ownership. The licences are issued by the regulator, OFWAT, which limits the prices that the privatised utilities can charge customers, based on a five-year adjustment cycle.

In other countries, however, the question will arise as to what basis the privatised utilities can use to charge customers for their services. This is especially the case for water services, which are usually a natural monopoly with no alternative choice for customers.

The first step is to determine what the value of the company inherently is. If the water utility had been privatised via a competitive bidding process, as might arise in emerging economies, then the highest price offered by bidders, plus any existing debt assumed by the privatised entity, could be stated as the equity value of the privatised utility.

The UK privatisation took place through a share flotation, so the equity value (termed the 'regulatory asset base' or RAB) was determined by taking the average daily market value for the newly privatised utility, as quoted on the London Stock Exchange, for the first 200 days, plus any existing debt assumed via the privatisation process.

Post-privatisation, the RAB was increased annually by an agreed index for inflation (eg, the UK Retail Price Index (RPI)), and this value together with the value, or cost, of any new capital investment, less depreciation of existing assets, gives the regulatory capital value (RCV). On occasion, the regulator applied an RPI – [x] inflation factor instead to the calculation to provide an incentive for the incumbent utility to gain more efficiencies in the use of existing assets.

In addition, the regulator may have a duty, as in the United Kingdom, to set tariffs at a level that enables the utilities to finance themselves. Where that is the case, the regulator allows the utilities to include their financing costs as part of the above tariff-setting formula.

To determine those costs, the regulator assumes a debt/equity ratio as for a notional water utility – say, 65/35. Using a model for weighted average cost of capital, and based on assumptions for the cost of debt and equity (using a capital asset pricing model), the financing component within the tariff is determined.

Each regulated utility produces its own business plan for the next pricing cycle (eg, five years). Against these cost forecasts and the number and type of customers in the privatised utilities market, the regulator can determine what is a reasonable tariff that the utility can change customers, both for clean water supply and sewerage services, while the utility owners are able to cover all their costs for operations and investment in new assets and debt, and make an acceptable equity return for investors.

Water utilities are long-term businesses operating in a stable marketplace and therefore raise much of their debt via the bond, rather than commercial bank loan, market. One of the additional conditions laid down by the regulator may be, as in the United Kingdom, that the privatised utilities must maintain an investment grade rating, as determined by Standard & Poor's and other credit rating agencies.

The above regulatory system has now been operational in the United Kingdom for almost 25 years. During that time, no UK water utility – nor, indeed, any UK power or gas transmission utility – has had its licence rescinded for breach of service or performance. That does not mean that the regulatory regime is perfect, but more comment will be made on that issue in the chapter on the UK infrastructure.

It is important, nevertheless, that any privatisation regime be dynamic and can adjust the demands on licensees as circumstances change. It has been noted, in this respect, that some countries impose a 'probity' test on public service utilities, which requires that such private utilities demonstrate that they are 'fit and proper persons' with respect to their suitability for owning public service assets and delivering public services. With the multinational nature of investment in the sector, such a condition has much merit.

In emerging markets, the scenario is often that the private sector is being asked to rehabilitate or upgrade an existing operational water system in a municipality. A number of issues arise:

- In such markets, the public is likely not attuned to paying economic tariffs for water services. Private financiers may therefore prefer the project to have, as customers, one or two creditworthy entities (municipalities) rather than the general public.
- The customer/municipality may not be creditworthy.
- It might be difficult to work out the cost of the new investment. There are rarely any recent asset registers to use as a reference to identify and assess the need for new investment. (This was the problem facing the London Underground Public-Private Partnership (PPP).)

As a result, the first step may be to contract an expert, often under a development bank technical assistance contract, which will assess the system and its management, and propose a plan as to what needs to be built and the steps to be taken to improve management and efficiency. This may take 12 to 18 months.

Given the limited number of water utilities operating as investors in international markets, there are relatively few companies which can assume the role of 'expert' on such occasion.

A plan is thus formulated, and the host government offers a tender for a PPP concession or decides to privatise the existing utility, again with development bank support. However, the expert is precluded from bidding under the procurement rules of development banks. Sadly, this has constrained the efficient development of water schemes in many emerging markets.

Apart from the above issues, investors will be aware of the need that any investment must exceed the minimum values to making private investment cost-effective.

A second, important point is that many such privatisations or PPP concessions are structured such that they may create contingent liabilities for the host municipality or government.

In conclusion, therefore, the opportunities for the use of private capital in water development projects is limited compared to some other sectors, but not impossible.

3. Waste management projects

3.1 Case histories

Waste management projects present many characteristics that are similar to water treatment plant investments. They can be effectively ring-fenced, technologically manageable, and achieve the minimum threshold for using private capital cost-effectively. Furthermore, their customer base is similar (ie, municipalities).

A key issue is that a waste management service is not free, and someone has to pay. Quite often, the public is averse to paying for the removal of their rubbish. The municipality therefore becomes the payor for the waste service delivered by the project, and the municipality charges the public via local taxes.

Another issue is: Who collects the rubbish from households, commercial outlets and industry? Sometimes it is the private waste management company, sometimes the municipality itself. There are examples of both.

The basis for payment, however, is on delivery of the rubbish to the private processor, termed 'gate fee' (usually quoted per tonne of waste).

The waste management process comprises four stages/areas:

- Waste collection – both household and industrial;
- Recovery and separation – mechanical sorting (glass, metal, plastics, paper, etc);
- Incineration – any resulting energy can be sold to the grid, while residue is passed on to landfill; and
- Recycling – for instance through mechanical biological treatment (MBT).

Incineration and MBT, mentioned above, consist respectively of burning waste to provide energy and heat, and a staged process to obtain stable product such as fuel or fertiliser.

Recycling waste can also be undertaken using a number of different processes, depending on the types of waste available:

- Gasification and pyrolysis – waste is heated to high temperature and converted into fuel;
- Auto-claving – waste is treated with steam to recover mixed organic waste;
- Anaerobic digestion – biodegradable material in waste is broken down in absence of oxygen; and
- Composting – waste is placed in rows ('windrows') and biodegrading takes place to form compost.

There are a number of precedents in Western Europe of privately funded waste management schemes. One major project was the Manchester Municipal Waste PPP (2009), which consisted of:

- a 420,000-tonne per annum MBT plant, producing 230,000-tonnes per annum of refuse-derived fuel (RDF); and
- a waste-to-energy (WTE) incinerator using as fuel 500,000 tonnes of RDF per annum.

The projects were structured as two separate special purpose vehicles that were, however, jointly funded. Overall cost was £640 million.

The shareholders were:

- for the MBT plant: Viridor (part of the Pennon Group) and John Laing Infrastructure Fund (50/50); and
- for the WTE plant: Viridor (37.5%), John Laing Infrastructure Fund (37.5%) and INEOS Chlor (25%).

The debt comprised a mix of commercial bank, EIB and UK government funding. As this was post-financial crisis, the 23.5-year bank loans included interest rate margins starting at 325 basis points (bps) over LIBOR, rising to 425bps at the rate of 10bps per annum from project completion, and a 50% cash sweep after Year 10. Average debt service cover ratio was 1.25, with a minimum of 1.2.

The prime customer was Manchester Municipality, one of the largest in the United Kingdom. The municipality itself also provided 270,000 tonnes of RDF, sourced from other plants that it operated, directly to the WTE plant to make up the balance of fuel supplies needed to achieve the full power generating capacity (36 megawatts) of the WTE plant.

The power and heat produced by incineration was sold to the INEOS plant nearby – a major consumer of electricity for the production of chlorine and other chemicals.

This deal was highly complex to structure and implement, and this was reflected in the number of project documents in the data room: reportedly, over 1,700.

Given the current EU requirements to reduce the volume of rubbish going to landfill sites, as well as the shortage of such sites, waste management projects of this type are becoming increasingly common. As for water projects, however, it is usually municipalities which are the payees for waste management projects, so the issues of creditworthiness and contingent liabilities arise.

Miscellaneous government services – schools, health, housing, offices, information technology, stadiums, prisons, defence

1. General features

Many of the projects considered in this chapter include accommodation in some form. In such projects, the private sector sponsors are building an accommodation asset and making it available for government to use in some way.

The risks are generally low, and many companies have experience of building such accommodation and managing the facilities. The payment regimes used, based on 'availability' requirements, have become well established, and there are many precedents to follow.

The financial risks can be relatively easily mitigated and managed, too. Projects may be highly leveraged – for instance, a debt/equity ratio of 80/20, or even 90/10 in some instances – and normal project financing terms and conditions apply.

Governments adopt this investment mechanism partly because it allows greater flexibility on the use of the asset – that is, if the government is not using the accommodation made available to it, a private sector owner is more likely to find someone else to use it, thus generating extra income.

Another reason why this funding mechanism may be preferred is that it offers greater certainty that the underlying assets will be properly maintained. In many countries, the track record of governments or municipalities maintaining government assets is poor, not least because government budgets may be often cut, whereas under a public-private partnership (PPP) mechanism the private party will receive no, or reduced, payment if the assets are not in the specified condition.

One of the major risk areas concerns the specification of the asset to be built and how it is to be used. Unfortunately, governments can find it difficult to define what asset is to be built and then, once they have decided, they may later change their mind.

Another risk area relates to potential changes in the underlying public service requirement. For example, how patients are treated in hospital today may be quite different from how they will be treated in 10 years' time. In other words, the underlying nature of the business may change.

If a project is funded by private financiers under some form of PPP concession, any change in the output specification of the service delivered under the concession will put the public sector concession grantor at a disadvantage in any negotiations to change the underlying contractual arrangements.

Lastly, the use of private capital for government accommodation projects invariably creates a contingent liability for the government department paying availability payments. This is often overlooked in government planning. A further issue for consideration in this regard is whether the contingent liability, so created, should or should not be on balance sheet for the government.

2. Case histories

2.1 Schools and advanced education

(a) *Glasgow Schools PPP*

This 30-year PPP-type concession was to rehabilitate 29 schools in Glasgow, Scotland, in 2000. Of these, 12 were new, to-be-built schools – 10 on existing school sites, two on new sites.

The investment cost was £225 million, plus £15 million for IT equipment. The concessionaire was a consortium made up of a construction contractor (Miller), a facilities management company (Amey) and a financial institution (Bank of Scotland).

Payments to the concessionaire were based on 'availability', against criteria such as maintenance, cleanliness and temperature of classrooms and school facilities, among others. The funding was highly leveraged (the debt/equity ratio was 87/13), supported by long-term bank loans.

(b) *Points to note*

- If funded individually, some of the school projects among the 29 would not have met the threshold which makes PPP financing cost-effective. Consequently, it made sense to develop them as a portfolio.
- Students use the schools for only 70% of the year. The schools are, therefore, made available for use by third parties outside school terms, providing a more economic outturn for the sponsors.
- The project also involved land which the schools did not use or need. This land was passed to the PPP concessionaire for residential development, adding to sponsor returns.
- Some 600 staff transferred their employment from municipalities to the concessionaire company under the UK regulations (known as TUPE) which protect employee rights and benefits under such transfer.
- Since 2006, schools PPP projects in Scotland, such as Argyle & Bute (£128 million), have been implemented under a not-for-profit concession structure.
- Similar PPP-type schools projects have been undertaken in Germany (Offenbach, 49 schools) and Belgium (Flemish, 211 schools, for €1.5 billion).
- The same funding structure has also been used at colleges and universities in the United Kingdom and elsewhere (eg, Zayed University, Abu Dhabi).

(c) *Further comments*

The construction and operation of schools by the private sector can have some unintended consequences:

- In private sector projects, financiers will expect to have the assets commercially insured. (Many public and municipal authorities may not insure their assets.)

  Under such insurance, classrooms may for instance have to have installed fire sprinklers as essential safeguard against fire. Such sprinklers can however be misused by students who set them off in class intentionally.
- Private sector sponsors of schools will wish to maximise revenues. Thus, many PPP schools initially installed vending machines, under contract with food suppliers, for chocolate, soft drinks, etc.

  Later, the state health authorities noted that too many students were obese. Vending machines were banned forthwith.

  However, as this constraint and resultant contract change had not been foreseen under the PPP Concession Agreement, the public authorities were forced to pay some compensation for lost income to the concessionaire.

2.2 Health and hospitals

(a) UCL Hospital, London

This project comprised the replacement of five existing hospitals in central London with a new 669-bed hospital (40 critical illness beds, 14 operating theatres and 96 consulting rooms) at a cost of £270 million in 2000.

The private consortium consisted of contractors (Amec and Balfour Beatty), plus a facilities manager (Building & Property Group). The funding was highly leveraged (90/10), funded with long-term (35-year maturity – this was pre-financial crisis) commercial bank loans.

Typical activities undertaken by the concessionaire include:

- ward and operating theatre availability maintenance;
- cleaning and temperature control throughout the hospital;
- catering;
- laundry;
- portering;
- telecommunication services;
- waste disposal; and
- helpdesk.

The major items of equipment (eg, CT scanners) are usually not included in such concessions, but rather funded and maintained by the manufacturers.

On rare occasions, PPP concessionaires have taken on clinical activities too (where they are paid a fee of [x] for, say, [x] hip replacement operations) as part of the concession, with unknown outcomes (eg, Braga PPP, Portugal).

(b) Points to note

- The payee for the availability payments for the UCL Hospital project was a London health trust – that is, a stand-alone government agency. As there was some concern as to the future creditworthiness of such an entity – could it go bankrupt? – a special government bill was required to assure financiers that, if such an event arose, the government would support the commercial obligations (ie, availability payments) of such trusts.

- The PPP concessionaire was able either to use or sell the land from the old hospitals for commercial or residential development.
- During the construction period, the National Health Service (NHS) updated the design of the beds to be used in all NHS hospitals throughout the United Kingdom. Unfortunately, the new beds were too wide for the doors to the wards in the new UCL Hospital, so all the doorframes had to be changed. The change of contract specification led to compensation to the concessionaire for implementing such change.

(c) ***Local Improvement Finance Trust schemes***

Because of the uncertainties stemming from the continuously evolving pattern of clinical treatment in hospitals, there has been a trend in recent years to building smaller medical centres, or clinics, which can treat patients locally for many ailments. Where that is not possible, the patients can be sent to specialist clinics or hospitals elsewhere.

One model which has been widely adopted in the United Kingdom for providing local medical services is called the Local Improvement Finance Trust (LIFT). Some 50 such LIFT schemes have been implemented in recent years.

Figure 21.1: LIFT (eg, local PPP health centres)

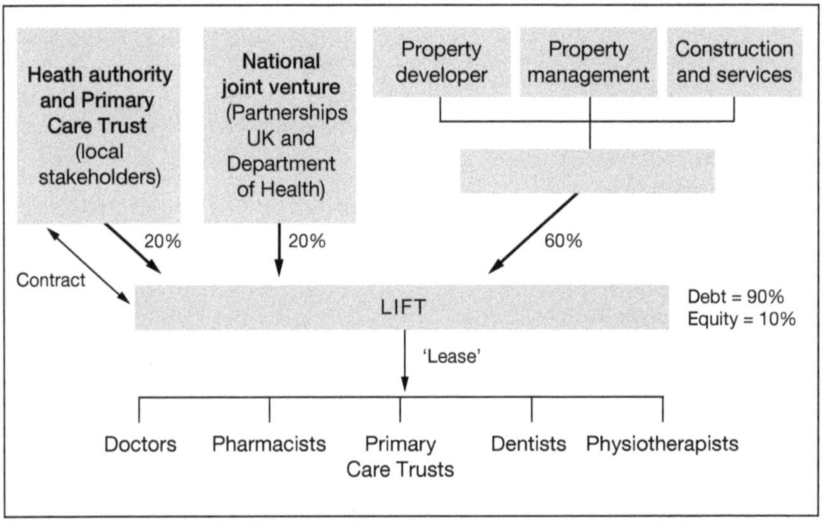

Source: author

A typical capital value could be £20–40 million, and the model is now well tested.

2.3 Government administration buildings

There have been many examples of UK government offices and buildings owned and operated by private sector PPP concessionaires – in particular, buildings for HM Revenue and HM Customs & Excise, which collect VAT, among other taxes.

One such example was the Mapeley STEPS, described as a PPP, which comprised the sale and leaseback of 600 buildings around the United Kingdom to a private property and investment company, Mapeley UK Ltd. The transaction value was £370 million, and Mapeley was able to provide the government with the flexible use of accommodation sought.

Shortly before financial close, it emerged that Mapeley UK was not a UK-domiciled company. Instead, it was based in a tax haven, which gave advantages, undisclosed until that point, to Mapeley UK should it wish to sell any of the properties its government clients did not need in the future. This highlights the fact that the ownership of the concessionaire to PPP-type ventures needs to be reviewed carefully.

A second example is the rebuilding of the National Physical Laboratory (NPL) in Teddington near London at a cost of £96 million, undertaken as a PPP by a contractor (J Laing) and a facilities manager (Serco) in 2006.

The NPL provides the government with testing and research facilities; one of its claims to fame is the broadcast of the Greenwich Time Signal (six short tones at one-second intervals, known as the 'six pips') on the BBC radio stations everyday from the NCP atomic clock.

As with many similar property-type PPPs, the concession also included the sale of spare land to the concessionaire for residential development.

However, major problems arose over the concessionaire being able to perform to the very exacting performance specification required by the NPL in its laboratories. In the end, both parties agreed that it was impossible, and the PPP concession was terminated, with the concessionaire receiving some compensation.

2.4 Housing

Many governments, particularly in emerging markets, attempt to use the PPP mechanism for social housing ventures. The results have not lived up to expectations.

In developed markets, governments have often already set up an institutional framework for this sector – for instance, via housing associations – whereby a government agency gains access to the long-term finance markets, supported by the government, and then uses such funding for social housing, managing and collecting rents from tenants accordingly. Arguably, in such circumstances the PPP mechanism brings no benefits.

A variant to this has been developed in Scotland in recent years, under the non-profit distribution model called the National Housing Trust. In essence, a private housing developer and management company partners with the government and local housing authorities to build and manage social housing estates, collecting rents accordingly to cover costs. After a certain number of years (eg, five to 10 years), the developer has the right to sell the houses and make, possibly, a capital gain.

2.5 Stadiums

In some countries, governments have built stadiums as national assets, rather than as centres of entertainment funded by the private sector. On such occasions, the lumpy nature of use of the stadiums (eg, to be used for football only at the weekends) makes them very speculative investments. Accordingly, where governments have developed these projects as PPPs, the private concessionaire has been paid on the basis of availability criteria; this is the case for the Lille and Le Mans stadiums in France, sponsored by the local municipalities.

2.6 IT projects

Information technology is a difficult area for PPP-type transactions. The underlying technology changes so rapidly, whereas PPPs are long-term ventures. Consequently, many deals in this sector are funded against corporate security.

One example of the difficulties encountered in this sector was one of the early UK private finance/PPP concessions for a computer-based, administration system for the Lord Chancellors Office (ie, the UK law courts), known as the Libra project.

A contract was awarded as a PPP concession to a major international computer software and hardware joint venture to develop and implement the system at a cost of €400 million.

There was no ready-made software package to use, so it had to be developed from scratch, and there were significant cost overruns in development, as it proved difficult to determine and fix the output specification.

The project failed and the concession was terminated (at some cost to the government).

As a result, IT projects are no longer promoted as PPPs.

It should be added, however, that there have been one or two attempts to use the PPP mechanism for implementing better infrastructure projects directly supporting IT operations (eg, mobile phone transmitters, masts, and broadband networks) as PPPs, but the technology risks remain significant.

2.7 Prisons

A number of countries – particularly the United States, the United Kingdom and South Africa – have adopted the PPP mechanism to build prisons, seen as secure accommodation projects. The underlying payment mechanism for such a PPP is, as usual, against availability, with specifications as to:

- ensuring a secure environment;
- maintaining order and discipline;
- providing decent conditions and ambience;
- providing positive regimes;
- preparing prisoners for release; and
- providing community access arrangements.

There are penalties for overcrowding and escape and, obviously, it is for the state to supply the prisoners.

There is some discussion as to whether such PPP prisons should be operated with privately rather than publicly employed guards, and there are arguments for both. However, the use of private resources will often lead to innovative security measures, such as the widespread use of CCTV in prison operations.

2.8 Defence

For many governments, the use of private capital for the provision of military services is a no-go area. However, the military can often be a good customer for the private sector.

There are many areas, and PPP precedents, where private investors, operators and PPP concessionaires can provide the service that the military requires at a much lower cost, particularly in the areas of:

- logistics – moving heavy military equipment (eg, tanks), providing a shipping fleet for equipment, or in-flight refuelling;
- warehousing – for the Navy at its bases;
- officer and staff training colleges and facilities;
- managing housing for military personnel and their families;
- water treatment plants for major military bases; and
- vehicle and aircraft maintenance.

UK infrastructure – issues and challenges

1. Introduction

In many ways, the United Kingdom is a pioneer in the modern world of private sector infrastructure financing and public-private partnerships (PPP). In the 1980s, the government of Margaret Thatcher privatised many of the country's public service utilities – airports, ports, power, electricity and gas transmission, water and telecoms – such that any new investments in these sectors had to be undertaken as privately funded, rather than state-funded, projects.

Some countries, by contrast – for example, the United States – already had a long history of privately owned or municipally owned public service utilities, but the corporate and governance structures imposed on such entities is well established, more highly regulated and more responsive to customers' demands than the regimes of their UK comparators.

Outside the public service sector, the United Kingdom has been at the vanguard of the development of mechanisms for procuring and funding other public assets with private capital, initially through what was called the Private Finance Initiative (PFI), which later became generically described as PPP. Indeed, the UK government has implemented between 800 and 900 such project investments over the past 20 years for schools, hospitals, prisons and offices.

The results have been mixed, with the failures attracting media attention and most successes passing unnoticed. Nevertheless, the reasons for the failures are as already described in Part 1 of this book:

- Channel Tunnel (Eurotunnel) – a financial disaster due to over-optimistic traffic forecasts and too much debt in the initial financial structure, whereas arguably the project has been a significant success economically;
- Channel Tunnel Rail Link (CTRL), now called 'HS1' after refinancing – an uncommitted private funding package at the outset, so the project had to be rescued by the government when private funding was not available;
- London Underground PPP – an overly complex concession contract (over 3,000 pages long), undefined investment programme, and no global precedent in the sector to follow; and
- PFI schools, hospitals, etc – arguably, the value-for-money assessments (as determined via an analysis using HM Treasury's Green Book) were artificially biased towards the PFI/PPP option, and underestimated the actual payments to be made by the PFI concession grantors.

Other problem areas that have affected the United Kingdom's programme of investment in key infrastructure assets in recent years include:

- a government objective to keep the financial commitments for infrastructure investment off balance sheet, if at all possible;
- a planning and decision-making process for major developments, which:
  - is institutionally and legally cumbersome;
  - is adversarial rather than collaborative in its approach to planning and consultation; and
  - lacks public confidence (eg, the compensation for compulsory purchase of land is arguably not equitable);
- a concentration of the UK population and economic development in the south of England, especially around London, which has led to overcrowding and congestion, thereby straining the infrastructure, while many of the sources for public service delivery (eg, power generation and water) are located in the north and west of the country; and
- the flawed arrangements for the privatisation of public service assets in the 1980s and 1990s, whereby the privatised entity became owner of the freehold of the land that it occupies but is not responsible for investment in any access infrastructure needed (eg, the rail and road connections to transport passengers and/or freight to and from the privatised terminal). This is in contrast to most other countries, which use the 'landlord model', whereby the government or state owns the freehold, and leases land to private entities to invest in and operate terminals – a model that leads to more holistic infrastructure planning and development.

The result has been sub-optimal investment in UK infrastructure over the past 50 years, and a somewhat incoherent and inconsistent approach to regional and sectorial initiatives.

By way of example:

- there have been no new vehicular bridges built over the River Thames – except for replacements when the old bridges fell down – inside the circle formed by the M25 motorway around London since the invention of the motor car;
- there are twice as many bridges in Paris crossing the River Seine within the area of the Boulevard Péripherique as there are within the London Inner Orbital road, when both the river distances and the populations living within these areas are comparable. Furthermore, most of the bridges in Paris are 2 × 2 lanes, whereas those in London are 1 × 1 lanes;
- more people pass through Waterloo Station each day than pass through Heathrow, yet Heathrow is commercially quite developed, while Waterloo (like other London train terminals for that matter) is not;
- there is only one, somewhat indirect, cross-London main railway line, whereas there are 10 mainline terminals. Most major international cities have cross-city rail links. In short, London offers sub-optimal east-west and north-south linkage by rail; and

- the main airport for London, Heathrow, is located to the west, the direction of the prevailing wind. Consequently, at most times the take-off and landing traffic over-flies highly populated central London, with all the environmental, air pollution, noise and accident risks that that brings.

This all makes any programme for future infrastructure investment in the United Kingdom daunting.

Unfortunately, the planners have generated and proposed a series of projects which, when viewed in the light of some of the financing criteria mentioned in earlier chapters, raise some significant challenges. These projects also arguably attempt to push boundaries beyond what some might consider financially prudent.

The case histories discussed later in this chapter describe some of the challenges faced. However, some explanation as to how UK utilities were privatised in the first place is pertinent at this point, as this had an impact on how some of the case histories developed.

2. UK privatised utilities and the Regulatory Asset Base model

The United Kingdom's infrastructure assets privatised in the late 1980s/early 1990s are as shown in Figure 22.1 on the next page.

It is clear from Figure 22.1 that, whereas all these assets were quoted on the London Stock Exchange following privatisation, today they are for the most part owned by private companies, themselves often controlled by unquoted, non-UK domiciled entities.

This raises issues of regulation, governance, transparency and probity, which are best described by examining, in detail, the process and outcomes for a specific sector (water) which represents a natural public service monopoly. All the other UK privatisations, however, followed a similar pattern, with comparable regulatory frameworks attached.

As alluded to above, no other major industrial nation has privatised its public service assets to the same extent as the United Kingdom.

2.1 UK water and wastewater industry

England and Wales water companies were privatised in 1989–91 by the Water Industries Act (1991). Scottish Water and Northern Ireland Water remained state-owned.

Under the act, a regulator (the Water Services Regulation Authority, or OFWAT) was created:

- to license water and sewage utilities (as 'undertakers' or 'appointees');
- to regulate the quality and standard of service to be delivered; and
- to set tariffs for customers such that the utilities can recover their costs, including the cost of operating and financing their ongoing (regulated) activities, plus the cost of enhancing the existing system and expansion.

How utilities finance their activities is left to the utilities themselves. Under the act, OFWAT has no remit to intervene in such matters.

Figure 22.1: Ownership of infrastructure assets

Sector (year of privatisation)	UK ownership	Non-UK ownership (including Channel Islands)
Airports (1986)	Manchester* Stansted* Newcastle* Cardiff*	Heathrow, Gatwick, AGS (Aberdeen, Glasgow, Southampton), Liverpool, Doncaster, Teesside, Bristol, Luton, Belfast City and International
Ports (1991)	Belfast* Bristol Newcastle/Tyne* London*	Association of British Ports (17 ports) London Gateway (2 ports) Forth Ports (4 ports) Hutchison Ports (3 ports) Peel Ports (4 ports) PD Teesport (4 ports)
Power (1990)	SSE ** Centrica**	EdF Powergen/E.ON Npower/RWE Scottish Power ENGIE
Power (high voltage transmission) (1990)	National Grid** SSE** Northern Ireland Government*	Scottish Power
Offshore transmission (2014)		Transmission Capital Partners Blue Transmission
Power distribution (1990)	SSE** Northern Ireland Government*	Scottish Power Networks UK Power networks NW Electricity Western Power Distribution Northern Powergrid
Gas transmission (1990)	National Grid** SSE**	Northern Gas Networks Wales & West Utilities
Water (1991)	Southwest** United utilities** Severn Trent** Scottish Water *	Thames Water, Affinity Water, Northumbria, Wessex, Yorkshire, Bournemouth, South East, Southern, Anglia, Bristol, Cambridge, Sutton and East Surrey
Railway operators (1994)	Stagecoach** First Group**	Arriva GoVia Abellio Heathrow Express Eurostar CTRL/HS1
Metros operators	Transport for London*	Manchester Nottingham Newcastle Crossrail 1 (under construction)

* municipal/state-owned ** London Stock Exchange-quoted

Source: author (2015)

Water and sewerage customers, if they are connected to a utility's network have, by law, to pay the water/sewerage bill, as and when presented. Hence, the privatised water/sewerage utilities are natural public service monopolies.

To represent customer interests more directly and to protect and promote their interests, the Water Industries Act created regional Consumer Councils for Water, to whom customers can relate locally (rather than to OFWAT) when customer problems arise.

Ongoing utilities providing a monopoly service are low risk enterprises, so much of their finance is raised as long-term debt via the bond markets. To encourage financial sustainability, all the water utilities, under Condition F of their licence (Paragraph 6A6(1)), are required to maintain an investment grade rating as defined by Standard & Poor's (S&P), Moody's and Fitch.

At privatisation (1991), most water utilities had S&P ratings of around AA- (ie, well into investment grade) and their balance sheets reflected less than 50% debt. Today (2017), the picture is quite different, with the average S&P rating significantly lower (BBB+), just above 'junk' bond status, with balance sheet debt between 65% and 80%, and even higher.

To date, though, no water utility has had its licence revoked for failure to achieve investment grade status. Indeed, rail franchises apart, no UK public service utility has had its licence revoked for unsatisfactory performance since privatisation 25 years ago. Some commentators argue that OFWAT sets water tariffs to ensure that utilities can achieve this financial status, rather than setting tariffs at levels that reflect the cost of the service provided.

Following privatisation, the privatised utilities were quoted on the London Stock Exchange, and thereby fell under the corporate and financial governance regime imposed by that market and public scrutiny of their affairs (eg, annual general meetings for shareholders, who could buy/sell shares on the market, when shareholders/customers could call directors to account and comment on executive pay).

Since 1991, however, 13 out of 17 major water utilities (one of which, Dwr Cymru, is now a not-for-profit entity) have become private companies and been withdrawn from the London Stock Exchange, so are unquoted.

Furthermore, most of these unquoted companies have, as their ultimate owners, non-UK investors or investment funds, many domiciled in offshore tax havens. In the latter case, OFWAT requires, under Condition P of the licence, that the licensee provide the identity and support of an accountable 'ultimate controller'. How effective this condition might be in case of failure or any significant event remains untested.

In setting tariffs, OFWAT requires the utilities to present every five years business plans and projections for the next five years. The utilities then negotiate and agree the tariffs to charge to customers with OFWAT.

As of December 2014, the tariffs for the 2015–19 price review ('PR14') were agreed and enacted. (For Thames Water, this process also included the tariffs to be paid to Tideway, the new utility charged with implementing the Thames Tideway Tunnel (see section 3 below).)

In calculating what it believes to be justifiable tariffs, OFWAT employs the Regulatory Asset Base (RAB) model. The origins of the RAB model go back to the privatisation of state-owned UK public service utilities in 1989–91.

At privatisation, the RAB for each utility was determined by the average market value of the privatised utility's shares on the London Stock Exchange for the first 200 days after privatisation, plus the book value (or market value, in the context of bonds) of the utility's outstanding long-term debt, to arrive at the value of the enterprise.

After the first year of privatisation, the RAB value for each utility was increased by the retail price index (RPI), which, together with the costs of new capital investment undertaken in that year, less depreciation on existing assets, determined the regulatory capital value (RCV), notionally representing the value of the utility.

Sometimes, OFWAT would, instead of using RPI as reflecting increases in prices and costs due to inflation, impose an annual RPI – [x] factor, as an incentive for the utility to become more efficient.

OFWAT also has a duty under the Water Industries Act to ensure that the utilities can finance their activities, so OFWAT allows the utilities to include, as a component of tariffs, an agreed return on capital based upon their individual RCV.

The return on capital is determined by applying a weighted average cost of capital (WACC) multiple to the RCV, the WACC being calculated by OFWAT assuming levels of debt and equity (ie, 'leverage', as defined by OFWAT) for a notionally efficient water utility, and using an econometric capital asset pricing model for the cost of debt and equity. An allowance for tax is also included.

2.2 Flaws of the RAB model

Overall, the RAB model displays flaws in the six areas discussed below.

(a) *Corporate governance*

Since 2000, many UK privatised water utilities have been taken over by investment funds and removed from the London Stock Exchange. Furthermore, OFWAT has no powers with regard to how the utilities arrange their affairs and finance themselves. Hence, such utilities can avoid certain aspects of governance and management accountability – for instance, they:

- adopt labyrinthine corporate structures. Thus, Anglian Water and Thames Water (and, indeed, Heathrow – see section 4 below) today both have seven to 10 corporate layers between the licensee and the shareholders, whereas after privatisation, when they were quoted companies, there were only up to two layers;
- adopt 'tax optimisation' structures, using shareholder loans at excessive interest rates to minimise tax liabilities (in effect, to extract dividends as interest payments before tax). Typically, shareholder loans, representing owners' equity injection, may be at 10%–15% interest, when market rates for debt are 5%–7%. The highest seen has been 21% for Wales & West Utilities, a UK gas transmission utility, in 2008–10;
- leverage their balance sheets to unsustainable levels, given that OFWAT cannot intervene in the utilities' finances; and

- may be owned and controlled by funds domiciled in tax havens such as Luxembourg (Thames Water) and Hong Kong/Cayman Islands (Northumbria and Anglia Water), which obscures share transfers and their values, as well as raises corporate governance issues.

Consequently, today such utilities are corporately weaker and less able to sustain downturns or exceptional events.

(b) ***Costs of finance***

In assessing the costs of finance which utilities incur for new investment projects, the leverage (or level of debt) assumed by OFWAT in its cost-of-capital (ie, WACC) calculations does not reflect the actual level of debt in the utilities' balance sheets.

OFWAT assumes a level of debt of, say, 60%–65%, as opposed to balance sheet debt proportions of 80%–90%. Arguably, the result is that OFWAT overestimates the WACC to the utilities' profit.

This issue is not unique to the UK water sector: it arises across the board for all UK utility sectors.

(c) ***Project completion***

In contrast to PFI/PPP investments, when payments are made to the private developer only when the PPP service is delivered (ie, when the project has been completed and is operational), for utilities funded under the RAB model customers pay financing costs during the construction period, as well as during service delivery. Such concept is contrary to normal private project investment principles. It is comparable to being asked in a restaurant to contribute towards the restaurant owner's financing of the dining room and kitchen equipment as soon as one sits down, rather than after a meal has been served – that is, after the service has been delivered.

In effect, therefore, under the RAB model much of the completion risk has been passed from the utility to its customers. The incentive for contractors to achieve project completion to time and cost specifications is now much diminished, if not eliminated. Furthermore, customers cannot manage, control or mitigate such risks. Overall, the RAB model represents a significant misallocation of risk.

(d) ***Funding commitment***

The RAB model neglects the need to have all the funding committed at the outset of construction – a fundamental principle of successful project financing (see the failure of the CTRL/HS1 project in this regard).

Furthermore, infrastructure projects never proceed to plan during construction, so the funding package needs to be flexible.

This is no problem for equity and bank debt, the latter's availability being assured through the payment of commitment fees and the funds drawn down, when needed. But this is not the case for bonds. The full amount of a bond issue becomes available for use at the date of issue, so any surpluses not used that day can only be put on deposit until required. This is financially inefficient and expensive.

(e) ***Environmental considerations***

Since the RAB model is designed to attract bond finance, environmental, social impact and climate change issues relating to the project, so funded, may be circumvented, or less stringently applied than when a project is funded with commercial bank loans, which must comply with the Equator Principles (a framework for determining, assessing and managing environmental and social risk in projects).

Any protection as provided via the UN Principles of Responsible Investment, to which many asset and pension fund managers are signatories, cover corporate governance issues only, with no, or little, impact on environmental, social and climate change issues. Any initiatives and accepted methodology to assign green ratings to bond issues, as for credit ratings, remain in their infancy, although the issue of 'green bonds' provides an initial step in this direction.

(f) ***Tax***

Over the past 10 to 20 years, UK governments have provided companies with a tax incentive to invest in assets of production by allowing them to 'bring forward', or accelerate, depreciation allowances – a cost that can be counted against tax – such that in the short term there is a reduction in corporation tax, but in the longer term, when this measure will reflect lower depreciation charges (and assuming corporation tax does not change in the interim), higher liabilities for tax will arise.

In balance sheet terms, this incentive is expressed as a 'deferred liability', and an analysis of UK water utilities shows such amounts to be significant – for instance, the deferred liability for Thames Water is just under £1 billion. Again, this characteristic does not apply to the UK water sector only, but to other private public services too.

Some commentators argue, however (and rightly so), that a (water) utility, whose investment programme should be dictated by the service obligations of its licence, does not need such an incentive at the taxpayers' expense.

3. Case history 1 – Thames Water and Thames Tideway Tunnel

3.1 Background

Historically, when it rained heavily in central London, the sewers – built in Victorian times – could not always cope with the extra volume of storm water. The proliferation of hard concrete surfaces in modern developments has not helped this phenomenon. As a result, such wet-weather flows, which may involve mostly rainwater rather than untreated effluent, were on occasion, when the sewers and the water treatment plants were full to capacity, passed into the Thames as combined sewer outflows.

In 2005–6 an expert team in water and flooding – comprising the utility Thames Water (TWUL), the Environment Agency, the Department for Environment Food & Rural Affairs (also known as Defra, the over-arching ministry for water services, TWUL and the Environment Agency), the Greater London Authority and private consultants, as well as OFWAT as observer – studied the problem and published its results in the Thames Tideway Strategic Study.

The conclusions recommended building the 25km west–east, 7.2m diameter Thames Tideway Tunnel under Central London to solve the problem of combined sewer outflows and to comply with the EU Urban Waste Water Treatment Directive.

The capital cost estimate was £1.7 billion, with expected economic benefits of £3–5 billion. This proposal represented the best answer to the problem considering the technologies available at the time.

As the project was in London, it was naturally the responsibility of TWUL, under its licence, to build the tunnel. However, TWUL failed to do so, and over subsequent years it became less able financially to support such a project, not least because of new debt it had raised to repay the acquisition debt used in the takeover by the Kemble/Macquarie consortium in 2006–7 (see below).

In addition, TWUL's inaction in building the tunnel over subsequent years raised the prospect that the EU Court of Justice would fine the UK government for breach of the EU Urban Waste Water Treatment Directive.

By 2010–12 it was clear that TWUL was significantly financially weaker than in 2005–6.

Figure 22.2: TWUL balance sheet values

Year	2005	2012	2015	2016*
Shareholder funds (£million)	1,661	1,401	1,439	3,113
Long-term debt (£million)	1,661	8,050	10,020	9,928

* = *first year under the International Financial Reporting Standards*

Some explanation, therefore, is pertinent as to how this deterioration in TWUL's finances came about.

TWUL is the company licensed by OFWAT to deliver water and sewage services in London and the Thames Valley. By a significant margin, TWUL is the largest England and Wales private water utility, with around 15 million customers.

In November 1989, TWUL was privatised and thereafter its shares were quoted on the London Stock Exchange. TWUL remained a quoted company until 2000, when RWE, the German power utility, acquired TWUL. Thereafter TWUL was removed from the exchange.

In December 2006, RWE sold TWUL for £5.1 billion cash to Kemble/Macquarie, a consortium of Macquarie Infrastructure Funds and other pension funds, domiciled in Luxembourg,

At the time, TWUL's debt stood at £2.9 billion, so this, with the £5.1 billion cash, gave TWUL an enterprise value of £8 billion. Following the sale to Kemble/Macquarie, the structure of TWUL became as shown in Figure 22.3, with 10 corporate layers between the shareholders and the licensed water company.

Figure 22.3: Thames Water Utilities (post-RWE sale 2006–2007)

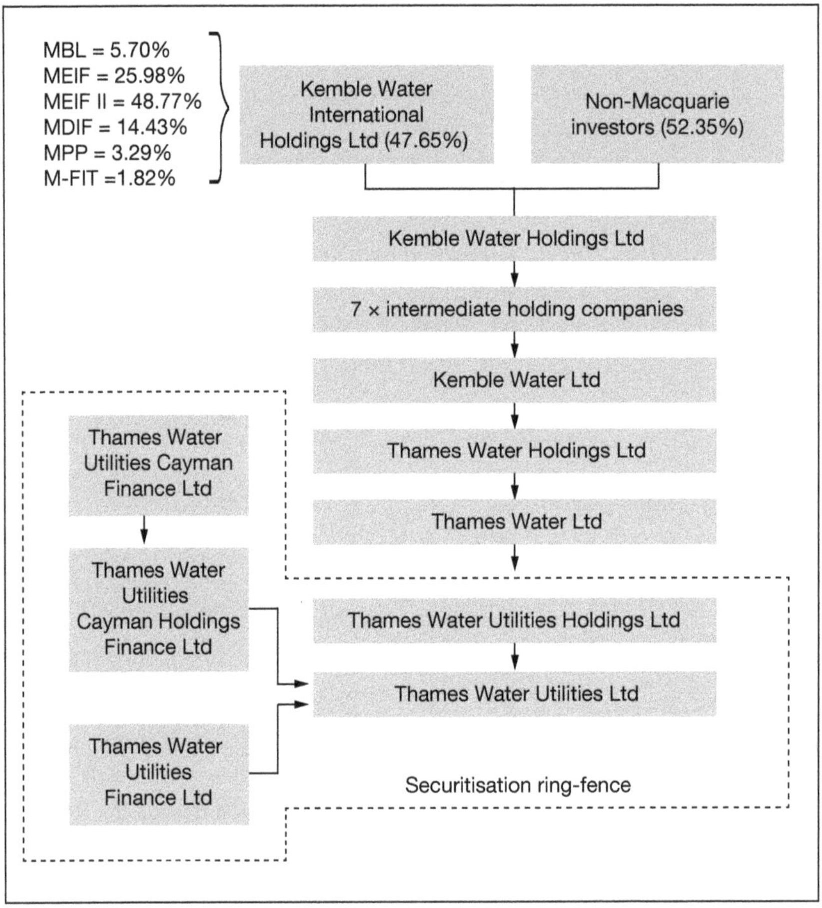

Source: OFWAT February 2007; Thames Water (Kemble) Finance plc – Floating Rate; Note (FRN) Prospectus 2012 (adapted by author)

Subsequently, it emerged that the £5.1 billion cash takeover of TWUL by Kemble/Macquarie had, in fact, been funded with £2.3 billion shareholder funds or equity (ie, cash), plus £2.8 billion of acquisition debt (from a third party). In effect, the takeover by Kemble/Macquarie had been a leveraged buy-out.

Further, in completing the TWUL takeover, Kemble/Macquarie had created a new TWUL subsidiary, Thames Water Utilities Cayman Finance Ltd, a Cayman-registered company (see Figure 22.3).

Then, TWUL's existing listed bonds, raised earlier by Thames Water Utilities Finance Ltd when owned by RWE, were migrated to Thames Water Cayman, and additional debt to repay the £2.8 billion acquisition debt was raised by Thames Water Cayman as bonds under a £10 billion 'securitisation' programme.

OFWAT was aware of this funding arrangement for the takeover, so to protect customers, it demanded that TWUL have its regulated activities ring-fenced, imposing the condition that the acquisition debt could be serviced (interest and repayment) only from TWUL dividends or unregulated TWUL cash flows (see securitisation ring-fence in Figure 22.3).

Notwithstanding the cash flow and rating covenants and ring-fences imposed by OFWAT, the Cayman company raised over £2 billion in bonds, using TWUL's credit status, over subsequent years to repay the debt used to purchase itself – a classic 'private equity' mechanism.

The outcome of this arrangement was that, when TWUL was being pressed by the UK government and the European Union in 2010–12 to build the Tideway Tunnel (five to seven years after failing to do so), TWUL was so indebted after repayment of the acquisition debt that it faced a dilemma.

TWUL could not fund the tunnel from its own resources, unless it strengthened its balance sheet by issuing more capital (an option rejected by TWUL's owners as it would weaken the return on investment), so TWUL turned to the government/Defra for help.

Meanwhile, by 2012 – six years on from the original Thames Tideway Strategic Study – no authoritative, independent assessment had been undertaken to confirm the need for the Tideway Tunnel. But by 2012–13, experts were arguing that the tunnel was unnecessary.

Indeed, with the investment that TWUL itself had made in the interim years on upgrading sewage treatment plants and the construction of the Lee Tunnel in East London (opened in 2015), the Tideway (the part of the River Thames subject to tides) was much cleaner and had not breached, at least significantly, if at all, Tideway-specific environmental standards for quality since the end of 2013, thereby complying with EU regulations. Furthermore, studies indicated that there appeared to be inconsistencies in the analytical model used by the government (Defra/Environment Agency) to justify the Tideway Tunnel.

(Note that:

- the Tideway Tunnel project serves only central London, downstream of Hammersmith;
- arguably, the population of this area of central London has not been growing since 2005–6; and
- by 2015–17 the consumption of water per head, and therefore demand for sewerage, had been decreasing as well.)

Rather than build the £4 billion tunnel, experts recommended that easier, lower risk and cheaper alternatives could be undertaken by TWUL, such as:

- separating sewers;
- controlling the sewer/interceptor connections in real time;
- using dispersed detention tanks;
- installing floating booms to collect rubbish; and
- adopting sustainable drainage systems throughout London, to preserve the quality of the Tideway.

However, both the government and TWUL consistently brushed aside such options, even though government wildlife experts had found that over 120 different species of fish and marine life were making their homes in the tidal Thames. The river's regeneration was confirmed by the Zoological Society of London, which received records of 2,732 mammals (seals, etc) sighted in the Thames between 2005 and 2015, commenting that "the river is springing back to life".

Nevertheless, TWUL and the government pressed ahead with plans for the Tideway Tunnel. It was then that the byzantine project structure for implementing the tunnel was devised, with OFWAT being directed by the government in August 2015 to issue a licence, following a bidding process, to Bazalgette Tunnel Ltd, named after the engineer who built much of London's sewers in Victorian times. Subsequently, Bazalgette assumed the public name of 'Tideway'.

3.2 The Tideway Tunnel's commercial and financial structure

The physical process of dealing with combined sewer outflows and the project structure for the Tideway Tunnel is as described below.

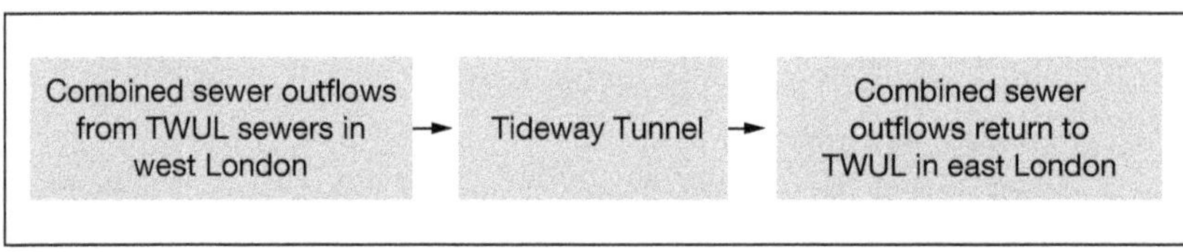

TWUL will physically deliver combined sewer outflows, which otherwise might be passed into the Thames, to the tunnel in west London (Acton), which will transport the outflows through the tunnel to Abbey Mills (25km away in east London), where TWUL will take them back again for treatment. Therefore, Tideway, as a public utility, has only one supplier, TWUL, and only one customer, TWUL.

In line with the project structure above, the commercial and payment structure for the project is as described below.

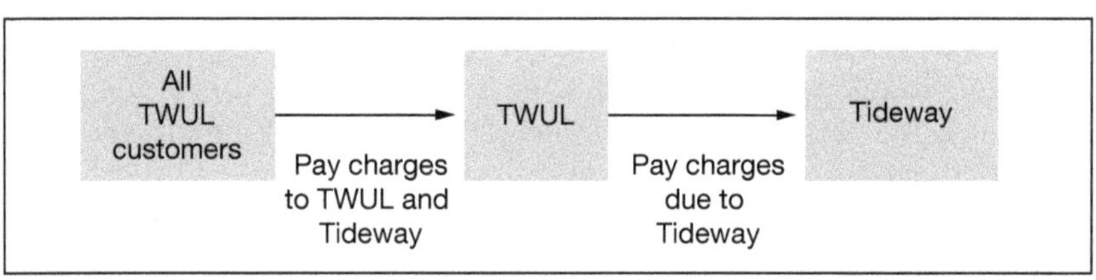

All TWUL customers, whether in London or not (eg, 50 miles away in Oxford and the Thames Valley), pay charges for the Tideway Tunnel to TWUL for onward passing to Tideway from 2016, even though the tunnel is not expected to be completed and in operation until 2023.

Initially, the charges for the tunnel were expected to be around £7 per annum per customer. However, it is expected that such costs will rise, increasing to a maximum of £70–80 per customer by 2023 and beyond.

Of the £4.2 billion (2011 prices) tunnel construction cost estimate, TWUL is responsible for funding £1.4 billion. Hence, Tideway will have to raise £2.8 billion, plus cost overruns, as a mix of shareholders' equity and loans or bonds, the latter possibly funded by pension funds.

The construction is expected to take seven years, much longer than most, if not all, private sector infrastructure projects undertaken anywhere.

Comment: This spilt of construction and completion responsibilities between Tideway and TWUL for a risky tunnelling project with a seven-year construction period raises significantly the inherent completion risks. A delay or problem for one party, which could easily arise in the interim, affects the other, even if they are corporately independent. This is a flawed structure. Furthermore, the actual construction of the tunnel is split between three contractors.

Tideway's plans for funding its part of the tunnel comprise equity (£1.2 billion estimate) made up of 40% pure equity and 60% shareholder loans (a UK tax break, as in the United Kingdom interest on such loans can be treated as a pre-tax cost), plus conventional debt. Hence, the leverage, assuming sub-debt as debt, is around 90%, whereas OFWAT assumed leverages of 65% under PR14 (its latest price review, see section 2.1 above).

Tideway's debt comprises a £1 billion revolving bank facility with 10-year maturity provided by six international banks (BTM, Crédit Agricole, Lloyds, RBC, Santander and SMBC). These banks, Santander apart, are all signatories to the Equator Principles. Arguably, however, the Tideway Tunnel financing is non-Principles compliant as it fails to address "consideration of feasible environmentally and socially preferable alternatives" as requested in Exhibit II, item b of the Principles) – unless one assumes the 2005–06 Thames Tideway Strategic Study as adequate. By contrast, the United Kingdom has 'designated status' under the Equator Principles, so could be viewed as exempt from such constraint.

The European Investment Bank has also agreed a £700 million loan to Tideway, the largest loan the bank has ever awarded in this sector.

Hence, the financing plan for Tideway uses a mix of equity and bank loan to cover early costs. Then, once a quantum of bank debt has been achieved, the bank debt will be refinanced with a series of long-term bond issues – that is, using the RAB model.

Comment: The flaws of the RAB model are (as discussed in section 2.2 above) that:

- the full project funding is not committed at the outset of construction;
- when it comes to refinancing the bank debt, the bond market may be unreceptive and the interest rate much higher than today;
- on such refinancing, Tideway bonds must achieve investment grade to comply with its licence. That may be impossible;
- given the interdependency of TWUL and Tideway's performance, any impact on Tideway's rating will affect TWUL's rating likewise, and vice versa; and
- such financing structure circumvents environmental, social impact and climate change constraints.

Further, in the event of any of the above outcomes, the committed bank debt, which is limited in amount, will be insufficient to complete the project.

To mitigate this problem in part, the UK government (via Defra) has provided a contingency funding facility (ie, a loan) for up to £500 million to provide funds in the event of a 'market disruption' event, which prevents investment grade Tideway bonds from being available or issued, and until markets are restored.

However, there is no fallback position or plan B for when the markets are not restored. The government could have to pick up the balance of cost to completion amounting to billions of pounds sterling, as well as have an outstanding loan to Tideway. This represents a potential liability for the government.

There is also a tripartite liaison agreement between Tideway, TWUL and Defra, under which Tideway can act only with the agreement of the other two parties. Consequently, Tideway is far from separate or independent. Any event which affects Tideway's ratings will impact on TWUL, and vice versa.

There are two additional project agreements:

- a support contract with Defra (Supplemental Compensation Agreement) for uninsurable risks; and
- a support contract with Defra (Contingency Equity Support) which provides additional equity in the event of excessive cost overruns requiring additional equity to support additional debt needs.

Overall, the suite of project/Tideway legal documents provided continuous employment for 20 to 40 lawyers for some months, if not years, for a situation (assuming that the tunnel is to be built) where a simple corporate funding, comprising an increase or issue of new TWUL equity, could have sufficed.

3.3 Conclusion

The result is a flawed corporate structure and an incomplete funding package for implementing the Tideway Tunnel. In effect, the construction/completion risk is being left with Tideway/TWUL customers, whereas the whole justification for privatising water services was for the private sector to carry such risks.

The project's contractual responsibilities, as opposed to risks, are spread between Tideway contractors, Tideway and TWUL. Failure in one could bring down all the others, leaving customers exposed.

Lastly, the funding structure leaves Defra and/or TWUL customers, plus UK taxpayers, with potentially huge contingent liabilities amounting to, possibly, billions of pounds sterling, when cost overruns or construction failures arise – all this when technical evidence now suggests that the project is an unnecessary risk and expense, when cheaper, lower risk alternatives are available.

4. Case history 2 – Heathrow Airport Expansion (Runway 3)

4.1 Background

In 1986 the British Airports Authority (BAA), which owned and controlled all the United Kingdom's major civil airports, was privatised under the Airports Act as BAA plc, which remained quoted on the London Stock Exchange until 2006. Accordingly, BAA was subject to public scrutiny and accountability (via annual general meetings, stock exchange rules, transparency on executive pay, etc).

In May 2006, a consortium led by Ferrovial (Spain), a major contractor and infrastructure concessionaire quoted on the Madrid Stock Exchange, paid £12 billion for BAA, a 78% premium (ie, £5 billion) on the BAA share price at the time. Ferrovial also inherited £4.3 billion of existing BAA debt and liabilities.

One reason why Ferrovial was prepared to pay such a high price was that the difference/premium (known as 'goodwill') could then be written off in Spain as a cost against tax in one year (this is now outlawed under EU law). (In the United Kingdom such goodwill is normally capitalised into the balance sheet over an extended period.)

Figure 22.4: Heathrow Airport (Gatwick and Edinburgh sold in 2011)

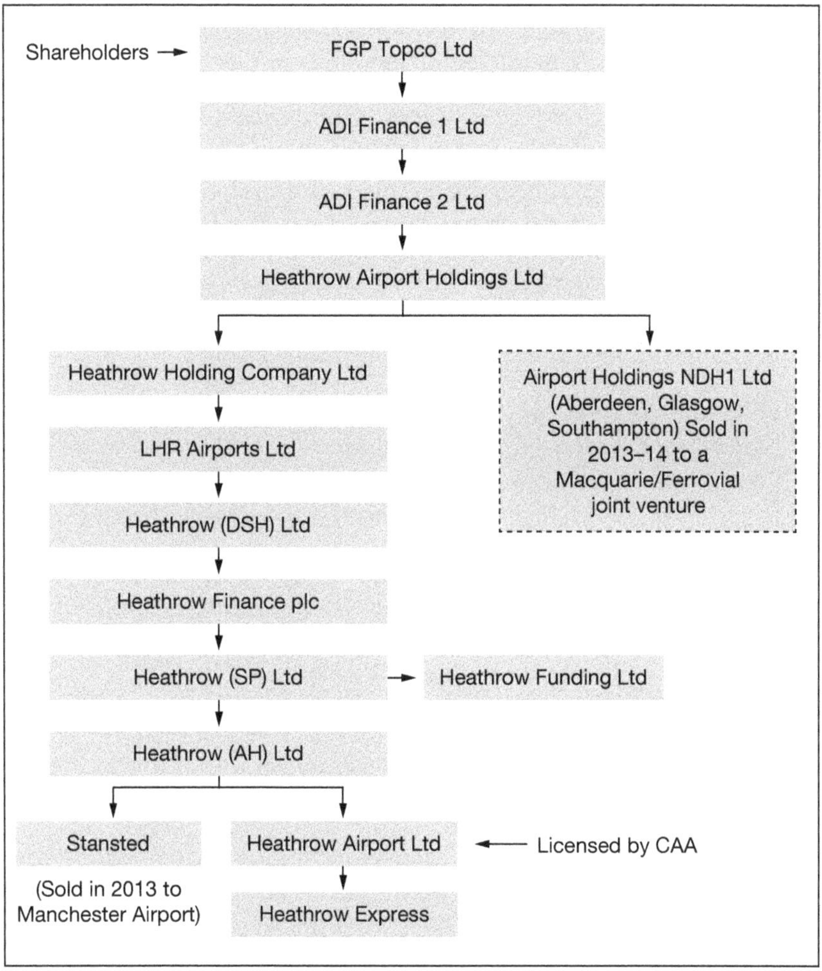

Source: Heathrow Finance plc – Prospectus, December 2012 (adapted by author)

The Ferrovial consortium (represented by FGP Topco in the corporate structure in Figure 22.4) comprised:

- Ferrovial, 62%;
- Caisse de Placement du Quebec, 28%; and
- GIC (Baker St), Singapore, 10%.

In the new multi-layer structure for BAA, there are 10 corporate layers between the shareholding company and the licensed BAA (see also in that regard Thames Water in section 3 above). Overall, such a structure is not conducive to transparency and normal corporate governance, and can be justified only as a construct to minimise tax.

As confirmation of this, before the acquisition by Ferrovial in 2006, BAA was paying £100–150 million per annum in corporation tax to the UK government. Since 2006, tax revenues have dropped off markedly, to the extent of providing BAA/Ferrovial with significant tax credits – that is, no tax liability, mainly due to the raising of new debt and increasing BAA's tax-deductible interest payments.

As with the Thames Water takeover by Kemble/ Macquarie, the BAA takeover was funded by £4.3 billion of 'cash' equity and £7.7 billion of acquisition debt and sub-debt. Overall, therefore, after the takeover BAA's debt burden had risen from £4.3 billion to around £9 billion, plus £3 billion of sub-debt and equivalent liabilities. Like Thames Water, the takeover had effectively been a leveraged buy-out.

While the takeover had no immediate impact on BAA's performance or quality of service, it more than doubled BAA's indebtedness and made the company less sustainable financially. Indeed, the financial markets became aware of this weakness, and for a time the future existence of BAA was in some doubt.

Over the next few years, BAA had to reduce its debt mountain (around £12 billion overall), especially as it was also under threat of losing its investment grade status on its bonds, a condition of its licence. Firstly, it refinanced its acquisition debt with longer-term funding. This did not in itself reduce BAA's debt exposure, but it spread out the repayments and reduced interest costs. However, dividends to shareholders were not paid in 2007/8.

In 2009, following an inquiry by the Competition Commission, BAA had to sell Gatwick Airport for £1.5 billion, and in addition raised £500 million of new equity. Against this, BAA had had ongoing capital expenditures of around £1 billion per year, so overall long-term debt did not decline.

In 2012–13, BAA, now known as Heathrow Airport Holdings, sold:

- Edinburgh Airport to GIP/City Airport for £807 million;
- Stansted Airport to Manchester Airport Group for £1.5 billion; and
- Aberdeen, Southampton and Glasgow Airports to a 50/50 joint venture between Ferrovial and Macquarie (AGS) for £1.045 billion.

Reviewing the finances of BAA/Heathrow for the period 2006–15 shows the following:

- In 2005 (pre-takeover), shareholder equity was £5.5 billion;
- In 2015, shareholder equity was £1.6 billion (29% of 2005 value);

- In 2005, BAA's long-term debt amounted to £4.3 billion; and
- In 2015, BAA/Heathrow Airport Holdings' long-term debt amounted to £12.7 billion.

By 2016, Heathrow Airport Holdings was owned by:

- Ferrovial, 25%;
- Qatar Holdings, 20%;
- Caisse de Placement du Quebec, 12.6%;
- GIC (Baker St), 11.2%;
- Alinda LP (US private equity), 11.2%;
- CIC (China), 10%; and
- Universities Superannuation Scheme (United Kingdom), 10%.

As with the UK water sector, the airports regulator (the Civil Aviation Authority or CAA) is not allowed under the law to intervene in the way airports fund themselves. Nevertheless, the Civil Aviation Act 2012 states that a primary duty of the CAA is to "carry out its functions under the Act in a manner which it considers will further the interest of users of air transport services regarding the range, availability, cost and quality of airport operation services".

Meanwhile, the UK government perceived in 2012 that the long-term prosperity of London, the Southeast and, indeed, the United Kingdom depended on increased airport capacity, and so set up the Airports Commission to review capacity and demand, and to come up with an effective and deliverable solution.

With Heathrow operating to capacity already and Gatwick approaching the same situation, it was concluded that there was a need for at least one new runway to be built near London by 2030.

The main options assessed included expansions at Heathrow, Gatwick and Stansted, and a new airport on the Isle of Grain in the Thames Estuary. These were reduced down to three options, following analysis:

- Heathrow Northwest Runway Expansion (Runway 3), at a cost of £17.6 billion, plus £5 billion for access infrastructure;
- Heathrow Extended Northern Runway, at a cost of £14.4 billion, plus £5.5 billion for access infrastructure; and
- Gatwick Second Runway, at a cost £7.1 billion, plus £0.8 billion in access infrastructure.

(Airports Commission Final Report, Paragraph 11.7. Costs at 2014 values)

In July 2015, the Airports Commission recommended Heathrow Runway 3 as the preferred option, and in September 2016 the government publicly supported that recommendation. The development now moves into the planning phase with local authority permissions, etc required before implementation.

4.2 Conclusion

As these airports are private companies, any financing of these options will have to be raised against their corporate credit. The government has already indicated that it will not provide financial support. Funding of the access infrastructure may, however, receive some, or all, government financial support.

The Airports Commission received advice that the recommended option, Heathrow Runway 3, was 'financeable' with private resources, but provided no further detail. It is understood, however, that Heathrow intends to use the RAB model, as for the Tideway Tunnel, for the expansion. Given Heathrow's financially indebted status, the only other option is to re-capitalise its balance sheet.

However, as has been shown earlier in this chapter, the RAB model misallocates risk. Other flaws, particularly with respect to environmental issues (eg, noise, air pollution) also arise. Heathrow's first-line customers, the airlines, have already stated they are not prepared to pay, as they would under the RAB model, until the new runway is available for use.

Hence, it is quite possible that the option chosen by the government may not come about due to lack of a viable funding mechanism.

As an aside, the analysis of the three final options was undertaken using the government's Green Book methodology (see the chapter on the options for governments in Part 1 of this book) and used the same optimism bias factor (20%) for all options. Given that the option chosen, Heathrow Runway 3, is significantly higher risk to execute, as well as more costly, such an assumption seems unbalanced.

5. Case history 3 – Hinkley Point C and other UK nuclear power plants

5.1 Background

The United Kingdom was one of the first countries to harness nuclear power in the 1960s. Overall, by the 1980s–1990s, nuclear power represented around 20% of the country's power generation capacity. As mentioned in the chapter on nuclear power, nuclear power generation is inflexible and, hence, used to provide cheap, base load capacity. Lastly, whereas the earlier nuclear power plants (NPPs) had typically a capacity of 600 megawatts (MW) per unit, the plants available today, using current technologies, are twice as big (eg, typically 1,200–1,500MW per unit), which at least doubles the construction costs. This raises significant financing problems if they are to be funded with private capital.

When built, NPPs usually receive a 30-year operational licence before they may be required to dismantle or decommission. Many NPPs built in the 1970s–1980s have reached or are reaching the end of their licence. For many units, on inspection at this milestone, the reactor core itself has been found to be in excellent condition, while the ancillary equipment is rather tired and needs replacing. Hence, many NPPs have been rehabilitated and given licence extensions, which puts off the day of costly decommissioning.

The United Kingdom built 19 NPPs, representing around 11,000MW of capacity, made up of:

- four units of the early, graphite-moderated (2 × 217MW and 2 x 490MW) Magnox type;
- 14 units (615MW each) of advanced gas reactors (AGRs); and
- one (1,198MW) pressurised water reactor (PWRs).

The Magnox reactors have been retired, and the remainder have forecast closure dates between 2023 and 2035.

The AGRs were effectively unique to the UK market: they included innovative online refuelling, but international sales were minimal. PWRs are the most common design internationally of that era, and many have been built and are still operational.

All the above NPPs were built under the ownership of the state-owned Central Electricity Generating Board. In 1990, the UK power generation and distribution sector was privatised, and the family of UK NPPs were vested into a new utility, British Energy, which was quoted on the London Stock Exchange.

All went well for a while, as much of British Energy's business was base load and enjoyed steady demand. However, after a while, the government started to introduce trading mechanisms, resulting in a 'pool' regime, which required generators to be much more flexible. This undermined British Energy's business and before long it was headed for bankruptcy.

Given the nature of British Energy's business, the government stepped in to help restructure the company. In due course, it was sold to state-controlled Electricité de France (EdF), the largest power utility in the world with 58 units operational in France.

Before long, the ageing AGRs were meeting their licence limitations, so it was decided to close down and decommission the existing AGRs and install replacements over a period.

To do so was, in cost terms, a significant investment in new plants. EdF was first off the mark with a planned new NPP at Hinkley Point, the site of an existing NPP, with two European pressurised reactor (EPR) units of 1,670MW each.

Two further projects have been proposed:

- NuGen (ENGIE and Toshiba) at Moorside, Cumbria with a capacity of 2 × 1,200MW AP1000 (Westinghouse/Toshiba technology); and
- Horizon (GE and Hitachi) at Wylfa and Oldbury (two AGR sites), with a capacity of 2 × 1,350MW advanced boiling water reactor.

5.2 Conclusion

EdF's Hinkley Point project is much more advanced than the other two, but they all face formidable financing problems. Such NPPs take at least six to seven years to build, and the RAB model, where financing costs are paid during construction (as for the Tideway Tunnel and, possibly, Heathrow) does not apply. The developers carry full completion risk.

To provide some risk mitigation, the government has agreed, in advance, that it will support Hinkley Point with a 'contracts for differences' sales contract, subject to EU state-aid approval, starting from 2025 (the estimated completion date) at a 'strike price' of £92.5 per megawatt hour (MWh). This compares with £75/MWh for the base load price in November 2016 and £150/MWh for offshore wind.

The government has also agreed to provide a £2 billion loan guarantee for the finance, although the overall investment cost for the two EPR units is estimated at around £16 billion.

Against this backdrop:

- it is clear that the balance of funding required for Hinkley Point remains daunting;
- with respect to equity funding from EdF, and possible partners, EdF's share price in 2017 is one-tenth of its pre-financial crisis level;
- EdF has closure/rehabilitation commitments to its existing 58 NPPs in France over the next few years; and
- to date, no EPR has been completed and is in operation. Completion of units in France (Flamanville) and Finland (Olkiluoto 3) have been delayed and are over budget, although two EPRs in China appear on target. Indeed, EdF has stated that it will not commit to build any more EPRs until Olkiluoto and Flamanville are complete.

In addition, the Hinkley Point investment by EdF has come under significant political opposition in France in recent months.

It comes as no surprise, therefore, that in February 2017 the UK Lords Economic Committee opined that the UK authorities should prepare a plan B. All three UK NPP developments face daunting financing challenges.

6. Case history 4 – HS2

6.1 Background

HS2 is a (very) high speed (up to 400kph, while France's *train à grande vitesse*, better known as TGV, peaks at 320kph) railway linking London, Birmingham, Manchester, Leeds and the East Midlands. The line is to be built in a 'y' configuration, with London at the bottom and Manchester and Leeds at the top, west and east respectively.

Construction on the first phase is expected to commence in 2017 between London and Birmingham with overall completion between 2027 and 2032.

In 2010, the cost estimates for the overall scheme were around £32 billion. By 2015, this had been revised upwards to £55 billion.

HS3 is another proposed high-speed link, cross-Pennine between Manchester and Leeds, to complement HS2. Cost estimates are elusive.

6.2 Conclusion

It is generally agreed that extra rail passenger capacity is required between London, the Midlands and the North. HS2 is expected to double, if not treble, that capacity, once completed.

However, high speed trains are expensive transport modes. They are expensive to build –possibly twice as much per kilometre built as conventional inter-city rail – and, again, twice as costly to maintain. Indeed, investment and operational costs may be higher still, because of the proposed HS2 speed.

Studies have shown that, for high speed rail to be economically beneficial, distances of 200–250 km between stations is required. Such circumstances do not prevail to justify HS2, as planned.

Are there alternatives which may sacrifice high speed for more capacity? After all, over £50 billion on a railway investment, which, once construction starts, will have to be completed if it is to serve any economic purpose, is a lot of money.

The studies underpinning the rationale for HS2 reflected many of the characteristics seen in previous case histories cited above. Optimism and engineering vanity prevail, when modesty might be a preferable virtue.

Commentators argue that:

- detailed examination of the possibility of installing double-decker passenger trains, as are used on many continental railways, might provide the extra capacity sought. Strengthening bridges, lowering track-beds and raising electrification gantries might provide a cheaper, lower risk alternative; and
- modern digital train control has been shown to allow up to 30%, possibly more, train throughput per kilometre than current control systems.

Will HS2 be another monument to engineering folly? One wonders.

Overall, UK infrastructure planners and decision makers have set some daunting technical and financial challenges with the above projects, which may leave future generations with economic nightmares and financial liabilities. Are such high risks justified?

Concluding comments

In summary, infrastructure project finance and public-private partnership (PPP) concessions:

- have long-term maturities – long-term business requires long-term funding;
- have most of their costs and revenues in local currency – to avoid currency exchange risk, it is worth maximising the funding in local currency;
- are transactions with complex detail – so the structure and terms of finance must by contrast be simple and transparent; and
- cover investment in public service assets and the delivery of a public service – investors and lenders should ensure that they maintain the highest standards of probity.

What follows are general guidelines and advice.

Firstly, for sponsors, lenders and investors in infrastructure project finance and PPP concessions:

- Use your common sense! Would you personally lend or invest in the deal under analysis?
- Work in teams. No one expert has all the experience and knowledge to assemble the commercial and financial packages necessary to support such deals.
- Learn from precedents, and learn when to say 'no'.
- Consider the debt/equity against the overall project risks.
- Seek contractual completion undertakings or guarantees.
- Review the long-term prospects and risks associated with sales.
- Review the alternative supply of essential project components.
- Comply with the UN Principles for Responsible Investment and the Equator Principles.
- If the opportunity arises, go and visit the project site.
- Monitor the deal closely after financial close.

Secondly, for governments:

- Choose carefully the sector and opportunity for when to use the PPP mechanism for acquiring private investment in public services.
- Be aware that some PPP structures create contingent, and possibly direct, liabilities for government.

Lastly, lenders to infrastructure project finance and PPP concessions must:

- ensure that all funding is committed and available at financial close;
- make provision for contingencies (ie, standby equity and debt);
- impose debt service triggers and benchmarks on borrowers;
- take security over the project assets;
- impose reserve accounts on project sponsors (debt service, maintenance and insurance);
- beware the risks of capital market instruments to mitigate risk;
- include international arbitration and sovereign immunity clauses in PPP concessions; and
- engender a spirit of partnership with counterparts. Such transactions represent long-term relationships.

To conclude, a motto for project finance practitioners could be:

You can have education.
You can have talent.
You can have genius.
But the most important human attributes are determination and persistence.

(Quoted by Margaret Thatcher, as related by Carol Thatcher.)

Index

Page references to figures or tables are in italics

A/B loan mechanism, 83, 96–97, 241
accommodation projects, 253–254
  defence, 259
  government administration buildings, 257
  health and hospitals projects, 255–256
  housing, 257
  information technology (IT) projects, 258
  prisons, 258–259
  schools and advanced education, 254–255
  stadiums, 258
AES, United States, 217
African Finance Corporation, 97
Aga Khan Foundation for Economic Development, 213, 217
air traffic control (ATC) projects, 37, 204–205
airports projects, 201
  access infrastructure risks, 202
  air traffic control, 204–205
  costs and completion risks, 201
  currency risks, 202
  in Ecuador, 203–204
  environmental risks, 202
  in Europe, 202, 203
  revenues risks, 201–202
  in Saudi Arabia, 204
  traffic risks, 201
  in United Kingdom, 202, 274–278
Almond Valley, Seafield & Esk Water Project, Scotland, 246
Alsthom, France, 180
Ambac, United States, 246
Anglian Water, United Kingdom, 266
Angola model, 92, 95
Aon plc, United Kingdom, 84
APG, Netherlands, 108, 174
Asian Development Bank, 156, 223
Assen–Zuidbroek highway project, 174
Aucoven, Mexico, 169–170
Australia, 228
  bridges and tunnels projects, 182
availability payments, 32, 48, 58, 75, 128, 145, 164, 170–173, 181, 213, 253, 254
  v cash tolls, 173–175
  points system, 171–172
Azerbaijan International Operating Company (AIOC), 240
Azerbaijan–Georgia–Turkey oil pipeline project, 240

Babcock & Brown of Australia, 89
Baku–Tbilisi–Ceyhan oil pipeline project, 240, 241
balance sheet, 26, 30, 33–34, 68, 80, 124–125
  issues, 48–50
  off balance sheet, 27, 28, 45, 48–50, 172, 174
  on balance sheet, 27, 28, 48, 49, 172, 254
Basel III guidelines, 30, 32, 33–34, 93, 175
BASF, Germany, 242
bid costs, 155–156
bid preparation and notices
  competitive dialogue, 155
  evaluation and detailed negotiation, 154–155
  pre-qualification, 154
  preparation, 154
  tendering, 154
Bina Istra highway project, Croatia, 172–173
Birmingham BioPower, United Kingdom, 236–237
Birmingham North Relief Road (BNRR), United Kingdom, 94, 167–168
Black Sea Development Bank, 97
Blue Stream gas pipeline project, Russia–Turkey, 241
Bogota Bus Way project, Colombia, 193
bonds, 29–30, 32–33, 60–61, 106–111, *107*, 187, 248, 266
  and bank funding, 174–175
  bond wraps, 109–110
  drawbacks, 107–108
  investment grade bonds, 108
  long-term, 29, 30, 60, 66, 188, 273
  performance bonds, 72, 140–141, 143
  ratings and ratings agencies, 108–109, *109*
  and regulatory asset base model, 267–268
Boyabat hydropower project, Turkey, 218
BP, Azerbaijan, 240
bridges and tunnels projects, 177
  in Australia, 182
  completion risks, 177
  currency risks, 178
  environmental risks, 177
  in Europe, 181
  international borders risks, 178
  land acquisition risks, 177
  traffic risks, 177
  in United Kingdom, 178–181
British Airports Authority (BAA), 274–277
British Energy, 222, 279
Bucharest, water project, Romania, 247
build, operate and transfer (BOT) projects, 27, 169
build, operate, own and transfer (BOOT) projects, 27, 29
Bujagali hydropower project, Uganda, 217–218
Bulgaria, hydropower projects, 218–219
bulk purchases markets, 208

business plan, 152–153
buyer credit, 99–101, *100*, *101*

CA Metro de Caracas, Venezuela, 191
Canada
air traffic control in, 37, 205
infrastructure project finance history, 30
capacity payment, 144
car parks, 163
risks for, 175
Caracas Metro project, Venezuela, 191
carbon credits, 226–227, 228–229
cash flow cascade, 43–44, *44*
cash flow model, 26–27, 41–45, *42*, 67, 92, 99, 101, 117, *117*, 131, 155
see also **project financing structure**
and export credit agencies, 101
and financial due diligence, 157
practical comments, 124–125
quantitative analysis *see* **quantitative analysis**
toll-road project (example), 125–129, *126–127*, *128*
cash sweeps, 32, 44, 79, 93
cash tolls, 46, 164, 165, 166, 168–169, 172–173, 180–181
v availability payment, 173–175
and debt service cover ratio, 128
Central Electricity Generating Board, 279
Central Europe, 29
roads and highways projects, 168–169
Centrale Thermique de Belle Vue, Mauritius, 236
certified emission reduction credits (CERs), 226–227, 228
Chad–Cameroon oil pipeline project, 240–241
Channel Tunnel (Eurotunnel) project, 27, 36, 166, 179–180, 261
Channel Tunnel Rail Link (CTRL) (HS1) project, 179, 187, 261
Chernobyl disaster, 223
Chevron, United States, 240
Chile, 29
roads and highways projects, 173
China, 95, 233, 280
nuclear power plants, 223
City bankers, 26
Civil Aviation Act (2012), 277
Civil Aviation Authority (CAA), 277
Clean Development Mechanism (CDM), Kyoto Protocol, 226–227
climate change issues, 77, 78, 222, 223
see also **environmental risks**
Colombia, 173
light rail and trams projects, 193
commercial bank loans, 33, 96, 103–106, 255, 268
and export credit agencies, 101
impact of financial crisis, 32
common terms agreement, 132–133
Commonwealth Development Corporation, 98
competitive dialogue, 155
complementary loan, 101
completion/construction risks
fixed project specification, 73
insuring physical asset risk, 74
penalty and incentive clauses in the construction contracts, 72–73
site acquisition and access, 73–74
turnkey contracts, 72
using experienced contractors, 73
concentrated solar power (CSP) systems, 233 234
concession agreement, 45–46, 66, 133–134, 136, 137, 139, 170, 171, 172
conditions precedent, 38, 105, 132, 143
conflicts of interest, 67, 159
construction contract
clauses of *see* **engineering, procurement and construction (EPC) contract, clauses**
general aspects, 139
Consumer Councils for Water, 265
contingency funds, 148
ContourGlobal renewable energy projects, Togo, 212, 236
contractors, selection of, 73
contracts
common terms agreement, 132–133
construction contract, 139–142
corporate identities and issues, 131–132
direct agreement, 133
implementation agreement, 133
inter-creditor agreement, 147–148
loan agreement, 146–147
operations and maintenance (O&M) contract, 142
penalty and incentive clauses in, 72–73
PPP concession agreement, 133–139
project engineer, 149
sales contract, 143–146
supply contract, 142–143
templates, 66
turnkey contracts, 72
contracts for difference (CfD), 75, 145, *146*
Convention of New York, 138, 139
Corporacion Andina de Fomento (CAF), 97
corporate debt financing, 26
see also **debt financing**
corporate governance, 82, 266–267, 268, 276
corporate guarantees, *39*, 39–41, 99, 258
assessment of creditworthiness of guarantor, 40–41
corporate identities, and contracts, 131–132
corporate tax, 132
coverage ratios, 122
Croatia, roads and highway projects, 169, 172–173
Cross City Tunnel project, Australia, 182
Cross-Israel cash toll highway, 173
cross-sector financial structures, 84–85
Crown Corporation model, Canada, 51
Croydon Tramlink project, United Kingdom, 192–193
cruise ship terminals projects, 198–199
currency convertibility and transfer, 92
currency risks, 80–81, *81*
currency swap, 81, *81*
Czech Republic, roads and highways projects, 168

Dartford Bridge project, United Kingdom, 27, 166, 178
Dartford-Thurrock Crossing Act (1998), 178
Dartford Tunnel project, United Kingdom, 178
DCT Gdansk Container Terminal, Poland, 197
debt financing, 29, 35, 48, 95

bonds, 106–111, *107*
commercial bank loans, 103–106
export credit agencies (ECAs), 98–103
international development banks, 95–97
Islamic finance, 111–112, *113–114*
leasing, 112, 115
national development banks, 97–98
offsets, 115–116
paying out by government before taking back and operating assets, 137
subordinate debt, 94
debt service cover ratio (DSCR), 78, 93, 106, 121, 124
debt-to-equity ratio, 36, 78
defaults, 32, 33, 34, 50, 102, 137
defence projects, 259
deferred liability, 268
deferred payments, 102
delivered service payment, 144, 145
design, build and finance deals, 55
design, build, finance and operate (DBFO) deals, 56, 166
design, build, finance, operate and maintain deals, 60
'designated status', 78, 273
development banks, 27, 32, 38, 89, 94, 222
see also **international financial institutions (IFIs); national development banks**
direct agreement, 133
Disi–Mudawarra water pipeline project, Jordan, 247
dividends, 41, 44, 66, 92–93, 94, 105
DONG Energy, Denmark, 242
Dubai Metro project, 192
Dubai Ports World (DPWorld), 198
due diligence, 56, 70, 82, 157, 209
see also **risks**
financial due diligence, 157
legal due diligence, 157
technical due diligence, 157
Dunkerque/Gravelines, France, 221

Earner Value Management System (EVMS), 158
earnings before interest, tax and debt amortisation (EBITDA), 41, 196
economic feasibility study, 53, 55
economic internal rate of return, 118
Ecuador, airport projects, 203–204
Electricité de France (EdF), 217, 279
EMASESA water project, Spain, 247
engineering, procurement and construction (EPC) contract, 37–38, 139–140, 145
and operations and maintenance contract, 142
engineering, procurement and construction (EPC) contract, clauses
assignment, 142
certification procedures, 140
change in law, 141
completion, 140
contract changes, 141
contract price, 140
defects liability, 141
definitions, 140
delays to completion, 140
dispute resolution, 142
early completion, 140
extensions to completion, 140
force majeure, 141
general contractor responsibilities, 141
governing law, 142
ground conditions and utilities, 141
insurances, 141
key subcontracts, 141
negotiate penalty and incentive, 72–73
payment and performance bonds, 140–141
performance warranties and liquidated damage, 140
price variations, 141
spare parts, 141
start and completion dates, 140
taxes, 141
termination, 142
transfer of title to assets, 140
enhanced property values, 186–187
Enron, United States, 108–109
environmental risks, 77–78
EON, Germany, 242
Equator Principles, 77–78, 216, 240, 268, 273
equity
in-kind contributions, 87–88
internal rate of return, 118, 120, *120*
investors, issues of, 92–94
new investment capital, 87
pinpoint, 132
private equity funds, *89*, 89–91, *90*
provided by the investors, 87
shares, 88
sovereign wealth funds, *91*, 91–92
ESA 95, 50
ESA 2010, 50
escrow account, 43, *44*, 47, 78
Eurocontrol, Belgium, 204
Europe
airport projects, 202, 203
bridges and tunnels projects, 181
infrastructure project finance history, 25–29
European Bank for Reconstruction and Development (EBRD), 169, 222–223
European Investment Bank (EIB), 48, 97, 174, 203, 241, 247, 273
project bond credit enhancement scheme, *110*, 111
European Union, 49, 174, 203, 228
Eurostar, 179
Eurostat, guidelines for public-private partnerships, 49–50
Eurotunnel, United Kingdom–France, 27, 46, 73, 75, 82, 139, 179–180, 186, 261
exit strategy, 93
export credit agencies (ECAs), 27, 32, 96, 98–103
buyer credit, 99–101, *100*, *101*
guarantees, 102
line of credit, 102, *103*
supplier credit, 102, *102*
Exxon/Mobil, United States, 240

FCC, Spain, 181
feed-in tariff (FiT), 229–230
feed-in tariff (FiT) Premium, 230
Ferrovial, Spain, 202, 275–276
finance lease, 115
see also **leasing**
finance sources, 87
debt financing *see* **debt financing**

equity *see* **equity**
financial adviser, 153–154
financial crisis, impact on public-private partnerships, 32–34, 174–175
financial due diligence, 157
financial engineering, 94
financial risks, 78–79, 253
financial structures
balance sheet issues, 48–50
corporate guarantees, *39*, 39–41, 99, 258
cross-sector, 84–85
government guarantees, *37*, 37–39, 96, 99, 132
not-for-profit companies/PICs, 50–51
project company, 35–37
project finance (cash flow) structures, 41–45
public-private partnerships (PPPs), 45–48
Finland, nuclear power plants, 221, 228
fit and proper person tests, 91, 135, 158, 249
Fitch Ratings Inc., 108, *109*, 265
fixed price contracts, 72, 164, 177, 208, 227
see also **turnkey contracts**
force majeure, 136–137, 141, 145, 246
France, 179, 186
cession Dailly acceptée mechanism, 188
nuclear power plants, 221
rail projects, 179, 186, 187–188, 288
Fukushima disaster, 223
funding availability, 93
funding structures
corporate guarantees, *39*, 39–41
government guarantees, *37*, 37–39
governments' choice, 53
sovereign guarantees, 38

G20 countries, 82
Gama Enerji, Turkey, 247
Gama Holdings, Turkey, 247
gate fee, 250
gateway decision-making process, 53, *54*
capital cost estimation, 56
cash revenues generation, 57–58
date for financial close, 56–57
demand certainty, 58
economic feasibility study, 53, 55
IT software-type projects, 55
law and regulation considerations, 55
PPP precedents, 57
private sector's role, 55
subsidies or subventions, 58
Gazprom, Russia, 241, 242
Gdynia, container terminal at, 197
geothermal power projects, 235
GGP Infrastructure Fund, 236
Glas Cymru, United Kingdom, 36–37
Glasgow Schools PPP, 254
government administration buildings projects, 257
government guarantees, *37*, 37–39, 96, 99, 132
governments, considerations for choosing public and private resources
common contractual terms and documents, 66
competition promotion, 65
completion and asset delivery, 64
conflicts of interest, 67
efficiency and operations, 64
employment issues, 65–66
institutional change, 64
institutional constraints, 67
maintenance regime lock-in, 64–65
national balance sheet issues, 68
political life cycle, 67–68
private sector investment, 64
refinancing gains, 66–67
short- to medium-term investment, 67
technologies, 64
timetable and complexity, 65
Greece, airport projects, 203
Green Book guide, 61, 278
Green Frog, United Kingdom, 212–213
Green Investment Bank, 236
grid connection risks
for hydropower projects, 216–217
for power generation, 210
for renewable energy projects, 232
Gulf countries, independent power producers or plants (IPPs), 211–212

health and hospitals projects, 255–256
Local Improvement Finance Trust (LIFT) schemes, 256, *256*
in London, 255
Heathrow Airport expansion project, 202, 274–278, *275*
highways projects *see* **roads and highways projects**
Hinkley Point C nuclear power station, United Kingdom, 278–280
hire purchase, 115
see also **leasing**
HKMTRC, Hong Kong, 186, 190
Hochtief, Germany, 203
Horizon project, United Kingdom, 279
housing projects, 257
HS1 project, United Kingdom, 179, 187, 261
HS2 project, United Kingdom, 280–281
HS3 project, United Kingdom, 280
HSL-Zuid project, France and the Netherlands, 188
Hungary, roads and highways projects
M1/M15 and M5, 168–169
hydropower projects, 215
access infrastructure risks, 216–217
in Bulgaria, 218–219
costs and completion risks, 215
environmental risks, 216
grid connection risks, 216–217
marine power, 219
revenues, currency and financial viability risks, 215–216
technological risks, 216
in Turkey, 218
in Uganda, 217–218

implementation agreement, 133
in-kind equity contributions, 87–88
independent power producers or plants (IPPs), *42*, 207, 235
in Africa, 235–236
emerging market, 210–211
general IPPs, 211
in Gulf countries, 211–212
in Mauritius, 236
in Morocco, 212
risks, 209

in Rwanda, 236
in Turkey, 218
in United Kingdom, 236–237
woodchip, 237
independent water and power projects (IWPPs), 211, 212
Indonesia, 29
roads and highways projects, 165
information technology (IT) projects, 258
infrastructure, definitions and interpretations, 23–25
infrastructure project finance
see also specific finance methods and projects
history of, 25–30, *26*
recent history of, 25
inherent capital balance, 93
initial public offering (IPO), 88
innovative proposals, 156, 203, 207
insurance, 74, 135, 141
life insurance, 28, 32–33, 67, 89, 90, 106, 108, 111, 196
monoline insurers, 109–110
and risk mitigation, 83–84
insurance reserve account, 74
Inter-American Development Bank (IADB), 156, 204
inter-city/high-speed rail (HSR) projects, 183
costs and completion risks, 183–184
environmental risks, 186
international borders risks, 186
land acquisition and planning risks, 186–187
traffic and financial liability risks, 184–186
inter-creditor agreement, 147–148
interest cover ratio, 122
interest rate risks, *79*, 79–80, *80*
interest rate swap, *79*, 79–80, *80*
internal rate of return (IRR), 92
economic IRR, 118
equity IRR, 118, 120, *120*
and present value, 118–120, *119*
project IRR, 118, *119*, 120
International Centre for Settlement of Investment Disputes (ICSID), 138, 170
International Chambers of Commerce, 138
International Civil Aviation Organisation (ICAO), 202, 204
international development banks *see* **international financial institutions (IFIs)**
international emissions trading, 227
International Finance Corporation (IFC), 77, 240
international financial institutions (IFIs), 95–97, 222
see also **development banks**
equity provision, 96
IFI A/B loans, 83, 96–97, 241
partial risk guarantees, 97
International Monetary Fund (IMF), 28, 49, 96
Ireland, 48, 174
bridges and tunnels projects, 181
irrevocable letter of credit (ILOC), 42, 43, 87, 141
Islamic finance, 111–112, *113–114*
Israel, roads and highways projects, 173
IT projects *see* **information technology (IT) projects**
joint implementation (JI) projects, Kyoto Protocol, 227
Jordan, water projects, 247
Jorf Lasfar IPP, 212

Kenya
geothermal power projects, 235–236
rail projects, 187
Kenya Power, 236
Kier, United Kingdom, 181
Kyoto Protocol, 222, 225, 228
Clean Development Mechanism (CDM), 226–227
joint implementation (JI) projects, 227

Labour party, 27
labyrinthine corporate structures, 266
land acquisition *see* **site acquisition and access**
landlord model, 195, 201
landslide risks, 196–197
Lane Cove Tunnel project, Australia, 182
Laos, hydropower project, 217–218
Le Mans stadium project, France, 258
leasing, 112, 115
finance lease, 115
hire purchase, 115
operating lease, 115
public lease, *31*
legal due diligence, 157
legal risks, 83
Lekki–Epe Expressway project, Lagos, 173
life insurance, 28, 32–33, 67, 89, 90, 106, 108, 111, 196
see also **insurance**
light rail and trams projects, 189
in Colombia, 193
risks, 192
in United Kingdom, 192–193
Lille stadium project, France, 258
Limerick Bridge project, Ireland, 181
limited partners, 90
limited recourse projects, 45
line of credit, 102, *103*
liquidated damages for under-performance, 76, 140, 143
loan agreement, clauses
conditions, 147
drawdown procedures, 146
fees, 146
inter-creditor issues, 147
interest payments, 146
introduction, 146
legal jurisdiction, 147
loan repayment, 147
loan and investor syndication, 81–82, *82*
loan life cover ratio (LLCR), 122, 123, *123*
Local Improvement Finance Trust (LIFT) schemes, 256, *256*
The London Courts of International Arbitration, 138
London Underground PPP, 50, 133, 139, 186, 190–191, 249, 261
Lord Foster-designed Milau Bridge project, France, 181

M1/M15 and M5, Hungary, 168–169
M6 Toll, United Kingdom, 167–168
Macquarie Bank, 89

Macquarie Infrastructure Group (MIG), 167
Malaysia, 29
  roads and highways projects, 165
management contract, *31*
management failure risks, 76
Manchester Municipal Waste PPP, 250–251
mandate letter, 157
Mapeley STEPS, United Kingdom, 257
marginal infrastructure projects, 23–24
Marsh, United Kingdom, 84
Mauritius, renewable energy project, 236
Medina Airport project, Saudi Arabia, 204
Melbourne City Link project, 182
merchant power pool, 208, 218, 222
Mersey Gateway project, United Kingdom, 181
Metronet consortium, 190, 191
metros and mass transit projects, 189
  costs and completion risks, 189
  in Dubai, 192
  financial viability risks, 189–190
  in Nigeria, 192
  in South Africa, 192
  traffic risks, 189
  in United Kingdom, 190
  in Venezuela, 191
Mexico, 27
  roads and highways projects, 166
mezzanine capital, 116
Midland Expressway project, United Kingdom, 94, 167–168
monoline insurers, 109–110
Moody's, 33, 108, *109*, 110, 265
Morocco, independent power producers or plants (IPPs), 212
motorway service areas, 163
  risks for, 175
Muharraq water project, Bahrain, 247
multi-layered corporate structures, 132
Multilateral Investment Guarantee Agency (MIGA), 84, 236
multinationals, 26, 41, 83, 115–116, 132, 240
municipal tax, 186
MWH, United States, 237

Nam Theun II run-of-river hydro project, Laos, 217–218
National Air Traffic Service (NATS), 204
national development banks, 84, 97–98
  see also **development banks**
National Grid plc, United Kingdom, 213
National Housing Trust, Scotland, 257
National Physical Laboratory (NPL) project, United Kingdom, 257
naval and military port projects, 199
NavCanada, 37, 205
net present value (NPV), 118
the Netherlands, 33, 230
  rail projects, 187–188
  roads and highways projects, 108, 174
Network Rail, United Kingdom, 49, 186
new investment capital, 87
Nexterra, United States/Canada, 237
Nigeria
  metros and mass transit projects, 192
  roads and highways projects, 173
'nominal' rate, 61, 62
non-recourse projects, 45
non-regulated projects, 24–25
Nord Stream project (Russia/Germany), 242–243
Nordic Development Bank, 97
North America, 32, 37
  Earner Value Management System (EVMS), 158
  infrastructure project finance history, 29–30
  private equity funds, 89–91
North Sea oil and gas resources, 26
not-for-profit companies, 49, 50–51, 98
nuclear power plants (NPPs) projects, 221–223
  advanced gas reactors (AGRs), 279
  in China, 223
  European pressurised reactor (EPR) units, 279, 280
  in Finland, 221, 228
  in France, 221
  future prospects, 223–224
  historical features, 221
  Magnox reactors, 279
  pressurised water reactor (PWRs), 279
  reactor types, 221
  in Russia, 223
  in United Kingdom, 278–280
  in United States, 221, 223
NuGen project, United Kingdom, 279

OECD Consensus Agreement, 99
offsets, 115–116
OFGEM, 213
OFWAT, 247, 263, 265–273
oil and gas pipelines projects, 239
  Azerbaijan–Georgia–Turkey pipeline, 240
  Chad–Cameroon oil pipeline, 240–241
  Russia–Germany gas pipeline, 242–243
  Russia–Turkey pipeline, 241
oil/gas/mineral terminals projects, 198
Olkaria Geothermal power project, Kenya, 235–236
Olkiluoto 3, Finland, 221
operating lease, 115
  see also **leasing**
operational risks
  management failure risks, 76
  operating cost risks, 75–76
  performance risks, 76
  revenue risks, 74–75
operations and maintenance (O&M) contract, 142
Oresund Bridge project (Sweden–Denmark), 49, 181
Ormat Industries, United States, 235
Overseas Private Investment Corporation (OPIC), United States, 204, 235

P3, 28
  see also **public-private partnerships (PPP)**
Pamir Energy Corp, United States, 213
Panama Canal project, 25
partial risk guarantees, 96
partnering, 27, 93
payback period analysis, *117*, 117–118
penalty points, and availability payment, 171–172
pension fund, 28, 32–33, 89, 90, 106, 108–109, 111, 173, 196
performance risks, 76
Petronas, Malaysia, 240

PFI (Project Finance Initiative) Executive, 166
photovoltaic (PV) systems project, 187, 233
physical asset risk, 74
physical risks, 78, 239
P&O, United Kingdom, 198
Poland
port projects, 197
roads and highways projects, 168
political risks, 61, 83, 94, 198, 216, 228
pool system, 207, 218, 222, 229, 279
ports projects, 195
access infrastructure risks, 196–197
container ports, 197–198
cost and completion risks, 195
cruise ship terminals, 198–199
currency risks, 196
environmental risks, 196
general purpose ports, 198
naval and military, 199
in the Netherlands, 198
oil/gas/mineral terminals, 198
political risks, 198
in Poland, 197
port services, 199
revenue risks, 196
traffic risks, 196
in United States, 198
Portugal, 48, 229
bridges and tunnels projects, 181
power and gas distribution projects, 239
applications and experiences, 239–240
power generation projects *see* **hydropower projects; nuclear power plants (NPPs) projects; renewable energy projects; thermal projects**
power purchase agreement (PPA), 209, 212, 217–218
power transmission projects, 239
applications and experiences, 239
PPP Arbiter, 190
preferred creditor status, 83
present value, and internal rates of return (IRR), 118–120, *119*, *120*
principles-compliant banks, 77
prisons projects, 258–259
private equity funds, 67, *89*, 89–91, *90*, 271
negative implications, 90
private finance initiatives (PFIs), 27–28, 55, 56, 62, 92, 110, 166, 261
see also **public-private partnerships (PPP)**
privatisation, 27, 261, 263–268
probity, 158–159
process project contracts, 144–145
procurement laws and infrastructure, 155
profitablity, changing over time, 92
project company, *35*, 35–37
project early repayment mechanism (PERM), 79
project engineer, 149
project financing structure, 41–45, *42*, 131, 283
see also **cash flow model**
general guidelines and advice, 283–284
project information memorandum (PIM), 152–153
project interest rate of return, 118, *119*, 120
project life cover ratio (PLCR), 122
project monitoring, 158
project process
bid costs, 155–156
bid preparation and notices, 154–155
business plan/project information memorandum (PIM), 152–153
conflicts of interest, 159
due diligence, 157
financial adviser, 153–154
fundraising, 156
innovative proposals, 156
mandate letter, 157
planning structure, 152, *152*
procurement laws and infrastructure, 155
project monitoring, 158
public-private partnership (PPP) unit, 151–152
standards of probity, 158–159
timetable, 155
project specification, fixed, 73
PSP, 23
see also **public-private partnerships (PPP)**
public interest companies (PICs), 36–37, 50–51
public lease, *31*
see also **leasing**
public-private partnership (PPP) concession agreement, clauses
see also **public-private partnerships (PPPs)**
access to land and utility, 134
assignment, 139
change in law, 136
completion, certification and start of operations, 134
concession, 133
concession period, 133–134
definitions and interpretations, 133
dispute resolution, 138
effectiveness, 134
employees, 135
expiry of the concession, 136
financial reporting and model, 135
force majeure, 136–137
governing law, 138
independent engineer, 134
information, rights of access and documents, 134
insurance, 135
law and authorisation, 134
maintenance fund, 135
materials and workmanship of the works, 135
modifications to the design, 134
obligations relating to public services delivered, 135
operations and maintenance costs benchmarking, 135
other issues, 139
payment regime, 134
records, 135
refinancing, 136
safety, 135
sovereign immunity, 138–139
specification, design and performance of the construction works, 134
subcontracts, 134
taxes, 135
termination, 137
public-private partnership (PPP) unit
aim and role of, 151–152
location of, 152

public relations, 152
staff, 152
public-private partnerships (PPPs), 45–46, 253, 283
concession agreement, 136, 137
see also **public-private partnership (PPP) concession agreement, clauses**
concessions, *31*
contracts, 27
and currency fluctuation, 23
definition of, 30–32
general guidelines and advice, 283–284
guidelines for, 49–50
impact of financial crisis on, 32–34
management contract, *31*
negative effects, 23
prisons projects, 258
public lease, *31*
recent history of, 25
service delivered to paying customer, *46*, 46–47, 131
service delivered to the public free, *47*, 47–48, 131
services contract, *31*
stand-alone concession, *31*
types of, 46–48
public sector comparator (PSC), *59*, 60
public services, 23
delivery of, 23–24, 27–28
publicly funded option *versus* private sector alternative, 58–64, *59*, *60*, *62*, *63*

quantitative analysis
cash flow model *see* **cash flow model**
coverage ratios, 122, *123*
debt service cover ratio (DSCR), 121, 124
interest cover ratio, 122
payback period, *117*, 117–118
present values and internal rates of return, 118–120, *119–120*
Quito Airport project, Ecuador, 156, 203–204
quota schemes, 228–229

rail projects
costs and completion risks, 183–184
environmental risks, 186
in France, 187–188
inter-city/high-speed rail, 183
international borders risks, 186
in Kenya/Uganda, 187
land acquisition and planning risks, 186–187
in the Netherlands, 187–188
rolling stock and vehicles, 183, 188
traffic and financial liability risks, 184–186
in United Kingdom, 187, 280–281
vertically integrated model, *184*, 184–185
vertically separated model, *185*, 185–186
Railtrack, United Kingdom, 185–186
RATP, France, 192
'real' rate, 61–62
recycling projects, 250
refinancing, 33, 66–67, 107–108, 136, 273, 276
regulated projects *see* **public services**
Regulatory Asset Base (RAB) model, 248, 266
corporate governance, 266–267
costs of finance, 267
environmental considerations, 268
flaws, 266–268, 273, 278
funding commitment, 267
project completion, 267
tax, 268
regulatory capital value (RCV), 248, 266
renegotiation, 45–46, 65, 80
renewable energy projects
clean development mechanism (CDM), 226–227
costs and completion risks, 227–228
geothermal power, 235
international emissions trading, 227
joint implementation (JI) projects, 227
in Kenya, 235–236
Kyoto Protocol, 222, 225–228
in Mauritius, 236
quota schemes or carbon credits, 228–229
revenue support mechanisms, 229–230
revenues, financial viability and political risks, 228–230
in Rwanda, 236
social power, 233–235
technological risks, 230
in United Kingdom, 236–237
wind power, 230–233
woodchip IPP, 237
Renewables Obligation Certificates (ROCs), 228
retail price index (RPI), 266
revenue risks, 74–75
revenue structure, 74–75
revenue support mechanisms
feed-in tariff (FiT), 229–230
feed-in tariff (FiT) Premium, 230
Rio-Antirion Bridge project, 181
risk analysis/assessment, 62–64
completion/construction risks, 72–74
currency risks, 80–81, *81*
environmental and social risks, 77–78
financial risks, 78–79
grid connection risks, 210, 216–217, 232
interest rate risks, 79–80
legal and political risks, 83, 94
loan and investor syndication, 81–82
operational risks *see* **operational risks**
projects *see* **airports projects; bridges and tunnels projects; hydropower projects; inter-city/high-speed rail (HSR) projects; light rail and trams projects; metros and mass transit projects; nuclear power plants (NPPs) projects; ports projects; rail projects; renewable energy projects; roads and highways projects; thermal projects**
risk matrix, *62*, 62–63
taxation risks, 82–83, 94, 132, 268
technical risks, 76–77
risks
definition of, 69–70
interest rate risks, *79*, 79–80, *80*
measurement of, 70–71
mitigation, 72–84
probability range, 70
sensitivity testing, 70, *71*
statistical probabilities, 70
roads and highways projects
availability payment, 170–173
car parks, 163, 175
in Central Europe, 168–169
completion risk, 164

currency risks, 165, 166
environmental risks, 165
highway projects, characteristics of, 163
land acquisition risks, 165
in Mexico, 166
motorway service areas, 163, 175
in Southeast Asia, 165
street lighting, 163, 175
traffic risks, 164, 166
in United Kingdom, 166–168
urban roads and road maintenance, 163, 175
in Venezuela, 169–170
rolling stock and vehicles, 183
risks, 188
Rotterdam World Gateway project, 198
Russia
nuclear power plants, 223
oil and gas pipeline project, 241
Russia–Germany gas pipeline project, 242–243
Rwanda, renewable energy projects, 236

SACE, Italy, 241
sales contract, 143–144
availability payments, 145
contracts for difference (CfD), 145, *146*
sales contract, clauses
process project contracts, 144–145
take-or-pay contracts, 144
tolling contracts, 145
Samsung, South Korea, 181
Saudi Arabia, airport project, 204
scheduled outages, 172
schools and advanced education projects, 254–255
Scotland
housing project, 257
Scottish Futures Trust programme, 36
water projects, 246
Scottish Water, 246
seaward side access risks, 197
SECO, Switzerland, 213
Second Tyne Tunnel project, United Kingdom, 181
secondary market, 93
self insurance, 74, 83
sensitivity testing, *128*, 128–129
services contract, *31*
Severn Bridge project, United Kingdom, 180
shadow tolls, 166
shareholder loan, 94, 132
shareholders
see also **equity**
types of, 88–89
Siemens, Germany, 180
site acquisition and access, 73–74
enhanced property values, 186–187
Sithe Global, United States, 217
skills shortage, 67
Skye Bridge project, United Kingdom, 180
SOCAR, Azerbaijan, 240
social risks, 77–78
solar power projects, 233–235
concentrated solar power (CSP) systems, 233–234
example, 234–235
photovoltaic (PV) systems, 187, 233
revenues, 234
South Africa
metros and mass transit projects, 192
prisons projects, 258
roads and highways projects, 173
Southeast Asia, 29
infrastructure financing project history, 27
roads and highways projects, 165
sovereign guarantees, 38, 96
sovereign wealth funds, *91*, 91–92
Spata Airport project, Greece, 203
special purpose project company *see* **project company**
St Petersburg, water project, 247
stadiums projects, 258
stand-alone projects, *31*, 45, 48, 57, 58, 132, 139, 207, 221, 225
Standard & Poor's (S&P), 108, 248, 265
state-owned enterprise, 37, 98, 184, 185
step-in rights, of lenders, 137
storage facility, 143
street lighting, 163
risks for, 175
subordinate debt, 94, 132
Suez Canal project, 25
Suez Environment, France, 247
Suez, Germany, 242
supplier credit, 102, *102*
supply contract, 142–143
swap payments, *79*, 79–80, *80*, 143
currency swaps, 81, *81*
interest rate swaps, *79*, 79–80, *80*
Swiss challenge procurement mechanism, 156, 203–204

Tajikistan, power generation projects, 213
take-or-pay contracts, 144, 217–218
TAQA, Abu Dhabi, 212
tax-free bonds, 29
tax optimisation structures, 266
taxation
corporate tax, 132
municipal tax, 186
taxation risks, 82–83, 94, 132, 268
technical due diligence, 157
technical risks, 76–77
tendering, 154
term sheet, 103–106
TGV (*train à grande vitesse*), France, 179, 186, 188, 280
Thailand, 29
roads and highways projects, 165
Thames Water, United Kingdom, 246, 266, 268
and Thames Tideway Tunnel, 268–274
Thatcher, Margaret, 27, 261
thermal projects, 207
access infrastructure risks, 210
costs and completion risks, 208
deregulated power system, *207*
emerging market IPP, 210–211
environmental risks, 210
general IPPs, 211
in Gulf countries, 211–212
market structures, *207*, 207–208
in Morocco, 212
power generation types, 208
revenues, currency and financial viability risks, 208–209
in Tajikistan, 213
technological risks, 209

in Togo, 212
in United Kingdom, 212–213
Three Mile Island disaster, 223
3P, 28
see also **public-private partnerships (PPP)**
Tideway Tunnel project, United Kingdom, 268–272
commercial and financial structure, 272–274
Togo, power generation projects, 212
toll roads projects, 27
see also **cash tolls**
tolling contracts, 145
Trafalgar House, United Kingdom, 166, 167, 178
traffic forecasts, 75
Trans-Manche Link JV, 179
Transport for London (TfL), 50, 190–191
transport projects *see* **airports projects; bridges and tunnels projects; light rail and trams projects; metros and mass transit projects; ports projects; rail projects; roads and highways projects**
trust/trustee, 43
see also **escrow account**
TubeLines, United Kingdom, 190, 191
Turkey, 27, 240, 241
hydropower projects, 218
turnkey contracts, 72, 128, 140, 183, 208, 221, 227
see also **fixed price contracts**

UCL Hospital project, United Kingdom, 255–256
Uganda
hydropower projects, 217–218
rail projects, 187
UK M6 Toll, 94
UN Commission on International Trade Law (UNCITRAL), 138
UN Principles of Responsible Investment, 78, 268
uncalled-for proposals, 156
unitary payment *see* **availability payments**
United Kingdom, 261–263
air traffic control in, 204
airport projects, 202, 274–278
areas affecting investment programmes, 262
bridges and tunnels projects, 178, 179–180, 181, 187
government administration building projects, 257
health and hospitals project, 255
infrastructure project financing history, 27
light rail and trams projects, 192–193
metros and mass transit projects, 190–191
National Air Traffic Service (NATS), 204
nuclear power plants projects, 278–280
power generation projects in, 212–213
prisons projects, 258
privatisation, 263–268, *264*
RAB model *see* **Regulatory Asset Base (RAB) model**
rail projects, 280–281
renewable energy projects, 236–237
roads and highways projects, 166–168, 167–168
sub-optimal investment in, 262–263
vertically separated railway system, 185–186
water and wastewater industry, 263–268, 268–274
water utilities, privatisation of, 247–249
United States, 92
air traffic control in, 204–205
bonds market, 106–107
infrastructure project finance history, 29–30
nuclear power plants, 221, 223
ports projects, 198
prisons projects, 258
urban roads and road maintenance, 163
risks for, 175

value for money (VfM), 58–64
Vasco Da Gama Bridge project, Portugal, 181
Venezuela
metros and mass transit projects, 191
roads and highways projects, 169–170
Vez Svoghe hydropower project, Bulgaria, 218–219
Virgin Rail, United Kingdom, 46

Wales & West Utilities, United Kingdom, 94, 266
Warnow Tunnel project, Germany, 181
warranties, 76, 136, 140
waste management projects, 245–246, 249
gate fee, 250
key issues, 249
process stages, 250
recycling, 250
in Western Europe, 250–251
Water Industries Act (1991), 263, 265, 266
water projects, 245, 247
in Jordan, 247
privatisation of water utilities, 247–249, 263–266
in Scotland, 246
in United Kingdom, 247–249
Water Services Regulation Authority, 263
watershed value, 56
weighted average cost of capital (WACC), 266
West Coast Mainline Rail Franchise, United Kingdom, 46
Willis Faber & Dumas, United Kingdom, 84
wind power projects, 230–233
wind farm, emerging market, 232–233
woodchip IPP, 237
World Bank, 96, 97, 217, 240
International Centre for Settlement of Investment Disputes (ICSID), 138, 170
International Finance Corporation (IFC), 213
negative pledge, 242

Zug, Switzerland, 243

About Globe Law and Business

Globe Law and Business was established in 2005 as an imprint of Globe Business Media Group. We set out to create law books which are sufficiently high level to be of real use to the experienced professional, yet still accessible and easy to navigate. Most of our authors are drawn from Magic Circle and other top commercial firms, both in the UK and internationally.

In Autumn 2015, we had an exciting turn in our history when Globe Law and Business was bought by a management team which includes my colleague Jim Smith and me, Sian O'Neill.

We love books, and our hardback titles are carefully produced, with the utmost attention paid to the editorial, design and production processes. We hope this results in high-quality titles which are easy to read, and a pleasure to own.

Our customers and authors are our most important concern, and as a smaller publisher, we are able to devote time and attention to each book, every author and our customers.

We'd very much like to hear from you with your thoughts on our titles or ideas for improving what we offer. Please do feel free to email me on sian@globelawandbusiness.com with your views.

Sian O'Neill
Managing director
Globe Law and Business

www.globelawandbusiness.com